Managing and Implementing Microsoft® SharePoint 2010 Projects

Geoff Evelyn

Published with the authorization of Microsoft Corporation by:
O'Reilly Media, Inc.
1005 Gravenstein Highway North
Sebastopol, California 95472

Printed and bound in the United States of America.

1 2 3 4 5 6 7 8 9 LSI 5 4 3 2 1 0

Microsoft Press titles may be purchased for educational, business or sales promotional use. Online editions are also available for most titles (*http://my.safaribooksonline.com*). For more information, contact our corporate/institutional sales department: (800) 998-9938 or *corporate@oreilly.com*. Visit our website at *microsoftpress.oreilly.com*. Send comments to *mspinput@microsoft.com*.

Microsoft, Microsoft Press, ActiveX, Excel, FrontPage, Internet Explorer, PowerPoint, SharePoint, Webdings, Windows, and Windows 7 are either registered trademarks or trademarks of Microsoft Corporation in the United States and/or other countries. Other product and company names mentioned herein may be the trademarks of their respective owners.

Unless otherwise noted, the example companies, organizations, products, domain names, e-mail addresses, logos, people, places, and events depicted herein are fictitious, and no association with any real company, organization, product, domain name, e-mail address, logo, person, place, or event is intended or should be inferred.

This book expresses the author's views and opinions. The information contained in this book is provided without any express, statutory, or implied warranties. Neither the author, O'Reilly Media, Inc., Microsoft Corporation, nor their respective resellers or distributors, will be held liable for any damages caused or alleged to be caused either directly or indirectly by such information.

Acquisitions and Development Editor: Kenyon Brown
Production Editor: Kristen Borg
Production Services: Octal Publishing, Inc.
Technical Reviewer: Troy Lanphier
Indexing: Seth Maislin
Cover: Karen Montgomery
Illustrator: Robert Romano

978-0-735-64870-8

To Kaye, Fifi, and Skye, the three most important people in my life.

To Max the dog, who sadly passed away early this year, this book is in remembrance of you.

Contents at a Glance

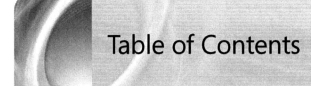

Table of Contents

What do you think of this book? We want to hear from you!

Microsoft is interested in hearing your feedback so we can continually improve our books and learning resources for you. To participate in a brief online survey, please visit:

www.microsoft.com/learning/booksurvey/

Chapter 3

Chapter 4

Chapter 5

Building Your SharePoint 2010 Team 87

Chapter 9

Chapter 10

Chapter 11

Chapter 15

What do you think of this book? We want to hear from you!

Microsoft is interested in hearing your feedback so we can continually improve our books and learning resources for you. To participate in a brief online survey, please visit:

www.microsoft.com/learning/booksurvey/

Acknowledgments

There are so many to thank and praise:

First and foremost, my greatest thanks go to my partner, Kaye, and my two daughters, Fifi and Skye; I am utterly blessed to have you in my life. The inspiration for this book came from them, and their support through the long evenings of writing was truly magnificent!

To Troy Lanphier, the technical editor for this book, my heartfelt thanks for your tireless work on keeping my thoughts on track and making sure I reworked and further defined sections of the book.

To Roger LeBlanc, who brilliantly copyedited the book, my hat's off to you, sir. Making the book really stand out in terms of formatting and ensuring my "grammar" was correct at all times was due to your awesomeness (if that's a word!)—many, many thanks.

To Sumita Mukherji and Kristen Borg at O'Reilly, thanks a ton for your aid in shepherding this book to the end! And, of course, Kenyon Brown, my acquisitions and development editor, who is the person most responsible for making this book happen; thank you for being there all the time to help me out, giving me guidance on format and style, and directing the book to the relevant people. This made the book a fantastic adventure, and I really hope we can work together again.

There must be loads of people at O'Reilly, all aiding this book, so thanks to all of them.

Of course, I did get inspiration, aid, and knowledgeable guidance from a host of people—all brilliant technologists, SharePoint champions, architects, administrators, developers, project, and program managers, all of whom I stand in awe. They have helped me properly structure my thoughts and given me guidance and knowledge in areas I could cover but needed review. Several are detailed in the book as well as in their blogs and mine.

Preface

What This Book Is About

Any SharePoint 2010 implementation, big or small, follows a process of engaging the client, the business, the support teams, and the users. The success of the implementation is based on the connection made between the business stakeholders and those technical teams responsible for the smooth running of the operation. By following a method that is understood by both parties, SharePoint 2010 implementation has focus and a history and is future proof.

This book will help you delve into SharePoint 2010 and determine the best way to get SharePoint up and running smoothly. With this practical guide, you'll gain project management best practices for implementing SharePoint in your organization and learn expert techniques for tuning your system to match the communication and collaboration needs of your users.

In this book, you will discover how to:

- Master SharePoint project governance

- Plan your SharePoint implementation and build your team

- Produce a system specification based on user requirements

- Determine the function, performance, interfaces, and design of your SharePoint system

- Optimize your hardware, software, and information architecture

- Take control of the documentation process during your SharePoint project

- Manage the implementation to respond to the evolving needs of your organization

To do this, this book will help you:

- Detail and understand the client's current business collaboration processes

- Define requirement specifications to match defined user requirements

- Design, plan and produce a system specification, including rules for management and governance

- Gather requirements from the users; for example, site premise, structure, information analysis, data content typing, organizational structure, and stakeholder management

- Design the solution; for example, taxonomy, metadata, content formatting, capacity, logical and physical design

- Define the implementation process; for example, procedures, guidelines for use, governance, testing, verification, validation, and customization

- Design the support environment; for example, create SLAs, backup and restore, disaster recovery and business continuity, staffing, and training processes

- Detail and carry out the installation and configuration of SharePoint 2010

- Create testing plans and verification exercises to ensure the resiliency and availability of the platform

- Define processes to ensure that you can educate and train the users to be productive with the SharePoint implementation

Who This Book Is For

If you are responsible for configuring, implementing, designing, or managing a SharePoint environment (or a combination of those roles), or if you are considering implementing SharePoint in your organization or for a client, this book is for you. If you are a project manager needing structured guidance on how to successfully implement SharePoint into an organization, then you should read this book. If you are a SharePoint architect and need to understand what you must do in order to provide a stable SharePoint environment, this book covers that. If you are a solutions architect and need to understand more about SharePoint in terms of governance, then there are areas in this book for you. If you are a SharePoint administrator and need to know where you fit into the implementation in terms of future support, then there are excellent sections in this book concerning monitoring management. Even if you are totally new to SharePoint and are simply considering using it in your company, and you need to know what it takes to get SharePoint properly implemented, this book is for you.

How This Book Is Organized

Chapter 1: Introduction

This chapter presents a basic historical look at project management and content management systems along with some successes and failures. It also contains a summary of how SharePoint is currently managed, its successes and failures, and why governance (management of SharePoint) needs to be high on the priority list for those who are implementing SharePoint. Finally, Chapter 1 presents a statement of what the book covers and its scope.

Chapter 2: SharePoint 2010 Project Mantra

This chapter lays out my take on what makes a good project-managed SharePoint implementation. It also describes how to combine procedure, objectives, enthusiasm, and what the initial steps are for those in charge of delivering the product.

Chapter 3: Content of Your SharePoint 2010 Project Plan

This chapter gives guidance on the content of a SharePoint project plan. It defines and describes the requirements of what makes up the project and applies to those new and old to project planning. Chapter 3 covers startup and closure; planning, milestones, dependencies, assumptions, risk planning, and more. Also described are the facets of where SharePoint implementation hooks into each of these and how the outputs lead onto further aspects concerning configuration management, acceptance, validation, and testing.

Chapter 4: SharePoint Planning and Control: Start As You Mean to Go

Chapter 4 describes the process for planning and controlling SharePoint implementation activities. It provides guidance on the procedures that are relevant to SharePoint deployment. This chapter focuses on and identifies those procedures that should be considered during a typical SharePoint project lifecycle.

Chapter 5: Building Your SharePoint Team

A successful implementation is achieved through a dedicated, skilled staff that is given clear goals. The most important thing in deploying SharePoint is to ensure your team is defined properly. This chapter lists the team members, their responsibilities, skillsets, and discusses how each of them contribute to the project.

Chapter 6: Building the Resources for Implementation: SharePoint Components and Sssociated Pieces

Key components are required to deliver SharePoint, and this chapter describes what they are and why they are required. Chapter 6 also describes the role of members of the team in collating this data and how the data should be used.

Chapter 7: The Business of SharePoint Architecture

Chapter 7 describes the concept of architecture and how it is applied to SharePoint. The principles of hardware, software, and information architecture are discussed in this chapter. Software architecture looks at the components of IIS, ASP.NET, Virtual Directories and how logically they are defined. Hardware architecture considers capacity, isolation, and sharing and looks at how the requirements for these can be defined. However, information architecture is discussed in detail since this is the foundation of providing the key requirements of hardware architecture planning and how software is then applied to it. The implementation of all of this is then listed as tasks and are slotted into the work breakdown schedule, including reasonings and how architecture agreements on Sharepoint also provides risk management detail.

Chapter 8: SharePoint Customization

This chapter details the "when and why" of SharePoint customization—the development and branding the priorities placed on implementation of SharePoint. It describes what the requirements are to carry out customization of the platform in terms of people and equipment; what the process is for ensuring that there is a split between development and production environments; the importantance of having a functional environment over its "look"; and when you should go for development and the responsibilities of the project manager to ensure that it is provided in a proper environment.

Chapter 9: SharePoint Governance

Extremely important to a successful implementation of SharePoint is its governance, by which we mean the strategy, rules, and support process provided to the user base. This chapter describes what SharePoint governance needs to be implemented from the outset, and how by having a structured environment, it can be continually maintained, monitored, standardized, and enhanced.

Chapter 10: SharePoint Configuration Management

This chapter addresses the configuration management of SharePoint and includes change control. Configuration management involves controlling the specifications, drawings, software, and related documentation that defines the functional and physical characteristics of a SharePoint implementation project, down to the lowest level required to ensure standardization. This chapter also describes the process and procedures so that the SharePoint project can provide a documented, traceable history, including any modifications or variants.

Chapter 11: Making Sure SharePoint Meets User Requirements

Chapter 11 provides the process under which the business can be asked questions that are relevant to their requirements. It demonstrates how the results of this investigation determine how SharePoint will meet those user requirements.

Chapter 12: Producing the System Specification

The main purpose of the SharePoint system specification for an organization is to expand the requirement specification to produce a clear, complete, and unambiguous set of documentation that describes the intended system in terms of its function, performance, interfaces, and design constraints. This chapter describes the benefits of producing a system specification for SharePoint 2010. It also goes into detail concerning the aspects of each of the report outputs. Additionally, areas concerning disaster recovery, fallback procedures, and lifecycle aspects are detailed. Further tasks concerning the actual build of the SharePoint platform is discussed in this chapter.

Chapter 13: Planning and Implementing the SharePoint One-Stop Shop

As the project takes hold and the business are getting engaged with SharePoint, so grows the need for knowledge transfer back to the business. All of this information needs to be stored and managed—what better place can you have than a centralized site called a "SharePoint One Stop Shop"?

Chapter 13 goes into detail on what exactly a SharePoint One Stop Shop is and why its implementation as part of the project is so vitally important.

Chapter 14: Releasing SharePoint to the Client

This chapter addresses key areas relevant to building the SharePoint development, test, stage, and production platforms. It includes information on testing and training the users.

Chapter 15: SharePoint Is Implemented, Now What?

This final chapter covers what it takes to ensure that SharePoint, once implemented, becomes part of the organizational lifecycle. This chapter describes the wrap-up procedures concerning archiving of project data and goes into detail concerning responsibilities of the team members and what they need to do to ensure that full handover is completed. The chapter concludes by discussing the importance of ensuring resources, governance, and other business-as-usual activities have been handed over satisfactorily.

Where to Find Additional Information and Updates

I started off my website way back in 2003, and since then, it's grown and I've tried to keep pace with the times. The current site runs on SharePoint 2010 Foundation, and it's great fun. Of course, there is a mountain of blogs that are relevant to this book—and quite a few of the links in this book point to blogs on the site. You will also find articles, links, and downloads related to SharePoint 2010, 2007 and 2003.

This site is:

http://www.sharepointgeoff.com

As for updates, just keep an eye on my website as I aim to publish more articles on SharePoint implementation, and of course, I welcome any input you might have. Please feel free to contact me using the contacts sheet on that site.

I do hope you enjoy my book.

Conventions and Features Used in This Book

This book uses special text and design conventions to make it eaer for you to find the information you need.

Text Conventions

Convention	Feature
Abbreviated menu commands	For your convenience, this book uses abbreviated menu commands. For example, "Choose Tools, Forms, Design A Form" means that you should click the Tools menu, point to Forms, and select the Design A Form command.
Boldface type	Boldface type is used to indicate text that you enter or type.
Initial Capital Letters	The first letters of the names of menus, dialog boxes, dialog box elements, and commands are capitalized. Example: The Save As dialog box.
Italicized type	Italicized type is used to indicate new terms.
Plus sign (+) in text	Keyboard shortcuts are indicated by a plus sign (+) separating two key names. For example, Shift+F9 means that you press the Shift and F9 keys at the same time.

Design Conventions

> **Note**
> Notes offer additional information related to the task being discussed.

Cross-references point you to other locations in the book that offer additional information on the topic being discussed.

> **CAUTION**
>
> Cautions identify potential problems that you should look out for when you're completing a task, or problems that you must address before you can complete a task.

INSIDE OUT This Statement Illustrates an Example of an "Inside Out" Problem Statement

These are the book's signature tips. In these tips, you'll get the straight scoop on what's going on with the software—inside information on why a feature works the way it does. You'll also find handy workarounds to different software problems.

TROUBLESHOOTING

This statement illustrates an example of a "Troubleshooting" problem statement.

Look for these sidebars to find solutions to common problems you might encounter. Troubleshooting sidebars appear next to related information in the chapters. You can also use the Troubleshooting Topics index at the back of the book to look up problems by topic.

Sidebar

The sidebars sprinkled throughout these chapters provide ancillary information on the topic being discussed. Go to sidebars to learn more about the technology or a feature.

Introduction

Project Planning in SharePoint

Microsoft SharePoint 2010 is a strategic technology that allows people to seamlessly connect with each other in terms of centralized content management. As a collaborative tool, SharePoint can be used by anyone, and it can be installed and configured quickly—usually to meet a "specific requirement." And this "specific requirement" is typically based on one person's perception that installing technology will solve a client request to get a product that allows teams to work closer together. But installation is not implementation.

Implementation of a product follows a plan. And that plan entails pulling in resources. You will need people, hardware, and software. You will need to define how SharePoint should be used by mapping it to user requirements, designing its physical structure, and then implementing it so that it will match those requirements.

To do this, you will need not only a strategy for planning, designing, building, and deploying SharePoint but you will also need a standardized method so that all SharePoint implementations follow the same route. Going down the route of installing SharePoint with little planning will produce a platform that is ineffective and unreliable, with low user acceptance.

The purpose of this book is to help you create a standardized approach for implementing SharePoint 2010, not directly from a technical perspective, but by explaining the required phases, the required people, the required resources, and wrapping this up using typical project management methods. Generally, technical people shy away because they want the nuts and bolts. Business people shy away because they want productivity. This book brings them both together to meet the common goal: true implementation of SharePoint.

Here is an example of how going down the route of providing SharePoint without planning courts disaster. I was working in a team whose purpose was to implement a content management system; this team was a mixture of IT professionals and technical staff. A meeting was held to choose the system of choice. A lot of administrators were there—server admins,

Active Directory admins, Microsoft Exchange admins—a lot of egos in one room. (Strangely but not surprisingly, no one from the business attended.) The meeting kicked off with gusto.

One member of the technical team—a Microsoft Windows Server admin—stood up and in a loud voice stated the following:

"Hey! We got SharePoint! It has got blogs, wikis, workspaces, team sites, search—let us have all of that. We don't need anyone to help us. It is easy to set up, and we'll just learn as we use it. We only need a site or two to store the documents in. If the users want in, we'll give them some sites to play with."

Does that sound okay? Well, what I explained was that the vast majority of SharePoint implementations have been based on exactly the scenario depicted by the admin's comments: project planning in a vacuum.

What's wrong with that? To best explain it, let's take that scenario and add a couple of months to it:

"Hey! We have 20 sites now. Lots of content. Not sure what we are doing. Not sure how it all connects together. We think we know how to manage it, though we don't know how big it will get. And we also can't control how big it gets because we are not entirely sure who is using it and why."

What's the Situation?

The situation described is that the technology is adopted without any analysis (known as *information architecture*) to define the requirements for using the technology within the organization and without *future-proofing* the technology.

Information Architecture is the study of how information, organizational structure, information flow, process flow and more are connected to user requirements. Without it, SharePoint is not defined to meet the client requirements, since Information Architecture leads to SharePoint user strategy in terms of content management. Information Architecture is further discussed in Chapter 7, "The Business of SharePoint Architecture." Future-proofing describes the exclusive process of trying to anticipate future developments, so that action can be taken to minimize possible negative consequences, and to seize opportunities. For example, you may want to make the platform easy to grow (to scale) so you add capacity to the system to accommodate it. You may want SharePoint to be easy to support, so you add more monitoring, performance tuning, even more people to look after the product as part of the implementation.

The preceding scenario simply describes the technology as having been put in blind (in other words, in a Wild West fashion). Of course, because no boundaries have been decided on and no use of technology has been defined, we head for an uncontrolled method of product implementation. Implementations that result from the given scenario rarely last as a proper platform for more than two months—they either become unsupportable, unmanageable, turn into white elephants (a platform whose expense has exceeded its usefulness), or have some combination of all these attributes.

So why don't we just correct the implementation? Surely it can be fixed? Although I love troubleshooting SharePoint environments, implementations devised in such a way are difficult to correct. Correcting the implementation at this point simply means you are shaping the implementation's future based on where the related company is now—and that is much more difficult because there is no audit trail showing how SharePoint was initially implemented. Planning SharePoint through to implementation means that you create information about its implementation as you go; and if that information is controlled and recorded correctly, you will have a project history. The following examples describe failures in implementation:

- Example 1: SharePoint is installed in an organization that has been using it for 2 years. There are 5000 users accessing over 200 sites and over 5 offices. They want to upgrade from their current SharePoint platform to the latest version. Unfortunately, the person who installed SharePoint left the organization half a year ago and there is no information on how the product was installed, or what changes had been made to the platform.

- Example 2: SharePoint is installed in a small organization of 10 people on a single server. They don't have a SharePoint person looking after SharePoint; they do it themselves. They want to now add another server to make SharePoint more resilient. They bring in a SharePoint "guru" contractor who then adds a secondary server in a week and then leaves. Three weeks later the secondary server develops a fault—they are forced to call in another SharePoint "guru" because they could not find the original person. Chaos ensues because there is no documentation found concerning the original, or the added server installation.

Adopting Project Governance in SharePoint Is Vital

Before I state why it is important that you have project governance, it is best to describe the key premise of project governance and the hurdles you must get over in implementing it. The first hurdle is that you must engage the stakeholders (the person or group in the organization affected or that has a direct interest in the project—also known as the *client*) on the topic. There is absolutely no point in explaining the wonderful aspects of SharePoint (and how it will sort out all of the company's woes by sharing data and establishing a framework for effective communication) unless the stakeholders have a grasp of what it means to have project governance. Stakeholder buy-in is the biggest factor concerning the adoption of SharePoint (or, in fact, any new technology).

Why is stakeholder buy-in important? All stakeholders need to know what's happening, when it's happening, and why it is happening. They need to be clear about who is involved, the stages of SharePoint implementation and what they entail, what needs to be achieved along the way, and how you'll reach key decisions and outcomes. It is crucial to remember the aims and objectives, protect the special qualities of the design, and hold on to the "golden thread" that will make the project successful and match the client's vision of SharePoint.

Some SharePoint project managers I have met are afraid to approach their clients to explain the concept of project governance; they feel the client will not want to implement Share-Point if doing so will alter the way people do things. Interestingly, it is not the implementation of SharePoint that invokes project governance, it is the implementation of SharePoint that allows people to work more productively.

A company called me up stating that they had been given SharePoint but had no idea how they got it or what to do with it. They were now having a nightmare controlling the management of the platform, especially since they wanted to rationalize their desktop technologies. I visited the company and found that technicians had decided to install it for a part of the organization where the users were not SharePoint trained, and now the entire organization had some use of SharePoint but that use was not quantified. Several weeks of discussion ensued about how it is important to engage with the organization in terms of gathering requirements first so that they are clear on who does what and why, and on what equipment and where, for a SharePoint implementation. Had this been done at the beginning (meaning the technicians had engaged with the organization) things would have been much better.

How Does SharePoint 2010 Help Project Management?

Effective SharePoint project management will work only if the client's aspirations map to the Project or Program Manager's (PM) understanding of their aspirations.

Through the use of project data management (using SharePoint 2010 features and tools such as reporting tools, data relevance, security, auditing, traceability, and centralization of data), the organization will be able to use SharePoint 2010 to increase team collaboration, create a standardized process, and ensure that the PM's project mantra is intact. (We'll have a look at *Project Mantra* later.)

SharePoint 2010 allows project managers and their teams to create sites that serve as a Project Management Office (PMO). This provides for the centralization of data and can be

Chapter 1

a massive win scenario for the client. Documents and other information in a PMO can be centrally stored and maintained, effectively standardizing and streamlining communications. Project managers can use document and list repositories to create a streamlined, one-stop shop for SharePoint documentation and communications. The goal is to carry out a good SharePoint implementation through a repeatable and standardized method of documentation control bound to project processes concerning document management. SharePoint 2010 is also directly integrated with Microsoft Office 2010 applications such as Microsoft Word, Excel, PowerPoint, Outlook, Access, Visio, and more. It is also directly integrated with the Windows operating system and with popular Web tools and technologies.

SharePoint 2010 has finely tuned access levels so that access to data can be limited. Permissions have been enhanced beyond the levels provided by SharePoint 2007 (for example, more out-of-the-box security permissioning, as well as an easier way to define and customize those permissions to suit the content being provided).

One of the most compelling aspects of SharePoint 2010 is the *unified infrastructure* approach, which entails having one platform with multiple solutions. This unified infrastructure results in easier integration and enhanced connectivity to multiple device and browser types.

What Is Project Governance in Relation to Content Management Systems?

Content management systems rely on project governance to deliver, support, and manage the platform. As a content management system, SharePoint makes project governance even more crucial because SharePoint is an enterprise system. It provides a technology platform that enables the organization to integrate and coordinate their business processes. It will provide a single system that is central to the organization and ensure that information can be shared across all functional levels and management hierarchies. It connects to all manner of Microsoft technologies and components. Additionally, these connected technologies and components could have their own project plans for implementation; they can also run on their own schedules that have been created and managed by their support and implementation teams.

Project governance techniques adopted in large organizations often use methodologies such as PRINCE, Agile, or Project Management Body of Knowledge (PMBOK). Unfortunately, when governance is applied to SharePoint, there is no standard methodology because SharePoint is based largely on the organization's understanding and application of the product. Companies rarely look (or will not take the time to look) for a standard method of deploying a product such as SharePoint, and they might often turn to external consultants and project managers to provide governance.

The only problem with this approach is that if the company does not understand the nature of project management and its application to SharePoint, the output of project governance probably will be meaningless, not clearly understood, not continually applied to the implemented product—or all three. And when that happens, the implemented product becomes a white elephant.

Content management systems such as SharePoint need to be designed, installed, configured, delivered, and managed. (Indeed, delivery and management may run in life cycles of their very own.) The project management methods of plan, control, risk, implementation, and signoff need to be cycled around these systems.

SharePoint Project Planning is a fine art. SharePoint projects are created by those who understand SharePoint. There is no point designing projects that look like this:

Phase 1:

1. Research the Market for SharePoint People

2. Get the SharePoint People

3. Purchase Vanilla Ice Cream

4. Install SharePoint

Those who do not understand SharePoint may even assume that the third step (Purchase Vanilla Ice Cream) "fits." A SharePoint project manager will demand not only the removal of that step, but also describe why it's wrong and ensure there are proper phases covering Investigation and Design, and Build and Deploy. In this book, we also describe who is required on a SharePoint implementation team, their roles, and typically what skills are required.

Project Management of SharePoint Provides Project Governance

Why is project management so important for SharePoint? Following are four main reasons.

Accountability

There are people who need to be assigned responsibility for actions, decisions, and policies concerning the management of the implementation and governance, all within the scope of their role within the project. In other words, someone puts SharePoint in place; and project management helps this by defining the what, when, why, and where of this implementation.

Chapter 1

Sustainability

While preserving the integrity of the platform delivered to the organization, the platform must meet present needs, but also future organizational requirements. SharePoint 2010 needs to be managed and governed to grow. By applying project management methodologies, SharePoint's economic (user requirements in terms of added features and products), social (the ability to enhance and connect people), and environmental (the infrastructure of SharePoint can be scaled, for example) aspects are protected and maintained.

Resiliency

A SharePoint implementation needs to be robust to survive. SharePoint must have the ability to provide and maintain an acceptable level of service in the face of faults and challenges to normal operation. Project management provides processes such as configuration management, planning for backup, disaster recovery, monitoring, and performance levels.

Supportability

SharePoint needs to be looked after. Project management defines the quality-control measures to be enacted by the team that is responsible for the SharePoint implementation.

As a Project Manager, you need to ensure that when describing the above four elements to the client, they understand there is a timeline to put in SharePoint. You cannot let the client put together the timeline themselves, because they will start by reasoning that anything they don't do is easy to do. Designing a SharePoint platform for worldwide operations cannot be completed in two weeks, for example.

I had a client who insisted that they wanted SharePoint in one week—yes, one week—for a team of 20 people in the company. I asked if any of the 20 people had ever seen SharePoint. No. I asked if any of the 20 people worked together on the same information as a team. No. I asked who would look after SharePoint when it was built. They said they would. I asked a bunch more questions. I think that the killer question was this one: who is going to manage SharePoint? Now, it's not to say you can't install SharePoint in a week, not to say that in the same week you could try to teach the very basics of SharePoint. But in terms of accountability, supportability, resiliency, and sustainability, you can't get that in a week. Those are continual processes, and to make sure you can apply those means planning through to implementation. How did I resolve that situation, review current process, educate the client, put together a plan, agree on the plan—its feasibility—through to implementation? The client got their SharePoint in one month and now, three years on, have scaled it to handle over 1000 people and manage their platform well.

A Historical Perspective on Project Governance with SharePoint

I've had some successes (and some failures) in gathering information concerning how projects historically implement SharePoint. SharePoint project planning is seen as time-consuming or as a nuisance, or it is just not generally understood or discussed. For a product that is so important to the growth of an organization in terms of communication and productivity, one would think it is very likely that project planning had been investigated or put into place.

Let's take a look at how SharePoint has been implemented thus far. By the way, this isn't just based on some techie talk such as "Hey, I downloaded it and installed it on a server." And it has little to do with the version implemented. Even though SharePoint 2003 has less functionality and fewer features than SharePoint 2007, which in turn has less functionality and fewer features than SharePoint 2010, a successful implementation of SharePoint is based on whether the planning through investigation and designing, building and then deploying was carried out correctly.

Failed Scenarios: When SharePoint Isn't Implemented Properly

Let's take a quick look at some scenarios where SharePoint is poorly implemented. Note that all of these implementations are examples of failures except for number 5.

1: By the Back Door

Someone in an organization downloads a copy of a beta version of SharePoint from Microsoft Developer Network (MSDN) or downloads the free version of Windows SharePoint Services (from Microsoft's Web site), installs it on a server, and begins using it. That someone then demonstrates SharePoint to some colleagues, who then show it to others (a process known as the *cascade effect*) and product usage grows within the organization.

2: By Stealth

Someone buys a copy of SharePoint after evaluating it for his department and sticks it on a server for his own use. Other departments begin to find out about the product, and they start using it.

3: By a "You Get It, I Got It" Approach

Someone tells the IT help desk that she wants to share documents online. The IT help desk, already overtaxed with other responsibilities, gets a copy of Windows SharePoint Server, and puts it on a server under their control. Users start using SharePoint, and they tell other users about it. Then those additional users start using SharePoint.

4: By an "Our Technology Is Old; We Want New Stuff, But We're Not Sure What. IT Help Desk, Please Help Us" Approach

In this scenario, an organization requires internal IT to provide a technology refresh of all the products under its control. This includes an upgrade of Microsoft Office. The IT help desk suggests introducing SharePoint into the mix, noting that better collaboration will result. Multiple products (including SharePoint) then get installed; users find out about these products and begin using them.

5: By a "We Want to Share, But We're Not Sure What; Let Us Find Out and Then We'll Decide" Approach

In this scenario, an organization involves internal and external people to investigate the organizations requirements and research which technology best fits the requirements. Although the help desk is definitely involved, business people and IT work together to decide on a product, and subsequently plan its implementation. They agree that SharePoint is one product that fulfills part of the objectives. Further work is done to build an implementation plan, resulting in the deployment of SharePoint. Users are then introduced to SharePoint and start using it.

Perspectives of Project Governance: What Is Wrong with Scenarios 1 Through 4

Let's examine the reasons that scenarios 1 through 4 lead to a poorly executed implementation of SharePoint.

1: By the Back Door

If SharePoint is implemented without governance from the outset, attempting to design and implement governance will take time and be more difficult because the users are accustomed to the Wild West approach. The culture will be one of "governance slows me down" and "the problems of SharePoint in the organization will sort themselves out." The back-door approach is usually the fastest method of getting the product, and the IT help desk is generally not involved.

2: By Stealth

If one department puts in SharePoint, the governance adopted will be based on the rules and processes in the department that first installed it. The governance will have nothing to do with a centralized approach by the company; hence, project governance in this approach will be stifled.

3: By a "You Get It, I Got It" Approach

In this scenario, the poor help desk is left to try to understand and support SharePoint. They are technicians and therefore are not suited to provide management rules, let alone review and audit them. Therefore, governance is very low on the priority list and seen as a nuisance—it gets in the way of trying to sort out a user issue—however, that's the problem. Because the help desk does not implement governance, it is highly unlikely the organization as a whole will, because they see the IT help desk as owners—after all, the organization was never directly involved with managing the product. There is no quality control.

4: By an "Our Technology Is Old; We Want New Stuff, But We're Not Sure What. IT Help Desk, Please Help Us" Approach

Aha! The organization speaks out and asks for new technology. The organization does it because it is generally not content with its current technology and wants to move to the next version. Unfortunately, this approach offers very little client involvement in determining what its processes are; therefore, not much insight is gained up front into how each of the technology upgrades will suit the client. The clients (because they are not asked) do not feel that they own any part of the technology and therefore don't need to own or be part of any project governance. This means there is no what or how—no project control and no project quality.

Project Governance Can Be Set Only by Establishing a Client SharePoint Context

The reason why scenario 5 will be a success is because there is a client involved in the SharePoint context. The client (business or technical) needs to understand that SharePoint is a collaborative technology that will help solve information challenges, but only if implemented using a structured, understood method, carried out by skilled implementers.

Project governance in a SharePoint implementation is not just a final step; it is a perpetual voyage. Once SharePoint is in use by an organization, it is vital that any further implementations of SharePoint refer to and are executed in the exact same method used for the original implementation. The same procedures concerning analysis, design, building, testing, and and deployment should be followed and understood. Of course, these procedures will be refined and enhanced over time, but the underlying process should continue to be used.

What This Book Is About

Writing a book detailing how to manage a SharePoint 2010 implementation is definitely not easy. This is because there are many types of implementations, ranging in scope from "I only want an evaluation done" to "I want a full-featured SharePoint presence for the entire organization." Therefore, this book has the following objectives:

- To be a source of steps that will help you implement a SharePoint 2010 presence for your organization

- To be a source of forms and procedures that will help your SharePoint 2010 project meet and exceed customer expectations and requirements

- To provide a project management implementation method that is repeatable and standardized for SharePoint 2010

- To logically connect business requirements to key SharePoint features

What This Book Is Not About

This book is not:

- A technical "How Do I" guide to building SharePoint physical server environments or connecting SharePoint to other environments

- A cookbook of development or third-party recipes

- A technical guide to fixing problems with SharePoint

- A statement that there is only a single, de facto method of implementing SharePoint

SharePoint 2010 Project Mantra

What Is the SharePoint 2010 Project Mantra?

S UPPOSE you have been chosen as the project manager of the Let Us Integrate Share-Point 2010 Into Company XYZ project. The first question you need to answer is, "why use SharePoint 2010?" There could be many reasons:

- The organization (or the client) has islands of information and applications.

- The organization has demonstrated slow responsiveness to business and user needs.

- The client is suffering from the effects of custom development and maintenance.

- There is currently poor information sharing inside and outside the organization.

- The client is having difficulty finding the right content, data, and people.

- There is increasing information management risk within the organization.

As a project manager, your task is to deliver your project on time and at the lowest possible cost. To do that requires combining the resources of both the business side of the organization and its technology department. *Business resources* are members of the organization who will provide details concerning the client vision; the information they provide is crucial to the format of SharePoint 2010. For example, they will determine how sites look, what the taxonomy is, and what metadata is associated with content. *Technical resources* refers to the equipment required: hardware (servers under which SharePoint 2010 operates and that it communicates with) and software (SharePoint 2010, Office 2010, and associated components and technologies), including third-party products. There will be business challenges, such as those brought about by changes in organizational structure, by the clients' vision, and by the clients' processes. There will be external challenges too—for example, those brought about by legal and economic issues.

Whatever these challenges, your SharePoint 2010 project mantra is critical. The project mantra shows how the project will evolve and align with your client's aspirations. It shows your enthusiasm about SharePoint 2010; your stakeholder group will likely feed off of that enthusiasm.

> ### Note
> A SharePoint project mantra is the combination of an enthusiastic and evangelistic approach to implementing SharePoint combined with a sound project approach that is repeatable, and gives the client confidence that the SharePoint implementation will succeed and meet their expectations. Your project mantra increases in accordance with the knowledge you have gained of what the client wants (their vision). Additionally, as the client's understanding of SharePoint grows in terms of how SharePoint will benefit their organization, the mantra increases.

A key part of making the mantra meaningful is adopting an evangelistic and realistic approach to implementing SharePoint 2010. Therefore, as project manager, you don't just need the typical organizational and scheduling skills (say, from a methodology such as Prince). You need to have an enthusiastic approach and appear to your peers and colleagues as having high-level skills in defining a collaborative environment that's responsive to change. This doesn't mean you need to have already implemented dozens of SharePoint 2010 projects and features. It means that you follow a specific method and that your SharePoint 2010 Quality Plan reflects that method.

The SharePoint 2010 Quality Plan is discussed in detail in Chapter 3, "Content of Your SharePoint 2010 Project Plan." To get the details required in the SharePoint 2010 Quality Plan, you need to address some important areas: your knowledge of the product, an understanding of the client's vision for SharePoint 2010, and the scope defining the client's requirements.

Your SharePoint 2010 project mantra helps you to easily describe the key features that SharePoint 2010 has and how they meet the full range of needs of employees, partners, customers, individuals, and teams. The features provided, for example, might include

MySites, team collaboration, department sites, enterprise intranet, and Internet presence, all aligned with an enterprise search facility.

The client should be left with no doubt that SharePoint 2010 will make information and knowledge sharing intuitive and easy. SharePoint 2010 includes smart live editing of text on the page; it has content controls, Visio Web integration, browser support, and the Office Ribbon. In short, it includes features that enable the client to control and reuse content while reducing information-management risk, which leads to faster and more insightful decision making.

The SharePoint 2010 project mantra involves understanding your client's SharePoint 2010 vision, understanding the product, and delivering the product in the most useful way for the client.

Your First Steps

You cannot easily implement SharePoint 2010 yourself because you will find (from reading this book for a start) that this requires you to carry out many pieces of work as well as control the timeframe and the client. You need a team to help you, and that team needs to be defined based on the scope the client has indicated.

The team ethos will ensure that the project focuses on defining, developing, and deploying SharePoint 2010 based on the client's requirements. (This is discussed further in Chapter 5, "Building Your SharePoint 2010 Team.") To build your team, you not only need to have an understanding of planning and controlling a SharePoint 2010 project, but an understanding of the client's organization.

By gaining this understanding, you are preparing both yourself and the client. Preparing yourself allows you to carry out investigations and build your team. Preparing the client allows you to understand their knowledge so that you both can define your collective expectations of SharePoint 2010.

For example, you need to determine whether your client has used SharePoint 2010 in the past or whether they are currently using SharePoint 2010. The answer to this question is critical, because it will give the project/program manager an immediate indication of the top-level project scope; therefore, the answer to this key question (and related questions) must be gathered at your first meeting with the client.

Table 2-1 lists key questions you might need to ask the client.

Table 2-1 **Key Questions**

Experience with SharePoint 2010	Key Questions to Ask
Never Used SharePoint 2010	Have you ever deployed it?
	Are there licenses available?
	Where is the client located?
	What is their size, industry, and revenue?
Currently using SharePoint 2010	Are there issues with the platform?
	Do you know the value of the platform?
	Are there any specific industry alterations?
	Has the organization grown since SharePoint was implemented?
Used SharePoint 2007, but it's currently not in use. Now looking to return to SharePoint with SharePoint 2010	When was SharePoint 2007 deployed?
	Why was it not used?
	What is its current state?

During this initial meeting, you will also need to find out whether or not the client has gone through SharePoint 2010 *implementation pain*. You must come to understand the client's experience of this pain because it influences how the users will view the platform going forward.

SharePoint 2010 implementation pain occurs when the relevant SharePoint 2010 plan did not succeed or issues came about seriously disrupting the SharePoint implementation, causing business disruption, financial loss, bad publicity, or any other consequences the client did not expect or desire. This pain could be caused by one or more of the following factors:

- The budget did not match the scope.

- The project scope could not be achieved.

- The project ran out of time.

- The project team ran away. (I've seen that happen!)

- The education of the users, team, or both did not succeed.

- The users missed the meaning of SharePoint 2010—the implementors failed to sufficiently educate the users and did not explain a definition of SharePoint (for example not even explaining to the users 'SharePoint is a collaborative technology that allows users to create and manage their own web sites.

By getting the client to divulge the details of these pains, you can itemize them and provide initial responses to the client to ensure the issues will be addressed or avoided in future projects. Additionally, the client might even indicate what they have done to prevent the problem from affecting them further—for example:

Company XYZ implemented SharePoint but did not manage to implement a requested feature because the project team ran out of time. The SharePoint project was then handed over to the business resources. The knowledge of the missing feature is detailed and known. However, the client is unable to use SharePoint to solve productivity issues because the feature is not available. This was the client's implementation pain. To prevent the client from experiencing this pain again, it was agreed to rigorously check the scope of all future SharePoint implementation projects and to provide alternatives or agree on a different method of working if user requirements cannot be met.

By meeting the client and gathering information so that you understand the current implementation level of SharePoint 2010 in the organization, you understand its basic usage within the organization and more. You have your first **boost** of SharePoint 2010 project mantra and you can make your first attempt to help the client create their vision of SharePoint 2010.

> **Note**
> Your SharePoint project mantra increases in accordance with the knowledge you have gained of what the client wants (their vision). Additionally, as the client's understanding of SharePoint grows in terms of how SharePoint will benefit their organization, the SharePoint project mantra increases.

The SharePoint project mantra ensures that the team doing the tasks are highly motivated and want what you want as the project manager: to succeed and to exceed expectations.

Know Your SharePoint 2010 Features

You need to have a grasp of what features are available in SharePoint 2010. This knowledge will help you focus the user requirements and find solutions to the organization's information and management collaboration challenges.

There is a mass of information available from Microsoft concerning the product scope for SharePoint 2010 (describing what SharePoint is). There is also a massive amount of support for the product from Microsoft, including information provided from articles written by SharePoint 2010 experts in the field.

There is a significant amount of information concerning SharePoint online. The best place to start with anything related to SharePoint is the SharePoint 2010 Home site at *http://share-point.microsoft.com/en-us/Pages/default.aspx.*

During the initial phases of your SharePoint 2010 implementation project, you will elicit information concerning what the user requirements are. These requirements then need to be mapped to key features so that detailed work concerning the configuration and deployment of those features can be pursued. The information gathered from the business analysis with the user base is used to drive the system specification, which is made up of the relevant features needed.

SharePoint 2010 has significant improvements over SharePoint 2007; however, I want to be clear—this book is not going to give you a list of these improvements. Neither is it going to detail how you should install those features. It will provide a list of SharePoint features so that you know what is available to meet a client's requirements.

> **Note**
>
> At the release of the 2010 version, SharePoint Technologies are no longer called Windows SharePoint Services (WSS) or Microsoft Office SharePoint Server (MOSS). WSS has been renamed Microsoft SharePoint Foundation 2010, and MOSS is now Microsoft SharePoint Server 2010. Microsoft SharePoint Server 2010 is available in either Standard or Enterprise versions, and there are versions for internal, extranet, and Internet sites. Additionally, the hardware requirements are now exclusively 64 bit (x64). There is no 32-bit (x86) version of the SharePoint 2010 Technologies; bear this in mind if your client wants to implement SharePoint 2010 but their core infrastructure uses 32-bit server environments.

Collaboration Features

Collaboration features include

- Social Networking Web Parts
- Wikis
- Blogs
- E-mail Integration

- Task Coordination

- Browser-Based Forms

- Centralized Forms Management and Control

- "Design Once" Development Model

- Form Import Wizard

- Integrated Deployment Model for "No-Code" Forms

- Compatibility Checker

- Site Manager

- Mobile Device Support

- Portal Site Templates

- SharePoint 2010 Sites and Documents Roll-up Web Parts

- Colleagues and Memberships Web Parts

- Integration with Microsoft Office and Applications 2010 and 2007 (Access, Excel, PowerPoint, Word, Outlook, Visio)

- Supports Tagging Content

- Enhanced Blog-Authoring Capabilities

- SharePoint 2010 Offline Abilities Enhanced in SharePoint 2010 Workspace

- Multicolumn Indexes, More View Control, Queries

- Visio Services. This lets users share and collaborate on Visio diagrams. A built-in viewer allows SharePoint 2010 users to view Visio files in their browser without having Visio directly installed on their system. Visio Services also retrieves and renders any external data used in the Visio diagrams.

If you're looking for additional resources that provide more in-depth coverage about Share-Point 2010 features, I recommend two books from Microsoft Press: ***Microsoft SharePoint Foundation 2010 Inside Out*** and ***Inside Microsoft SharePoint 2010***. Visit *http://microsoft-press.oreilly.com/?cmp=il-orm-msp-hp* for more information.

Chapter 2

Search and Management Features

Search and management features include the following:

- People Search

- Social Search

- Extension of Search Through Customization (Using Business Connectivity Services) and Other Federated Search Options

  Visit *http://msdn.microsoft.com/en-us/library/ee534979(office.14).aspx* to read *What's New: Business Connectivity Services* to learn more about these enhanced capabilities.

- Business Data Search (with Enterprise CAL only)

- Re-parenting. Search automatically updates when content is rearranged—for example, a SharePoint 2010 site is moved or changed in a hierarchical structure.

- Integration with FAST Search Server 2010, providing thumbnails, previews, visual best bets, result counts, sorting, tunable relevance ranking, and more.

- Usage reporting and logging is vastly improved; it uses a new database, specifically designed to support usage reporting and logging. This information is extensive, allowing third-party vendors to create custom reports based on the information it contains.

- Disaster recovery features at both the farm and granular backup level.

- Windows PowerShell. This administrative functionality is truly a massive improvement over the STSADM toolset and provides much more scope for managing SharePoint 2010.

Content Management Features

Content management features include the following:

- Business Document Workflow Support

- Document Management Site Templates

- Integration with Microsoft Information Rights Management (IRM)

- Document Information Panel

- Document Action Bar

- Retention and Auditing Policies

- Records Repository

- E-mail Content as Records

- Legal Holds

- High-Fidelity Web Sites with Consistent Branding

- Navigation Controls

- Content Authoring

- Content Publishing and Deployment

- Slide Libraries

- WYSIWYG Web Content Editor. SharePoint 2010 includes Live Editing of text on the page and includes content controls and the Office 2010 Ribbon

- Site Variations

- Page Layouts

- Policies, Auditing, and Compliance

- Browser Support (covers XHTML browsers such as Firefox and Safari as well as Internet Explorer versions 7 and 8). Note that Internet Explorer 6 is not supported in SharePoint 2010.

- Social Media. Status integration with My Sites, My Network, and newsfeeds. Massive improvement to the Profile Area, covering Organization, Content, Tags, Notes, Memberships, and Colleagues. Includes a personal TAG Cloud.

Visit *http://msdn.microsoft.com/en-us/library/ee537015(v=office.14).aspx* to read *What's New: Workflow Enhancements* and learn more about how you can build rich workflows that can accommodate complex business scenarios.

Business Intelligence Features

Business intelligence features include the following:

- Integrated, Flexible Spreadsheet Publishing

- Ability to Share, Manage, and Control Spreadsheets

- Data Connection Libraries

- Web-Based Business Intelligence Using Excel Services

- Business Connectivity Services, which allows SharePoint 2010 to connect to sources of external data (also included in Office 2010)

- Business Data Catalog

- Business Data Web Parts

- Business Data Actions

- Integrated Business Intelligence Dashboards

- Report Center

- Key Performance Indicators

- Filter Web Parts

Platform Features

Platform features include the following:

- Alert Filtering

- Field Types

- Site Columns

- List Indexing

- Content Types

- Workflow

- Tree View

- RSS Feeds

- Recycle Bin

- Property Bags

- Web Services

- Alert Customization

- Event Receivers

- Feature Framework

- Solution Deployment Model

- Excel Spreadsheet Developer Reuse and Extensibility

- Major and Minor Version Tracking

- Folder-Level and Item-Level Access Controls

- Rights-Trimmed User Interface

- Subsite Promotion

- Consistent User Experience

- Virtual Server Security Policies

- Pluggable Authentication

- LDAP Pluggable Authentication Provider

- Common Search Technology and Infrastructure

- Backup/Restore Support for VSS (Volume Shadow Copy Service)

- Large-List and Cross-List Indexing Automatic Breadcrumb Bar

- Append-Only and Multivalue Lookup Fields

- Support for ASP.NET 2.0

- ASP.NET Master Pages

- Content Type Settings

- Folders in Lists

- Folder Metadata

- Cross-List Queries

- WSRP

- Change Logs

- Job Service

This is very important—don't just look at the SharePoint 2010 features, also look at the client applications used in the organization. This is a good place to start looking to see what project management tools are in use.

In the past with SharePoint implementation projects, Microsoft Project wasn't easy to integrate, so project managers had to collaborate with the client stakeholder and other teams using either Project Server or e-mail to move the project plan around. Additionally, a project plan on a SharePoint site could not be viewed graphically as one would do using Microsoft Project. One of the major points you need to make in terms of communicating the program schedule is that all companies run projects and if they are going to use SharePoint as their collaborative tool, they should review their current project management processes. For example, do they store their project management guidelines online? Are they accessible to staff? How do they manage projects centrally? Do they use shared project plans? And so on.

Most companies have a Project Management Office (PMO), which is a team responsible for project management or an individual whose role is the kingpin project manager. The tools that these individuals use should be examined.

One of the major features of SharePoint 2010 is the integration of Microsoft Project and SharePoint 2010. You now get full integration with SharePoint 2010 lists, and the interface is the same. Also, the team planner is integrated, the data grid is revamped, and much more.

> **Note**
>
> It can be very embarrassing if you demonstrate features of SharePoint 2010 in front of the client and are unable to provide solutions or voice alternatives when the client has a query or request. Additionally, it will be acutely embarrassing if you attempt to hype the features of SharePoint without fully understanding what the client wants, or more importantly, not educating the client about the benefits and features of SharePoint that would apply to the client's organization. Your reviews with the client add to acceptance and respect of your skills by the client, and helps the client feel comfortable that you as Project Manager can deliver. Do not be afraid to suggest methods where the current client's work processes could improve with the adoption of SharePoint. Also, do not be afraid to simply state you "do not know" or "SharePoint will not be able to do XYZ".

Engage the Right People

There are two types of client personnel you need to engage for performing the implementation of SharePoint 2010: business and technical. These are the key stakeholders and decision makers. The business client provides the vision. The technical client provides the infrastructure. They both have requirements. This is the same for nearly all product installations—they require technical and business input.

Later, you will discover that you need more than one person to implement SharePoint 2010 properly. To assist you, you need someone who deeply understands SharePoint 2010, and you need someone who can quickly come to grips with and understand the organization, as well as translate business requirements into technical requirements.

The technical client (also known as the *technical authority*) will be interested in the infrastructure side of SharePoint 2010, including the following topics:

- How responsive is the product?

- How is it going to reduce installation issues and make it easier to train the support team?

- How is it going to reduce the cost in the mid-term? For example, will more servers be needed as the requirement gets bigger? And how much does the software cost?

The business client will be interested in whether SharePoint 2010 will solve productivity, information, and management challenges concerning collaboration and sharing data. The issues this person will likely want to examine are the following:

- Can the users come to grips with SharePoint? Can they build their own sites, and then work and distribute their content easily?

- Can the users learn the product quickly and re-apply things they know from using the current tools in a SharePoint 2010 environment?

- Is SharePoint 2010 easy to use?

- Is SharePoint going to help automate work processes?

- Is SharePoint going to secure content?

- How do you control SharePoint 2010 (or at least be advised how to control it)?

As detailed in the section "Your First Steps" on page 15, your initial meetings with these two clients will help you understand the nature of their environment and, at the same time, get a feeling for their requirements.

Ask the Right Questions

In asking the right questions concerning what the client wants for the SharePoint 2010 implementation, you are setting the scope for the top-level part of project, refining the project plan, recording key user requirements, and scoping the infrastructure.

The kind of questions you ask are based on the client's organizational objectives, the content they carry, the applications they use, and how searching for content is carried out. You also need to look at how content is formatted and how information is structured.

This is further discussed in Chapter 11, "Making Sure SharePoint 2010 Meets User Requirements," to help you gauge and identify SharePoint 2010 features that can solve specific challenges.

How to Perform an Effective SharePoint 2010 Implementation

An effective SharePoint 2010 implementation has a quality plan, a project plan, a configuration plan, testing, validation, and scope details. All of these elements describe to the client (both business and technical) what the SharePoint 2010 implementation is and what has been agreed and signed off on by all parties addressed in the implementation plan.

The implementation plan has a number of facets, described in Chapter 3, "Content of Your SharePoint 2010 Plan."

In essence, all the relevant procedures associated with the SharePoint 2010 installation are known or adhered to. In addition, as the project manager, you need to sell SharePoint 2010, and to do that you need to do the following:

- Find SharePoint 2010 case studies.

- Identify the client's Microsoft licensing model.

- Engage with the client, carry out reviews of the organization, find out what the client wants to achieve with SharePoint, ascertain the technical infrastructure, find out how the client's users collaborate, find out how users work with Web content, and find out how users search for data. This is called "gathering user requirements."

- Plan your deployment carefully.

- Educate and demonstrate. This fosters client adoption.

Successful SharePoint 2010 implementations can be guaranteed to have quite a few of the following attributes:

- They have a good proposal.

- They start with a good work plan and assume minor changes will occur.

- They are structured into smaller projects for the timeframe and ensure that the scope of the project does not blow out of proportion.

- They make the SharePoint 2010 project sound like fun.

- They have a resourceful SharePoint 2010 architect.

- They strike a balance between planning and doing.

- They have contingency plans and plan for the worst case in performing critical tasks.

- The team members are clear about objectives and their terms of reference.

The SharePoint 2010 implementation realizes and addresses three areas of productivity:

- **Organizational Productivity**   Addresses process automation, information access, and roles

- **Personal and Team Productivity**   Addresses user enablement, user adoption, and ease of use

- **Infrastructure Productivity**   Addresses responsiveness, reduced complexity, and cost reduction

Negotiate an Appropriate Scope

When I say "scope" here, I am not talking about a SharePoint 2010 technical term. This book concentrates on the setting up of SharePoint 2010 from a business perspective; therefore, don't expect that the word "scope" is about searching scopes in the SharePoint 2010 Search Crawling feature!

A SharePoint 2010 project scope can be described as follows:

The work that has to be carried out in order to deliver SharePoint 2010, its services, and specified features and functions; it is the definition of what the project is to accomplish as well as the budget (time and money) that has been created to achieve the objectives.

Chapter 2

A good scope needs to be clear and concise. The project name is a good place to begin. Lack of planning in SharePoint 2010 often results in a failed implementation, and that lack of planning is often due to a poorly designed project scope.

An effective SharePoint 2010 project name that reads something like "Create a SharePoint 2010 environment to enhance collaborative working in Company XYZ" is much better than "SharePoint 2010 Environment Project." More concise is not always more clear. The aim of the SharePoint 2010 project name is to document the project so that everyone is aware of what is expected during the life of the project. It also helps provide a vision of where the project is headed and is the projection of your project mantra.

Here's the scenario: you get a requirement to provide SharePoint 2010 to a company, and you have just been appointed to be the SharePoint 2010 project manager. The client has already looked at the product, but they don't really know what they want. They are sure they want a branded My Site, an extranet, and an intranet, and they think they will want document management features from SharePoint 2010 Enterprise edition. When asked for the scope, the client states it is to "Build and deliver a SharePoint 2010 instance."

Clearly that is not a good scope. To correct this as project manager, you need to create that SharePoint 2010 project mantra and to get the client to review the scope. What is missing is the Quality Plan, which describes the how and why of the project. This is a direct output of the SharePoint 2010 project mantra.

There are three critical parts to quality planning that relate directly to the work you are expected to do, and these are contained in the Quality Plan that management will sign off on. The Quality Plan defines the product scope. For example, a product scope for Share-Point 2010 to the organization would be similar to the following statement:

A collaborative technology that enables people to easily create and manage their own Web sites.

> **Note**
> Creating an appropriate project scope ensures that the client understands what they are going to get and why they are using SharePoint 2010 to solve the myriad issues that have been stated. You should try to showcase successful SharePoint 2010 implementations and review Microsoft case studies as part of the project scope. You will find many examples at *http://www.microsoft.com/casestudies*.

Deciding What Not to Do Is As Important As Deciding What to Do

A famous quote regarding SharePoint 2010 is, "If you need to have something happen in SharePoint 2010, the answer is never 'No.' The question is, 'Do you have money to spend if you get to a No situation?'." Here's an example of how this observation might play out:

Company A wants to adopt a feature to enhance People Search in SharePoint so that when someone searches for an individual, the results display a small list of recent documents that person has created. The reason the company wants this particular search behavior is that it likes to have open access to documents created and to be transparent with regard to who has authored the documents. The company doesn't have any internal developers familiar with SharePoint, and the budget is tight. However, the client is adamant about having this feature in place.

This functionality isn't available out of the box. You must do some investigating to find out how best to implement this new feature. You should start by examining the company's technological resources to find out whether there's a way it can be done in house—of course, that's not possible in this case. So you need to move on to the second option: determine whether it's possible to bring in a developer.

But wait a minute.

By doing this, you are already passing the point of project planning!

Here's another example.

Company B has hired a SharePoint team to implement SharePoint 2010. That team has a connection to a third-party development company that will build numerous features for the product to meet a specific client requirement.

While building the tool, the development company adds additional features that are not required by the client. It did this because the team wanted to prove they could do it and go beyond client expectations. Unfortunately, in doing this, they created a bigger collection of user documentation to cover the unneeded features and the additional training and support requirements that go along with them.

This scenario is infamously known as *feature-scope creep*. It means one or more features not originally contemplated by the client have been added in. The preceding scenario is a combination of two types of feature-scope creep—customer-pleasing and gold-plating—

because there is a desire to please or impress the customer by adding product features beyond what was requested.

Avoid Biting Off More Than You Can Chew

The SharePoint 2010 feature set is so large that failing to carefully manage the scope can easily push you to your limits as a project manager. There are so many interesting things to do in SharePoint 2010 while working on a particular problem that it's easy to become distracted. As well, solutions you put in place in a SharePoint 2010 implementation might require you to work in maybe three or four areas of the platform. One can easily fall into the trap of discovering lots of interesting and fun things to do.

For example, suppose that as project manager you must provide the ability for information from the user directory to be available in SharePoint 2010. You think, "OK, that's an easy one. I'll focus on the User Profiles section of SharePoint 2010." Be careful—there's a lot going on in that area, more than just putting in some fancy user properties and working with user metadata. Before long, you'll find yourself falling into the following traps:

- Working extremely long hours

- Running into a brick wall because some customization is required

- Charging out for developers

These actions add increased costs to the project and increase project timeframe. And you might be tempted to justify this to the client as exceeding the scope. But remember, that the objective of the project manager is to deliver what the client wants on time and at the lowest possible cost. You can do this by keeping the following guidelines in mind:

- **Pace yourself**   Don't get stressed and don't overwork. Doing that will lead to fatigue, which doesn't make for an effective SharePoint 2010 evangelist!

- **If you are in trouble, renegotiate the deadline**   Tell the client what is going on. Ensure that they know what you need and why you need it. The client will understand.

- **You are not the god or goddess of your SharePoint 2010 implementation clan**   There are enormous areas to work with in SharePoint 2010. If you are in trouble, get help. Don't attempt to sort it out yourself because that might only increase the project timeframe. Don't gloss over an obstacle by believing that you will get to it later. If you do that, you are not even following a schedule. If you don't delegate tasks and manage them, it will just cause you more stress!

- **Regroup** This book describes procedures that ensure you schedule time to find out where you are while you are running your SharePoint 2010 project. A well-structured SharePoint 2010 has a *regroup day*, once per week. On this day, the project team takes a rest from implementation, and as such, you take a rest. Use this time to reassess the workload and adjust the schedule.

Renegotiate the Scope If Necessary

You might find that renegotiating the scope is required for the following reasons:

- You are in trouble because you have bitten off more than you can chew (as mentioned in the previous section).

- A particular client requirement, while possible to accomplish, might require purchasing a third-party product or developing a feature, which would push the implementation over budget.

- Similar to the preceding point,acheiving a particular client requirement might not be possible within the timeframe established for the product going live.

- Delivering a particular client requirement might introduce unwarranted risks into the implementation.

To give you a picture of how you might end up in one of these situations, let's look at an example that illustrates the final point in the list.

Client A has requested that the SharePoint 2010 implementation include a record to show views to sites, documents, lists, and any additions or deletions made. As a SharePoint 2010 practitioner, you suggest using either the SharePoint 2010 auditing feature or the analytics feature in SharePoint 2010 at the site level. The only problem is that the available hardware is a single server with a single SQL box without much hard disk space.

You explain to the client that the hardware might not be up to the challenge and that it might be necessary to take one or more of the following actions before the desired functionality can be implemented:

- The hardware must be sufficiently upgraded (which requires more money and more configuration time).

- A third-party product must be procured and connected to SharePoint 2010 at a later stage. (This doesn't directly affect immediate implementation of some functions, but it does introduce additional support issues, costs, and most likely implementing a separate product.)

Chapter 2

- Commit to the client request, but have the client agree to accept the risks to the hardware.

- Omit the feature or features that result in extra costs (time or money), and push those features into a category of items to be investigated at a later date.

What you have just done is carried out a quick evaluation and weighted the outcomes of each alternative. The key thing here is that the client is involved and has a say in which of the alternatives is satisfactory. This is an example of renegotiating the scope, and it should be done for every key aspect of the implementation plan.

Let's analyze a few other reasons you might need to renegotiate the project scope:

- **Hardware**   The existing hardware might be a reason to renegotiate scope if the SharePoint 2010 implementation is going to be a medium farm (more than one front-end server, application server, and attached to an SQL cluster) and you find that there is simply not enough capacity in the infrastructure (meaning not enough servers are available or the available servers are not up to the job).

- **People**   The proposal to install SharePoint 2010 includes managing the implementation going forward. If you find that the people assigned to the task are not capable of managing a SharePoint 2010 implementation, you need to ensure that the project scope addresses this shortcoming.

- **Budget**   Your project is underway. Your SharePoint 2010 implementation is taking shape. The farm is in place, and some development efforts are underway. The client indicates there is a change in the budget for the project. In this case, the scope must be re-evaluated to ensure that the project goals are aligned with the new budget.

Avoid Having to Whittle Your Scope Down to Nothing

The scope of your project to implement SharePoint 2010 is crucial. It states the agreement between you and the client.

The one, overriding scope we're discussing here is the one for implementing SharePoint 2010 according to the client's requirements; however, most projects have more than one scope because there are at least four stages to implementing SharePoint 2010:

- **Stage 1: Content Assessment and Architecture Review**   An assessment is conducted of the way the organization works with data and how individuals work together.

  ○ **Scope 1:** Develop a hierarchy that facilitates information management and solves information challenges.

- **Stage 2: SharePoint 2010 Site Development**   A basic SharePoint 2010 site structure is developed that provides a practical foundation to address the business and technology issues identified during the content assessment and architecture review.

  ○ **Scope 2:** Design a physical site framework and taxonomy, and build relevant SharePoint 2010 portal sites.

- **Stage 3: Portal Pilot**   SharePoint 2010 is installed; the solution is implemented and tested in the environment.

  ○ **Scope 3:** Provide training and awareness sessions to users and support teams.

- **Stage 4: The SharePoint 2010 portal is operational.**

  ○ **Scope 4:** Provide best practices for management and governance.

Even though there are scopes at every stage of this implementation, it is important to state clearly and without ambiguity the absolute lowest level of what you can achieve. For example, consider the scope of Stage 1 of a SharePoint 2010 implementation which is somewhat nebulous:

"Develop a hierarchy that facilitates information management and solves information challenges."

We need to examine that scope closely. The real meaning of that scope is the you're an investigation of the current work processes of the organization (that is, an understanding of how the client personnel communicate and collaborate with content). Based on understanding these processes, your stated scope identifies how SharePoint 2010 will be implemented to solve the client's information challenges.

For example, suppose that the client needs to get SharePoint 2010 up and running as quickly as possible. Because of the time constraints, the client suggests removing the Stage 1 scope. If this scope is removed, there is a serious risk that SharePoint 2010 will not be implemented around any well-planned design or in a way that aligns with any client work processes. Without this scope, the scopes for stages 2, 3, and 4 become either redundant or meaningless. Scope 2 (technically design and implement SharePoint 2010) would then have to be revisited because the processes of the client are unknown. If the client performs a large amount of Excel reporting and uses external services through SQL, and Scope 1 is ignored, how will you know that you should install Excel Services and investigate and implement Business Connectivity Services to enhance the use of SQL data connectivity?

Be careful not to heavily whittle down or eliminate your scopes. At the same time, ensure that the scopes you do put in place are fully understood by the client.

Your Best Project Tool Is Your Plan

Installing SharePoint 2010 requires a skilled and multifaceted technical team. From a business perspective, SharePoint requires careful implementation for a client new to content collaboration and sharing. It is therefore important that you have a plan that reflects all the aspects of the installation so that the client understands what is being done, when it is being done, who is doing it, and how much it costs.

There is little point in assuming there is a project plan when installing SharePoint 2010 and the client asks "Hey, how is the SharePoint 2010 installation going?"

And the reply is "No problem. It is all in my head."

Amazing as it might sound, I've seen that happen.

There's good project engineering and bad project engineering. Good project engineering leads to tangible progress. Bad project engineering hinders progress.

In the past, project managers have generally used e-mail as the top collaborative tool. So you were likely to hear conversations like the following:

"Where is that business case?"

"Check my e-mail."

"What about those project risks?"

"Ahh, let's check my e-mail."

"Can you give me your status report on the project, please?"

"No problem. Let me check my e-mail."

That approach can work, I suppose. However, if you are running a project team where information needs to be updated, collated, and reviewed by more than one person, that is not a great way to run your project. So ensure that you have the necessary tools available for proper communication. SharePoint 2010 is perfect for this because it enables you to centralize, share, and manage all aspects of your project. This functionality can be show-cased to your client as you work together on the project.

Remember that your SharePoint 2010 Project Plan defines the what, when, and why on the project. In Chapter 3, "Content of Your SharePoint Project Plan," I will describe the elements of your plan and how you can place your SharePoint 2010 Project Plan on an Implementation site, managing it using SharePoint 2010 features and functionality.

SharePoint 2010 provides you with tools that ensure your project can be managed effectively. SharePoint 2010 helps you accomplish this in the following ways:

- **By centralizing your project documents and project communication**   You can easily create document libraries to store key project items such as the Business Case, Project Quality Plans, Risk Management Lists, and Configuration Management Plans. In fact, every form and procedure in this book can be created as a list of information.

- **By integrating existing project management tools (for example, Project Professional 2010)**   SharePoint 2010 integrates with Project Professional 2010 so that working on a Work Breakdown Schedule (WBS) is easy.

> **Note**
> Project Professional 2010 is designed to assist project managers in developing plans, assigning resources to tasks, tracking progress, managing budgets and analyzing workloads. The application creates critical path schedules, although critical chain and event chain methodology third-party add-ons are available. Schedules can be resource leveled, and chains are visualized in a Gantt chart. Additionally, it can recognize different classes of users. These different classes of users can have differing access levels to projects, views, and other data. Custom objects such as calendars, views, tables, filters and fields are stored in an enterprise global which is shared by all users.

- **By providing tools to automate project management processes**   For example, you can create a Risk And Issues log and have automated alert processing for it. In this case, when a project member submits a risk it can be automatically e-mailed to the project manager for action and then routed as part of the Quality Plan document in a document library. Risk items in a SharePoint 2010 list can be connected to physical data in a document library.

- **By providing project reporting using dashboards**   SharePoint 2010 provides rich and detailed information by graphically reporting content information using built-in charts.

> **Note**
>
> A *dashboard* is an executive information system user interface that (similar to an automobile's dashboard) is designed to present information in an easy-to-read format. For example, SharePoint can obtain information from one or more applications that may be running, and from one or more remote sites on the Web and present it as though it all came from the same source on a SharePoint site. SharePoint can provide Business Intelligence Dashboards and Key Performance Indicators using internal data from lists, or from Excel Spread-sheets, Access, Visio, SQL Reporting Services, and much more. For more information, see this screencast: *http://channel9.msdn.com/shows/In+the+Office/Using-Microsoft-Office-SharePoint-Server-to-Create-BI-Dashboards-and-KPIs/.*

All of these tools improve team collaboration (which is the heart of SharePoint 2010). Later in this book, I'll show you the methods by which these tools can be used in your SharePoint 2010 one-stop shop.

Summary

The SharePoint 2010 project mantra is about knowing the product, knowing what your client vision is, knowing how the organization operates, and being enthusiastic and evangelistic in your approach to providing the platform. Your client feeds off this mantra, and from it you will both have a shared vision of how SharePoint 2010 will look, feel, and work in the organization.

A well-planned project includes an appropriate scope. This scope defines the implementation, and a good implementation comes from proper planning. Planning is the key element—I'll revisit the topic in more detail later in the book. For now, here are a few planning tips:

- Come up with an accurate and detailed plan (one that includes tasks and Gantt chart).

- Review your plan weekly. Use your Gantt chart to gauge your long-term progress.

- Revise and rewrite your plan on a weekly basis in the form of a to-do list.

- State your plan as a high-level WBS, and then group it into several tasks per grouped area.

- Use your to-do list to manage your week-to-week activities.

- Assess your progress weekly, even if only to measure what you haven't done.

CHAPTER 3

Content of Your SharePoint 2010 Project Plan

Before You Get Started

Y ou need to understand the concept of a SharePoint Implementation Plan. A SharePoint Quality Plan and SharePoint Project Plan make up a SharePoint Implementation Plan. The Quality Plan and Project Plan are separate documents, and this chapter will explain the contents of each and how they are connected. The combined output of these creates a SharePoint Implementation Plan. The Quality Plan details the *who* and *how* of a SharePoint 2010 implementation. The Project Plan details the *what* and *when*. You cannot have a Project Plan without a Quality Plan, because the Quality Plan describes, at the very least, the people who will be carrying out the project tasks detailed in the Project Plan.

The project manager must be aware of the procedures that are included in the life cycle of a SharePoint 2010 implementation project and of the forms that need to be collated and managed. Figure 3-1 shows the procedures and how they are connected.

This chapter concentrates on the production of the various plans and the administrative activities related to those plans. By the end of this chapter, you should have a thorough understanding of the content of a SharePoint 2010 Implementation Plan and the procedures, forms, and tools required to support it.

To support your adventure through these procedures, you need to create two key forms: the Project Startup Checklist and the Project Closure Checklist. Figure 3-2 illustrates the Project Startup Checklist.

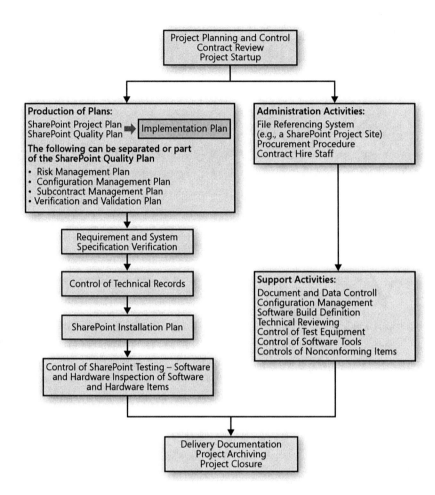

Figure 3-1 SharePoint 2010 Project planning and control life cycle.

SharePoint Project Startup Checklist

SharePoint Project Title				Project Number

Considerations	Y	N	N/A	Reference
Review Contract Requirements				
Have the commercial aspects been addressed?				
Have the technical aspects been addressed?				
Have the quality aspects been addressed?				
Has the client acknowledged the contract receipt?				
Is the client familiar with the contract requirements?				
Appointment of Staff				
Have the "technical authority" individual(s) been identified?				
Has the Project Team been recruited?				
Have the "Terms of Reference" been generated for the project team?				
Have the approval and authorization authorities been identified?				
Have the resource requirements been identified?				
Establish Project Interfaces				
Have the commercial and purchasing procedures been identified?				
Are the computer facilities for the project team established?				
Has the project documentation policy been created?				
Has the filing policy (document and data control) been established?				
Produce Plans				
Has the SharePoint Quality plan been produced?				
Has the SharePoint Project plan been produced?				
Has the Subcontractor Management plan been produced?				
Has the Risk Management plan been produced?				
Has the Configuration Management plan been produced?				
Verify and Validate				
Have technical reviews and internal testing plans been identified?				
Are the subcontractor SharePoint deliverables acceptable?				
Has the client accepted the SharePoint deliverables?				

Project Manager Name				Date

Figure 3-2 Project Startup Checklist.

As you can see, each section of this checklist relates to the plan you are drawing up and is used as a guide to ensure you are ready to carry out the work. The checklist also informs the client what pieces of work have been done, have not been done, and do not need to be done. The Project Closure Checklist will be detailed in Chapter 15, "SharePoint 2010 Is Implemented, Now What?"

Create the SharePoint 2010 Quality Plan

The SharePoint 2010 Project Plan (which we will examine in detail in the section "Introducing the SharePoint Project Plan," on page 51) should ensure that the contractual requirements of the project are completely fulfilled. On a large project, a project plan might be produced for each identified subsystem that is part of the overall product.

The SharePoint 2010 Project Plan complements the SharePoint 2010 Quality Plan and duplication of information or instructions from one plan to the other should be avoided. In simple terms, the SharePoint 2010 Project Plan details the what, why, where, and when aspects. The Quality Plan determines the project policies and the aspects of who and how.

During your initial meetings with the client, you should identify the client's requirements. These requirements are then used to produce the SharePoint 2010 Quality Plan. This plan details the business requirements and specifies how the project will deliver these requirements.

Here's a real-life example of the importance of a Quality Plan. I was called to fix a Share-Point implementation project where the project manager (who was no longer with the company) decided that the only thing required was a couple of technicians, a list of instructions on how to install SharePoint, and someone to sign off on the installation. Because no scoping of the project was done to find out how SharePoint should be used, how it would grow with the organization, how it should be controlled, or what should be done if there were problems in meeting future client requirements, the SharePoint delivery failed to perform as the client felt it should and the users did not accept it. They blamed SharePoint for virtually every problem because it was an easy target—no one liked it. I was successful in fixing the implementation, but it was a slow and painful process for the organization. The users had to re-engage with SharePoint, but through the process of gathering user requirements, they felt more empowered. Stressing the need for a Quality Plan to bolster a carefully defined Project Plan that includes design tasks (for example, gathering user requirements) is key to a successful SharePoint implementation. The SharePoint 2010 Quality Plan includes the following:

- Project organization and responsibilities

- Risk management

- Subcontract management

- Design and development life cycle

- Configuration management

- Verification and validation plans

- Acceptance and delivery

You might be thinking, "OK, when I install SharePoint 2010, I can do all of that at the same time or ignore it." If you choose to proceed this way, you will be responsible for signing off on all the implementation to the client's satisfaction, or you will be assuming the client does not need to be satisfied. I think that's a mistake. You would be very unlucky if you were pushed to provide a companywide SharePoint 2010 solution and there's no team currently looking after the technology and no person who knows about it and how it was designed in the first place. Things are not going to go very well if you adopt that method!

For example, an exasperated client once called me to help them properly engage with a SharePoint installation. The installation was carried out by a SharePoint consultant who delivered SharePoint to the company and then left the company without handing over SharePoint to the company technical team. The technical team members had no training in SharePoint and were very busy managing other technologies. Users were accessing the SharePoint installation but were concerned about the lack of support. A Quality Plan defines who will look after SharePoint and who will deliver it, and the Project Plan defines when it will take place and who takes control of SharePoint in terms of support, including training.

To build a SharePoint 2010 Quality Plan, you need to use the Project Startup Checklist (see Figure 3-2). You can find the Quality Plan on the checklist in the section "Produce Plans." Once a Quality Plan draft is completed, you should indicate a Y (for "yes") in the Y column and give an identifier so that people can locate the Quality Plan in the reference column. So continuing on from the headings given earlier, you would be able to create a Quality Plan.

Project Organization and Responsibilities

The SharePoint 2010 Quality Plan needs to be clearly defined with the help of the business stakeholders. To do this, you need to delineate the relevant areas of the business—first, you identify who the key stakeholders are, and then identify who on the project team needs to interface with the technical and business teams that will be supporting the product.

Technical teams include the people who administer SharePoint and manage the servers that provide SharePoint services. Business teams are the people who support SharePoint team sites and the content on those sites. These business and technical teams have the responsibilities shown in the checklist. For example, one technical team could be called the *SQL Database Team*. In this case, one of the specific responsibilities the team has related to the SharePoint implementation is looking after the SharePoint SQL databases. Likewise, business teams also have responsibilities. For example, you might have a business team responsible for testing a SharePoint site or a SharePoint feature. Responsibilities create the objectives (for example, in order for the business team to test SharePoint, team members need SharePoint training). You should make a point of recording the responsibilities and objectives of each member in the project organization. To formulate a work schedule, you need to ensure that you know who is responsible for what in the business. For SharePoint 2010, there are two camps you must deal with. The first camp includes personnel who look after and support the technical infrastructure—for example, Active Directory, Microsoft SQL Server, Microsoft Exchange, the firewall and security elements, and so on. This is the *technical camp*. Then there is the *business camp*. The people in the business camp will shape your SharePoint 2010 environment; they will tell you what needs to be in the environment, how it will function, who will own the implementation, who will test it, and so on.

First let's make a list of groups within those two camps, and then list the name of the person accountable for a particular service in one of the groups, as well as their contact details. This is the first step toward forming the Project Startup Checklist.

Table 3-1 is an example of a list you can compile if you need to ascertain who the stakeholders are and who the business and technical leads are. You can also include (as I have done) key people who have a stake in the back-end connectivity to SharePoint 2010 or people who are good contacts to have. Note that you need to update this list regularly and ensure that all parties listed know who is on this list. Once this list is created, you need to use it in your Project Plan Work Breakdown Structure (which is where you list the tasks and who should be assigned those tasks).

Table 3-1 Project Title: SharePoint 2010 Implementation Project XYZ

Name	Job Title	Responsibilities
Walter Harp	Head of Company	Stakeholder
Kim Akers	Communications	Stakeholder
David Pelton	Technical Manager	Decision Maker
Charlie Herb	Business Manager	Decision Maker
Katie Jordan	SQL Lead	Database
Kevin Kelly	AD Lead	Active Directory
Jerry Orman	Messaging Lead	Exchange
Howard Gonzalez	Infrastructure Lead	Servers

Once you have identified who is responsible for what in the company, it is time to start involving your own team (meaning yourself, the architect, the business analyst, and others). The Project Startup Checklist refers to your team-building efforts as the "Appointment of Project Staff." This information is used to construct the Project Responsibilities column shown in Table 3-1.

Note that you do not need to list everyone on the technical team because it's the responsibility of the technical manager, as the decision maker, to identify who they are. For SharePoint 2010, you must know who is currently responsible for the infrastructure (including security), messaging, user data store, and database. And because we are talking about SharePoint 2010, the infrastructure includes technologies such as SQL Server, Exchange Server, Active Directory, and Forefront TMG.

After this exercise, your team list could look like Table 3-2.

Table 3-2 Project Title: SharePoint 2010 Implementation Project XYZ

Name	Job Title	Responsibilities
Walter Harp	Head of Company	Stakeholder
Kim Akers	Communications	Stakeholder
David Pelton	Technical Manager	Decision Maker
Charlie Herb	Business Manager	Decision Maker
Katie Jordan	SQL Lead	Database
Kevin Kelly	AD Lead	Active Directory
Jerry Orman	Messaging Lead	Exchange
Howard Gonzalez	Infrastructure Lead	Servers
Your Name	Project Manager	Project Team
Holly Dickson	SharePoint 2010 Architect	Project Team

Chapter 3

Risk Management

You need to systematically identify and assess the potential risks to the project. By this, I mean risks to the entire project, not to some internal and technical component of Share-Point 2010 (which is covered in the section "Configuration Management," on page 48). Risks to the implementation of the project are not the same as risks related to SharePoint Governance. For example, a lack of content audit compliancy or inadequate levels of SharePoint content access are borne out of a lack of SharePoint Governance. Methods ensuring structured SharePoint Governance are discussed in detail in Chapter 9, "SharePoint Governance."

As you might recall from the project mantra mentioned in Chapter 2, the client has a *vision* of the SharePoint 2010 implementation as benefitting the organization by providing a boost in *productivity*. If there is a risk that any of the following client benefits cannot be attained, it must be communicated to everyone in the list of stakeholders (listed in the section "Project Organization and Responsibilities" on page 42).

- **Operational Productivity** Addresses process automation, information access, and roles. This is a client-productivity goal—individuals in the organization should be able to work more efficiently using SharePoint 2010.

  Example: Individuals intend to automate several activities concerning document retention and expiration. They want to be able to control access to documents and set up permissions to access relevant documents. This is a key objective of the organization using SharePoint 2010. Without this in place, there is a serious risk to the effectiveness of the platform and its usefulness.

- **Personal and Team Productivity** Addresses user enablement, user adoption, and ease of use. This is a client-productivity goal—individuals in the organization should be able to quickly understand how to use SharePoint in meeting their information objectives.

  Example: Users have never seen SharePoint 2010. If the users are not trained in the platform, there is a serious risk that they will not be able to easily manage their electronic data or sites holding that data.

- **Infrastructure Productivity** Addresses responsiveness, reduced complexity, and reduced Total Cost of Ownership (TCO). This is a client and technical authority productivity goal. SharePoint as a platform should be responsive and resilient, and it should reduce TCO—for example, reduce hardware and software (licensing) costs.

  Example: The client expects a high level of performance concerning the SharePoint infrastructure—for example, the client expects the percentage of users who can be active on SharePoint is on target—as well as concurrency, and they expect that Share-Point 2010 can handle an agreed-upon user load. If SharePoint does not perform to the agreed-upon target, there is a question as to how effective the solution will be to the organization.

In any organization where SharePoint 2010 is implemented, you need to adopt a risk management process, and a document stating that the process should be referenced in the "Risk Management" section of the Quality Plan.

A risk management procedure for SharePoint 2010 is available at *http://spsrisk.geoffevelyn.com.*

The section of the SharePoint 2010 Quality Plan titled "Risk Management" details the top-level risks and what strategy will be taken to mitigate these risks.

Subcontract Management

At some point in the implementation of SharePoint 2010, you might require third-party aid. For example, you might want to bring in a developer team to customize SharePoint 2010, or you might need to provide a third-party feature for backup tasks, restore functions, and so forth.

Before going down this route, you need to ensure that there is a need to bring in a party outside of the selected project team. Don't get caught in the syndrome known as "developing beyond SharePoint 2010." In any uncontrolled development, whether software or hardware, falling prey to such a syndrome can have a serious negative impact on the productivity of the platform, resulting in SharePoint 2010 implementation pain to the client.

The topic of SharePoint 2010 subcontracts is normally raised when it is considered, for whatever reasons, more effective to place discrete packages of work relating to an existing SharePoint 2010 environment in the hands of a company outside of the organization. The Share-Point 2010 Quality Plan needs to state that it will or will not advocate the use of these services as part of the implementation. If the service is required, this section of the Quality Plan needs to state the nature of the engagement with the subcontracts and specify that the project manager will follow organizational principles and rules governing the hire of such contracts.

You'll find a blog article that discusses a Subcontract Management procedure that can be applied to SharePoint at *http://spssubcontract.geoffevelyn.com.*

Design and Development Life Cycle

A number of factors can discourage the design and development of a SharePoint 2010 implementation: it costs money, it consumes the time of the most highly skilled people, the time spent in producing the plan can delay the start of using it, the life cycle could cause inflexibility in the implementation approach, and estimation of the life cycle is difficult. These objections should not detract from the importance of proper design and development.

The requirement for SharePoint could be as simple as this:

The installation of a SharePoint 2010 environment, which can be accessed via the Internet by a company worker.

According to this statement, the basic design delivers a SharePoint 2010 extranet. To complete the design and development, you have to review security features of SharePoint 2010, and you need advice from the Information Security team in the organization regarding Internet access policies.

Further investigation *is always required* to document and provide *a detailed* design.

The detailed design of the SharePoint platform would not go into the SharePoint 2010. The SharePoint 2010 Quality Plan merely lists the various design aspects the client requires as these become work schedules in the Project Plan. Design and development of SharePoint 2010 is a two-stage process. First, you need to detail the client aspirations using the three productivity statements: Operational Productivity, Personal and Team Productivity, and Infrastructure Productivity. These are described in the section "Risk Management," on page 44. You can map these statements to the following questions put to the client, and complete the "Design and Development" section of the Quality Plan:

- Collaboration Questions (Operational Productivity)

    - What kind of data do you produce?

    - Do you want users to create their own sites?

    - Do you have any geographical regions or any regions overseas?

    - Are there any governance concerns, such as branding or storage?

- Technical Questions (Infrastructure Productivity)

    - Where are your data centers? How are they connected? Are they in house, separated geographically, or by building?

    - Is there a Change Management process that ensures standardised methods and procedures are used to handle modifications to hardware and software?

    - Is there a Procurement process concerning the buying of hardware and software? Who is responsible for the process in the organization?

    - Is there an Installation process concerning the installation of software, hotfixes, or patches? Who is responsible for that process in the organization?

    - Where is data backed up to? Who is responsible for the backups, and what level of backup are required?

- Is there a need for a developer environment so that programmers can extend and customize the SharePoint environment?

- Is there a closed environment where SharePoint can be set up for test purposes?

- Content Questions (Personal and Team Productivity)

  - What Web content do you have?

  - How do you manage publishing online content?

  - Who are the key content managers (note this is needed for the user requirement gathering)?

- Search Questions

  - What do you want to include in the search?

  - How big is the content you want to search?

  - Who can access these locations?

  - What should be excluded?

  - What kind of data should be crawled?

> **Note**
>
> When gathering answers to the above questions, the client may need to draw on the expertise of someone who would have knowledge in specific areas. For example, the technical questions are best answered by an individual assigned by the client known as the **Technical Authority**. As a project manager, you may require the skills of a SharePoint Architect to ensure you get quality answers at a technical level. Further investigations covering the Search, Content and Collaborative question areas can be carried out by a combination of your Business Analysts and Information Analysts. (See Chapter 5, "Building Your SharePoint Team," for more information on the Technical Authority, Business Analysts and Information Analysts.)

The second stage of design and development requires the gathering of detailed user requirements and technical requirements. The process for carrying this out is covered in the Chapter 11, "Making Sure SharePoint 2010 Meets User Requirements" and Chapter 12, "Producing the System Specification."

The "Design and Development" section of the SharePoint 2010 Quality Plan, therefore, requires the following:

- A statement concerning what kind of SharePoint platform is needed

- A paragraph describing the high-level design options

- A paragraph describing the references to the user and technical requirements

> **Note**
> Make sure that you include a reference to the "User Requirements and System Specification" in the "Design and Development" section of your SharePoint 2010 Quality Plan.

Configuration Management

Configuration management for SharePoint is a process that includes the detailed recording and updating of information that describes the hardware and software that make up the organization's SharePoint platform. Configuration management enables you to record information concerning versions and updates that have been applied.

The "Configuration Management" section in your SharePoint Quality Plan should briefly describe the nature of the configuration management system your organization uses and who will bear the responsibility of updating the system. (Typically, this is a specifically assigned individual, but it can also be assigned to each member of the project team. However, this means training them on how to use the configuration management system!) If there is a process, policy, or procedure regarding configuration management, it needs to be referenced.

Configuration management is crucial because it allows, for example, a SharePoint administrator to find out what is currently installed on a particular SharePoint server or what version of a third-party application is installed.

This topic is so important that an entire chapter has been dedicated to it. (See Chapter 10, "SharePoint 2010 Configuration Management.")

What kind of information should be captured in configuration management?

- Makeup of the infrastructure (for example, farm topology, server physical nature, Windows operating system, and connected systems).

- Software and hardware assets (SharePoint 2010 version, connected systems versions— for example, location of binaries, hardware details, serial numbers, MAC addresses, service accounts, and so forth).

- Modification and procurement (including details about alterations to the hardware or software and any information concerning how or where they were obtained). For example, in SharePoint 2010, it includes details about the specific configuration carried out.

- Tracking and audit (including details concerning installation, alteration, and who carried out the installation or alteration).

In order to assure standardization, configuration management involves controlling the specifications, drawings, software, and the related documentation that define the functional and physical characteristics of SharePoint 2010 down to the lowest level. Configuration management provides a documented, traceable history, including any modifications or variants. You absolutely must have configuration history for SharePoint 2010.

Some configuration management systems are connected to a change management or service desk system. These are systems that allow people to record requests and incidents and raise requests for changing hardware, software, or a setting in an production environment. For example, if any modification of the platform is required, an individual (or nominated person) raises a service or change request to ensure the work went through the correct approval and other processes before being done.

Collection of information that needs to be recorded in your configuration management system is a continual process, and the information is not recorded in the SharePoint 2010 Quality Plan's "Configuration Management" section. Only the details about the location of the relevant policy, who is responsible for configuration management, and referred documentation that describes the configuration management plan, policy, or procedure is needed.

Verification and Validation Plans

To fulfill the client requirements, you would ensure, of course, that there is an agreement on what constitutes a completed SharePoint 2010 implementation. To do this, you need to prepare a Verification and Validation (known as V&V) plan. In this plan, you might be required to provide specific acceptance tests to ensure that SharePoint 2010 meets the client's requirements. (This can include, for example, not only the client's acceptance of the physical environment, but also items such as branding, functionality, resiliency, and so forth.) These acceptance tests can be considered the final stage of validation and require careful planning.

The SharePoint 2010 implementation should be subject to V&V activities to confirm that the logical planning put in place matches the physical environment. This is carried out at the server level and then at the component level, ending with being applied at the Share-Point 2010 application level. The scale of the V&V activities should be appropriate for the size of the SharePoint 2010 installation and the nature of the installation. V&V activities must be planned, documented, and systematically managed in accordance with contract requirements. The V&V activities are all listed within the V&V plan. These activities must be conducted at discrete stages of the project and the following information recorded:

- Acceptance testing of the product

- Third-party products to be added to the SharePoint 2010 environment

- Internally developed tools to be added to the SharePoint 2010 environment

- Modifications that will affect the SharePoint 2010 environment

- Impacts to the disaster recovery or business continuity aspects of SharePoint 2010

The Acceptance and Delivery section in the SharePoint 2010 Quality Plan references the V&V plan and its location.

Acceptance and Delivery

The "Acceptance and Delivery" section of the SharePoint 2010 Quality Plan states who is going to be responsible for signing off on the project as completed, and it includes a statement of what constitutes a successful SharePoint 2010 implementation based on the project scope. Additionally, it also states how SharePoint 2010 will be handed over to the client. You can't simply say, "Hey, I've installed SharePoint 2010 on your servers. Now I'll leave you to it. Let me know if it works."

You must ensure that SharePoint 2010 has been fully tested (a process known as acceptance testing), from its lowest level (accessing SharePoint 2010) to the various advanced features that have been deployed. In Chapter 14, "Releasing SharePoint 2010 to the Client," I cover the procedures that make up SharePoint 2010 testing, how to best carry out the procedures, and how to get the client to correctly sign off on the project's completion.

Introducing the SharePoint Project Plan

This chapter gives guidance on developing the content of the SharePoint 2010 Project Plan. Your Project Plan is a document that should contain the following sections:

- Project Overview

- Milestones and Deliverables

- External Dependencies

- Assumptions and Restrictions

- Work Breakdown Structure

- Program Schedule

- Resource Requirements

- Project Reporting

For every SharePoint 2010 implementation, each topic in the preceding list should be addressed, although the size and nature of the project will determine the level of detail in each section.

> **Note**
> The use of Microsoft Project Professional 2010 is recommended to support various sections of the Project Plan. This tool is particularly relevant on larger projects because schedules are subject to a continual change, review, and update process, which can be a time-consuming and costly task. The use of a SharePoint 2010 site to hold the Project Plan and related material is vital.

Project Overview

By the time you get around to writing the Project Overview section of the Project Plan, you will have built most of your SharePoint 2010 Quality Plan, if not all of it. Recall that the SharePoint 2010 Project Plan defines the what, why, where, and when aspects of the implementation.

Before we continue, I should remind you that your SharePoint 2010 Project Plan and SharePoint 2010 Quality Plan are separate but linked documents. They are devised as separate documents so that the focus of how and why (SharePoint 2010 Quality Plan) are separated from the concerns of what, when, where, and who (SharePoint 2010 Project Plan). For example, in the Project Plan you would have a task called Plan Server Configuration for SharePoint 2010. The Plan Server Configuration task states the what; the date it is to take place is when; the individual assigned to the task is who. Further notes relevant to the task would even specify in some cases where the task was to take place.

After creating the Plan Server Configuration task, you need to define the subtasks. You then need to determine the normal load on the servers from roles and usage patterns; estimate the index size; find out the number of documents stored and document the store size, growth rate, peak load, caching, and any load balancing required; determine the need for growth; determine a future scale-out approach; and then draw the system architecture.

Should you really put that in a SharePoint 2010 Quality Document for the client to read? No, you should not, because the client is unlikely to read it and that kind of information is likely to blur the client vision defined in the document. Neither is the technology team likely to read the business data. However, both teams will read it if you structure each plan as a separate document and have them reference one another. The result is that in the Project Plans you do not indicate who will be doing the work; you do this in the Quality Plan. Likewise, you don't say what tasks will take place in the Quality Plan; you do this in the Project Plan.

The first section of the SharePoint 2010 Project Plan should be a brief overview that includes the following items:

- The SharePoint 2010 project title and the client name (and, if applicable job number, the contract number)

- A brief description of the overall task of the project, giving an outline of the system, hardware, and providing relevant background detail where appropriate

- An overview of major milestones and deliverables

- Major issues (for example, high-risk tasks or tight timeframes and so forth)

- Major subcontractors, which you can get by referring back to the "Project Organization" section in the SharePoint 2010 Quality Plan

- Team arrangements

- Client dependencies

- The scope of the plan in relation to the whole project (high-level or low-level). For example, the SharePoint Implementation Plan might be part of a program. The organization might be going for a full technology refresh program, such as upgrading desktops and software. SharePoint is simply part of this program. Therefore, the scope needs to reflect that the plan is a lower level plan. Another example is that you might have to use a third party who provides a project plan to deliver SharePoint training as part of the implementation. The project plan for the SharePoint training is therefore a lower level plan of the project to implement SharePoint. The hierarchical structure of the project planning documentation, which you should provide so that all associated plans can be identified.

Although the Project Plan might appear to overlap with parts of other documents, it is useful for giving participants a brief description of the work involved, providing background information, listing major events and issues involved, and providing the reader with some appreciation of the detail that is shown later.

Before moving on, note that the preceding list sets out the project in terms of what has been included in the SharePoint 2010 Quality Plan, along with the following:

- A buying vision from the client. This vision statement should indicate that the budget has been established and mitigation statements have been drafted to cover possible required alterations to the budget. Any alteration to the budget changes the Share-Point 2010 implementation scope.

- Affirmation that the client is willing to explore SharePoint 2010. The client's attitude should not just be, "Hey, let's put up a SharePoint 2010 site, build some document libraries, and we are done." The client needs to have a deeper understanding of SharePoint 2010. That knowledge will allow the client to explore various areas of the product to solve information and management challenges that arise.

> **Note**
> There are many ways of getting the client to better understand SharePoint 2010. For instance, provide examples of successful implementations, describe the product, demonstrate SharePoint 2010 sites and features, or walk personnel from various parts of the company's organizational structure through a topology exercise. What's important is that the client gets to understand the product.

This topic is also covered in Chapter 11, "Making Sure SharePoint 2010 Meets User Requirements."

- Know the client and the respective decision makers. Identify the organizational "chain of command"; find out who the business unit leaders are so that you can ensure you get decisions agreed and supported by the client.

- Come to a clear agreement on the timeframe of the SharePoint implementation, and the scope. What is the SharePoint implementation going to deliver? When someone says, "Give me SharePoint 2010, please," I ask two questions: "What is going to be in it?" and "When would you like it?" I never ask, "How much money do you have?"

  You'll find a blog article that discusses the importance of Schedule, Timeframe, and Budgets at *http:// spsscopeschedule.geoffevelyn.com.*

- SharePoint 2010 is a good fit against the current client tools being used in the organization. If SharePoint is the only product required, how well will it interface with the current tools being used by the users?

Milestones and Deliverables

External milestones might be dictated by the client—for example, a fixed date for a particular deliverable. External milestones that are related to payments for the completion of certain stages of the project should have a clear definition of the precise requirements necessary before the payment will be made. This level of detail provides visibility to all staff and the client of their respective responsibilities for meeting the milestones. Tangible internal deliverables should also be specified so that there is no doubt that a particular milestone has been reached.

An unambiguous statement of each deliverable will clarify the contractual requirements. If the client has to authorize the Project Plan, he or she will have no doubt as to what the output of the project will be. Project members will also understand the output from the project, and this will put into context the tasks required to achieve this output.

A statement of all deliverables expected from any subcontractors must also be included in this section, and it must be done so in the same unambiguous manner, with the text taken from the subcontractor's own Project Plan!

When setting the milestone dates, ensure that the agreed timeframe has been included in the estimates of work leading to the milestone. Client plans will be based on these milestone dates, so you must aim to complete every one successfully by the indicated dates to avoid embarrassment!

There are four phases to a SharePoint 2010 Project Plan (Client Vision, Plan, Build, and Operate):

- **Client Vision**   This phase includes the client evaluation of SharePoint 2010 features, evaluation of corporate objectives, client needs (productivity goals), cost/benefit analysis, project scope (lab environments, pilot, geographical deployment, coexistence), confirmation of major milestones, funding, and sponsorship. This requires using your

SharePoint project mantra. (For more information, see Chapter 2, "SharePoint 2010 Project Mantra.")

- **Plan**   This phase includes team building, technical investigations, test labs, security, performance, governance, and so forth.

- **Build**   This phase includes pilot and production platforms (from test labs conversion to user acceptance, or UAT). This is carried out using the configuration management process to ensure the steps carried out to deploy are recorded and managed.

    See Chapter 14 for more information on UAT.

- **Operate**   This final phase marks the completion of deploying SharePoint. Here, the SharePoint project is reviewed as part of a closure process. Maintenance, establishing governance, and ensuring resources match the implementation is also completed here. Once this phase is finished, SharePoint can be handed over to the client as successfully implemented, and the SharePoint environments can be placed into the "Business As Usual" category.

Each of these phases has at least one deliverable; therefore, you need to produce a statement concerning each one.

External Dependencies

External tasks that the project will rely on to be completed (and completed on time) are recorded in the Project Plan; and the Project Manager is responsible for ensuring this takes place. Listing these items helps the client and internal management appreciate their respective responsibilities and the possible consequences if their particular dependency target date is not met. You should record the dependencies at the detailed planning stage. As part of this list, you should include the risk factor of dependencies not being met, the possible outcome of the external tasks, and what actions might be taken.

External tasks are those that are not controlled directly by the project manager. For example, they might be tasks that are under the control of a subcontracted company or an internal interfacing team. For example, consider the provision of service accounts in SharePoint. These accounts are used to ensure accountability of certain features in SharePoint. Certain services, such as User Profile Services in SharePoint, require separate service accounts. These accounts are created by interfacing teams that are not under the control of the project manager. So, if there was a task called "Configure User Profile Services," there would be an external dependency called "Create Associated Service Accounts." Okay, that's a much more detailed area.

Here's another example. A subcontracted company is made responsible for providing SharePoint training. There is also a task in the Project Plan called "Launch Production

SharePoint Site." The client has requested that this task requires that the users can operate the relevant site. This means the users need to be trained before using the new production SharePoint site, and they will need to be trained by the subcontractor. Therefore, the Launch Production SharePoint Site task has an external dependency called "Train Users" that is the responsibility of the subcontractor.

Timeframes must be allowed for client authorization of project documentation. As you saw in this chapter, there are already several sets of documentation that require creation, and the last phase of the project (Operate) requires review and sign-off by the client (for example, Quality Plan, Project Plan, User Requirements, System Specification, and so on). Typical examples of external dependencies for SharePoint 2010 include:

- Server procurement process

- Communication Room availability (as well as building facilities availability)

- Disaster-recovery planning (including geographical and time-difference factors)

- Security constraints (for example, access to data centers, access to the client building, access to resources for the project team—for example, desktops, laptops, or any equipment provided by the client)

- Third-party software lead time and installation

Assumptions and Restrictions

No plan can be produced without some basic assumptions being made or some restrictions being imposed. This section details typical assumptions and restrictions. In the Project Plan, you should provide to both management and staff visibility of factors that have an impact on the project's ability to meet customer requirements. The client must agree to the assumptions on which the program is based by authorizing the Project Plan in advance of its execution.

Figure 3-3 shows what these assumptions might look like in a SharePoint 2010 Project Plan.

Assumptions and restrictions are likely to cover technical and management aspects of the project and can also include factors about methodologies used. Any subsequent planning might be seriously affected if these two factors are not recorded accurately. A complete list should be generated and kept up to date when the Project Plan is revised. If any of these assumptions or restrictions becomes invalid, the Project Plan can be re-assessed at a later date.

If the significant factors are recorded, there is less chance of staff being pressured into accepting an ill-advised change. Another important assumption to be documented is the resource profile and the anticipated level of skill or security upon which the plan is being based.

No.	Assumption	Validated By	Status	Comments
1	The Portal site will be available to all users in the company	Kim Akers	Confirmed	Completed by Intranet team
2	Development resources will be available at start of project to provide support	David Pelton	Open	Need to confirm number and cost of resources
3	Content will auto-populate Stage environment on a daily basis	Charlie Herb	Open	Need to complete validation by SharePoint project team

Figure 3-3 SharePoint 2010 Project Plan table of assumptions.

Work Breakdown Structure

A Work Breakdown Structure (WBS) is a key entity of a SharePoint Project Plan. It is a separate document and is referenced by the SharePoint Project Plan. The WBS describes the project activities in a top-down manner; it has a structured format in which groups of related tasks are broken down into levels of increasing detail, each with unique identifiers. Each task identified in the WBS should have a defined output or milestone that is related to a project deliverable. These milestones allow progress on the project to be monitored against clearly defined goals.

Major tasks, leading to a milestone, must be fully defined so that all the activities can be identified and the resources required planned for in the project schedule. Sufficient information should be contained in each description so that the project manager can write an appropriate instruction for completion of that task. Each task should be capable of being subjected to the following analysis:

- Whether the entry conditions are fully definable

- Whether the activities required are fully definable or defined

- Whether the validation necessary to confirm that the task has been completed satis-factorily exists

- Whether the deliverable from the task is clearly identifiable

Each major task should be as autonomous as possible because the absence of interrelating dependencies significantly eases the management of the work.

After the WBS has been generated, a program schedule can be created. The program schedule is a list of key WBS headers.

Consider this example. You need to detail technical requirements for SharePoint. To do this, you have to carry out several tasks leading to documenting those requirements and achieving sign off. Therefore, detailing technical requirements for SharePoint 2010 becomes a WBS header, while the tasks required to achieve that task are subtasks. All of these sub-tasks make up a WBS called "Detail Technical Requirements," and all WBS header tasks col-lectively make up the WBS for the entire SharePoint implementation, comprised of three phases.

Each major task on the WBS should be assigned to a sole responsible person identified on the project organization chart. This chart and the project staff responsibilities should be detailed in (or referenced from) the SharePoint 2010 Quality Plan, in the "Project Organiza-tion and Responsibilities" section.

A referencing scheme should be adopted for the WBS to make it easier to read. This refer-encing scheme should align with the headers in the SharePoint 2010 Quality Plan.

The WBS details the tasks of the four phases, and each phase is made up of a list of tasks ending in a milestone. The phases are Client Vision, Plan, Build, and Operate. The Client Vision phase is encompassed into your SharePoint Quality Plan and the SharePoint Proj-ect Plan (please see the sections "Risk Management" on page 44, and "Project Overview" on page 51). For more information on the Client Vision phase, see Chapter 2, in which I describe the Plan, Build, and Operate phases.

> **Note**
>
> Before beginning any of these phases, remember your SharePoint 2010 project mantra. Remember also that you cannot do all of this yourself (as mentioned earlier and in the section titled "Resource Requirements" on page 64). A good way to lose that mantra is to introduce SharePoint 2010 implementation pain to the client, and basically fail at your SharePoint 2010 implementation plan is by assuming you can do everything yourself without any aid. Make sure you get help—it is not a sign of weakness to request help (and you are likely to need it at the early stage). Make sure the client knows you need human resources to succeed.

The Plan Phase

The Plan phase takes the results of the vision statements and details the SharePoint 2010 environment, reviews the client's use of content, reviews security, details the user technology, plans how best to integrate them, and much more. It is without a doubt the most important phase, and no build of SharePoint 2010 should be attempted until you have completed this phase.

The SharePoint 2010 Plan phase is very important, so much so that a significant part of this book is dedicated to aspects of the Plan phase. For more information, you can read Chapter 5, "Building Your SharePoint 2010 Team," Chapter 6, "Gathering the Resources for SharePoint Implementation," Chapter 9, "SharePoint 2010 Governance," Chapter 10, "SharePoint 2010 Configuration Management," and Chapter 11, "Making Sure SharePoint 2010 Meets User Requirements."

The Build Phase

The Build phase kicks off once the Plan phase is completed and signed off on as acceptable by the client. The purpose of this phase is to manufacture and deploy the SharePoint 2010 environments. Here the test environment and production environment are created, including the relevant software (and testing of it).

This phase can include multiple build tasks—for example, creating a staging environment (also known as a User Acceptance phase, or UAT), a disaster recovery environment, a development environment, or an extranet environment. Each of these environments carries different criteria for success, so ensure that they are stated in your SharePoint 2010 Quality Plan. If they are not, steer away from using these subphases because they are not scoped. They would be better categorized as separate projects in their own right.

> ### Best Practice in SharePoint 2010 Organization Implementation
>
> You create three environments in which the topology design is identical: Test, Stage, and Production. The Test environment is always created first and then documented, reviewed, and tested. Then the Stage environment is created. The Production environment is created last and mirrored from the Stage environment. The Stage environment is used as part of change management to ensure that anything taken to production has configuration management history. Additionally, the Stage environment is backed up before changes destined for the Production environment are applied to Stage. The Test environment is used to ensure that the client has an area to try out SharePoint 2010. It also provides an area to demonstrate the features without forcing changes to the Production environment. Please note that this book does not describe how to install SharePoint 2010, but it does guide you through the production of a software specification so that you have the details you need to carry out a successful implementation.

More details on this subject are covered in Chapter 12.

The Operate Phase

After the Build-phase deployments are completed, you need to ensure the resiliency of the SharePoint 2010 environments and to vet your client requirements from the SharePoint 2010 Quality Plan. (See the section "Risk Management" on page 44 for a description of the three pieces: organization, personal/team, and infrastructure.) Hence, the Operate phase marks a review, post implementation, and optimization of the SharePoint 2010 Deploy phase. This phase is where governance is established and reviewed, and where the company can embrace SharePoint governance based on the Plan phase. Also, it is where your SharePoint 2010 administrators step in. Most importantly, it's where training can be carried out and reviewed.

The final part of this phase is full hand off and project closure. The Project Closure Checklist is described in Chapter 15.

Program Schedules

Time to dust off Microsoft Project—this is where you take the top-level tasks identified through the WBS and detail them on a plan.

A Program Schedule is a list of the WBS header tasks. The WBS is the detail of the Program Schedule and based on a Gantt Chart.

The schedules for each task should show the timeframe for all activities and their inter-dependencies. The "WBS" and "Program Schedule" sections of the Project Plan are both subject to frequent review or change and should be separate documents. The emphasis on updating project progress can be carried out in the WBS using, for instance, Microsoft Project. The key milestones from the WBS are entered as the Program Schedule and this is what the client sees. Of course, if there are alterations in the timescale for the WBS milestones that also appear in the Program Schedule these must be updated. The reason for making these separate is that the client and other people who may need to see the Project Plan are not concerned with the details in the WBS, but will want to know that key milestones have been reached and that progress is at a high level.

The guidance given in the following subsections should not trivialize the complex processes involved when planning a task; instead, it is presented to emphasize the need to have some structure to the planning process and provide guidance in this area. The Project Plan is a living document and often the subject of frequent review and update.

The program schedule is created to specify the human resources you have on your project team and what tasks they will perform—for example:

- A business analyst will review the current business and end user requirements.

- Your SharePoint architect and the SQL DBA will detail the capacity planning for SharePoint 2010.

- Your firewall team and SharePoint architect will review the security arrangements for SharePoint 2010 to be accessible from the Internet.

Examples of the SharePoint 2010 Plan phase tasks include the following:

- Form the project teams, and define the terms of reference.

- Determine the technical requirements.

- Determine user and business requirements.

- Determine the preliminary design.

- Determine coexistence detail.

- Create the test lab environment.

- Perform risk assessment.

- Determine communication strategy.

- Determine education and training strategies.

Chapter 3

- Evaluate client software and hardware.

- Perform governance planning.

- Determine server configuration.

- Determine security and Performance.

- Determine local area network (LAN) and wide area network (WAN) considerations.

- Determine failover and disaster recovery plans.

- Determine localization, integration with current organization key applications, and maintenance (how maintenance will be operated and by whom).

- Determine the content and navigation structure.

- Sign off the Plan phase as completed.

The Build phase tasks include the following:

- Deploy the test system.

- Deploy the production system.

- Deploy other SharePoint 2010 environments.

- Perform the User Acceptance tests and business tests.

- Sign off the Build phase as completed.

The Operate phase tasks include the following:

- Confirm backup arrangements.

- Test disaster recovery and business continuity.

- Ensure monitoring is in place.

- Review deployed environment(s) with users.

- Review deployed environment(s) with technology support.

- Review deployed environment(s) with client.

- Educate and train administrators and users.

- Sign off Operate phase (this completes SharePoint implementation).

How to Establish a Program Schedule

How do you establish basic premises for planning the execution of a SharePoint 2010 project? Here's a list of tasks related to doing this:

- Set up the WBS from the top down to the lowest level task that can be confidently estimated. As a guide, the lowest level tasks on the WBS should consist of activities of approximately five days duration (to be executed in the near future).

- Define the scope of the identified blocks from the top down and their relationship to each other.

- Identify dependencies, both internal and external, and identify the assumptions and restrictions that must be considered.

- Draw up a relational time-dependent network, preferably using a Gantt chart and the resource-planning facilities of Microsoft Project 2010.

- Time-analyze the network. Identify any shortcomings, the critical path, the initial time contingency, any overlap of start and end dates, and so forth.

- Resource-analyze the network. Identify resource loading, obtain a staffing profile, identify levels of expertise, and so forth.

- Repeat the process until the whole plan contains all the elements required to produce the deliverables on time and within the budget.

- Obtain approval or authorization after reviewing the plan with the client and technical authority, and recording authorization.

- The old adage of "Plan, plan, and stick to the plan" is still true; however, the plan must be subject to regular review. The project manager is responsible for ensuring that any changes within the project are reflected in the current Project Plan.

Chapter 3

Resource Requirements

The resource requirements should provide a full summary of the staff needed for the SharePoint 2010 project. The level of detail specified should be equivalent to that given for the tasks identified in the relevant WBSs. The resources needed for future phases of the project that have not been planned in detail need only be outlined; a future staffing profile can be used to identify where and when specific skills are needed. The resources required will include some or all of the following, depending on the size of the SharePoint 2010 implementation project:

- Project manager

- SharePoint 2010 architect, who will be responsible for the design and creation of the SharePoint 2010 environments (and who is not just a Web designer or Web developer)

- SharePoint 2010 engineer staff for SharePoint 2010 production, integration, and testing

- SharePoint 2010 developers, including staff for software development, and specification through to delivery (which are programming tasks and not required at the same time as installing SharePoint 2010)

- SharePoint 2010 business analysts, who are staff members who investigate the current technology, people, and organization and document these findings as part of the Plan phase

- Support staff for Active Directory, the firewall and proxy, SQL Server, Exchange, Office Communicator, and desktop support (and for any client tools seen as a critical integrated element for SharePoint 2010

- Support staff, including staff for the communication rooms, data centers, and server infrastructure

- Computer resources (including a SharePoint 2010 site for the team)

- Tools and specialized facilities

- Software packages that need to be procured

There are other resource requirements, but they are outside the scope of SharePoint 2010 and assigned to project management of human resources.

Consideration must be given to where resources are to be obtained. The decisions must be documented in the SharePoint 2010 Quality Plan in the "Project Organization and Responsibilities" section.

You also need to obtain the commitment of the "owner" of such resources to provide the resources to the SharePoint 2010 project at the right time. You should never just hope or assume that just because these resources are listed that they are available.

Summary

The content of your SharePoint 2010 Project Plan defines the nature of what you will achieve and the agreed-upon client requirements as documented in the SharePoint 2010 Quality Plan.

You will not be able to produce all of the required plans and documents yourself. Therefore, you should identify at an early stage what kind of resources you will need, where they will come from, and what they will do.

The following chapters go into further details about resources, configuration management, governance, and specification building, which lead up to the chapters that cover the implementation of SharePoint 2010.

SharePoint Planning and Control: Start As You Mean to Go

P LANNING and control is a process that requires good communications, both within the project manager's team and across the organization that's installing Microsoft SharePoint 2010. We're now going to discuss how using uniform procedures will make this process easy to manage.

Planning and control are as much an issue for small SharePoint 2010 install projects as large ones. Experience shows that small projects are more likely to overrun their budgets, time constraints, scope, or a combination of all of these. This can be caused by any of several factors, including company priorities, or the inability of the project manager to control the implementation project.

The key to planning the SharePoint implementation is control. Without this, scopes will change, the resources will be unmanaged, and the work schedule will be ignored. The planning and control process commences at the bidding (proposal) phase of the project.

Remember the Project Startup Checklist back in Chapter 3, "Content of Your SharePoint 2010 Project Plan"? You're going to need it now. (See Figure 3-2.)

Using the first section of the checklist, "Review Contract Requirements and Terms and Conditions," you have already addressed the following issues through your initial strategy meetings with the client:

- **Commercial aspects**   You are clear on the budget, the client's willingness to spend on the contract, and you have documented and agreed upon the financial risks. You have a rough idea of the worth of your SharePoint instance because you have carried out a cost-benefit analysis.

- **Technical aspects**   You have an understanding of the organization's current technical level and abilities. From a business goal perspective, you are able to list SharePoint 2010 features and benefits, as well as Microsoft Office 2010 system features and benefits, so that the client has a basic understanding of how these can fulfill their vision. You are also able to indicate infrastructure optimization features and benefits, as well as identified risks with the current technology (and also risks in adopting the new platform!).

- **Quality aspects**   In terms of your role as a project manager, you know how you will deliver SharePoint 2010 to the business and who is going to carry out each aspect of the work. You have created a basic SharePoint 2010 Project Plan and have referenced this against your SharePoint 2010 Quality Plan.

If you have addressed the preceding issues, go to the checklist and mark off the first section.

> **Note**
>
> The Reference column in the checklist can be used so that if you have other documentation you want to associate with the Quality Plan you can enter the reference code of that document in the relevant checklist column. This is used so that you know where all documentation is associated with the implementation plan.

The Project Startup Checklist should be used to ensure that you maintain control of the implementation. It communicates to the client the initial stages and progress made to date, and it identifies to everyone associated with the implementation where all the associated documentation is. The following list describes the other sections of the Project Startup Checklist:

- **Appointment of Staff**   A SharePoint implementation requires people to help create the implementation, consisting of the project manager, technical authority (representing the business), SharePoint architects, administrators, business analysts, information analysts, and so on. You will need to list resources (for example, desktops, laptops, software, places to work, and so on). You also carry out the creation of the Terms of Reference stating what each team member is responsible for, as well as specifying who is responsible for approving and authorizing recruitment and payment (as necessary). This is described further in the section "The Project Manager's Responsibilities," on page 70, and in Chapter 5, "Building Your SharePoint 2010 Team."

- **Establishment of Project Interfaces** A project manager for a SharePoint implementation needs to understand how to obtain hardware and software, how to locate resources for the team, where documentation is to be housed, how that documentation is to be filed, and the current organization referencing or numbering scheme, including any templates that must be adhered to.

- **Production of Documentation** A SharePoint Quality Plan and Project Plan must be created, including a subcontractor plan, a risk management plan, and a configuration management plan. The Quality and Project Plans are covered in Chapter 3, and project planning is covered in "All SharePoint 2010 Projects Must Be Planned and Controlled to Ensure Success," on page 69.

- **Verify and Validate** A SharePoint implementation must be tested and reviewed, and subcontractor deliverables need to be marked as acceptable to the client. The client needs to agree with the deliverables of the project. Together, these four sections of the Project Startup Checklist aid in the design of SharePoint 2010 for the client by forming a process I call "SharePoint 2010 Planning and Control."

SharePoint 2010 Planning and Control is used to help design the features of SharePoint 2010 required by the client, map these to the business needs of the client, and then describe the supporting physical design that is required to support the business needs. Therefore, through planning and controlling this phase, you can identify several critical areas of the SharePoint 2010 implementation:

- Review the information and management challenges to be met—for example, maybe you're not just implementing SharePoint 2010; maybe this is just part of a technology refresh for the organization (that is, Microsoft Exchange, Office Communicator, and Office software gets replaced as well). This means a business review of the client's day-to-day working processes.

- Conduct a functional review of the features through architectural design.

- Provide a proof of concept, which is wrapped into the SharePoint Quality Plan.

- Provide a physical design of SharePoint 2010.

All SharePoint 2010 Projects Must Be Planned and Controlled to Ensure Success

The planning and control procedure addresses the planning and control of all customer contracts related to the platform and formally authorized work. All SharePoint 2010 projects must be subject to formal project planning and control procedures appropriate to the type, size, duration, and risks involved. This procedure is associated with the SharePoint 2010 Quality Plan, the SharePoint 2010 Project Plan, and the SharePoint 2010 Project Startup Checklist.

The Project Manager's Responsibilities

The client provides the project manager with his or her Terms of Reference (TOR). The TOR must include the following statement:

The project manager is responsible for the planning and implementation of SharePoint 2010 and will engage his or her SharePoint 2010 team to deliver the client's requirements.

The project manager needs to appoint other team members and generate their TORs (see Chapter 3, Figure 3-2 for the Project Startup Checklist). You can also refer to Chapter 5 for more help in identifying the rest of the team and their TORs.

Both Project Manager and Technical Authority Are Essential

As well as a project manager, a technical authority is absolutely critical to the successful implementation of SharePoint 2010 and supports the project manager. The technical authority to plan and implement the project is delegated to the technical authority by the client through a TOR generated by the project manager.

The technical authority is there to ensure that there is a connection between project management and technical resources, and also to ensure that the delivery of SharePoint 2010 can be implemented and supported by the organization. The technical authority also ensures the relevant technical resources are available within the organization to support the project. The technical authority is not a project manager for SharePoint, but rather, a coordinator of technical resources by the business and signs off on the delivery of SharePoint (from a technical perspective) on behalf of the client.

The project manager is essential. A SharePoint implementation project cannot exist without a project manager. The project manager is not a SharePoint architect (though in small projects you could have the same person be the architect and project manager if the SharePoint architect can interface with both the technical and business aspects of the project.

The principal areas addressed by the project manager are these:

- Planning and authorizing the execution of the project—for example, the work required to collate business requirements; the work required to map those requirements to a SharePoint 2010 solution; the work required to build a SharePoint 2010 instance, including relevant features such as the training of the client and handover of SharePoint 2010 to the client.

- Defining the tasking procedures by which SharePoint 2010 is implemented—for example, capacity planning, configuration management, and so on. These tasks are then taken on by the SharePoint 2010 architect.

- Defining and implementing the appropriate progress-monitoring procedures—for example, a SharePoint 2010 One-Stop Shop, procedures to manage SharePoint 2010 after it is live.

- Maintaining the project records.

- Ensuring the project has been set as "Started" and "Closed" when required.

Although the project manager is delegated commercial authority on the project, it is recommended that support is given to her concerning the issues of major purchases (for example, servers, SharePoint 2010 user licenses, contract amendments, and so on).

If the project manager needs to exercise her responsibility in a different manner to that allowed by the procedures referenced, this circumstance must be identified in the Share-Point 2010 Quality Plan and the Quality Plan must be authorized by the business manager.

The preceding guidance is very important. A SharePoint 2010 implementation needs to be treated carefully so that the project does not go out of scope or out of budget when implementing features.

Let's explain that with an example: The project manager of company XYZ gets a contract to install SharePoint 2010 and is provided a TOR explaining his responsibilities by the client. The business leaves the project manager to deliver the project. The project goes over budget, but this is not spotted by the business manager. The project manager, exasperated, goes to means outside of the TOR to get further funds for the project.

In this scenario, the project manager likely will lose face with the business manager. As such, the project is bound to fail or introduce significant SharePoint implementation pain.

The SharePoint 2010 Architect Is Approved by the Project Manager and Technical Authority

It is vital that when providing SharePoint 2010, you enlist individuals who have a thorough understanding of SharePoint 2010 and who can describe how features of the product can be applied.

In my experience, there has been confusion between the purpose of an architect and the purpose of a developer. To me, a developer *builds* things. An architect *designs* things. That's not to say that a developer cannot be an architect and vice versa.

I had a client who needed a SharePoint environment that was a simple installation for a small business of five people. I spent half a day with them, gathering information concerning their pain points, what they currently do, and how they want to improve what they do. They kept stressing that all they needed was somewhere to share information. I described the features of SharePoint concerning document management, upload, download, retention, and archiving, and they got pretty excited. At the end of the meeting, they said, "We really like all the stuff to do with content management in SharePoint, and we need to embrace that in our work process. We have a number of paper-based processes that we would like to get automated. Can we do that?"

"Of course," I said.

Now, does that answer "Of course" mean that you bring in a developer right away? No. Because you are not customizing anything yet. You are designing. You have not even looked at whether certain features in SharePoint will meet the requirement. An architect with a developer's hat on could determine whether that is or is not the case and, if necessary, suggest to the project manager that resources are required to carry it out.

Let me clarify the top-level roles for a SharePoint implementation again. There are two sides: client and project. The client side is represented by the client (aha!), typically by someone acting as the technical authority representing the client's technical infrastructure. This person is usually the service delivery manager or a technical lead responsible for all of the other technical leads who will interface with the technical teams within the SharePoint project team. The project side is represented by the project manager and a SharePoint architect. When bringing in a SharePoint architect, it is important that this person, who also embraces the Design Authority role on SharePoint 2010, shall be made by the project manager in conjunction with the technical authority appointed by the client. By doing this, it further ensures that the technical authority's vision of SharePoint 2010 can be realized.

Why?

Because the SharePoint 2010 architect is there to ensure the SharePoint 2010 feature set is mapped to the infrastructure of the business.

Other Authorities Required Within the Project Organization

For SharePoint 2010 implementation projects requiring large teams or involving multidisciplinary groups, the project manager should prepare a project organization chart, linking it into the company structure. In addition to listing the project manager and the SharePoint 2010 architect, the chart should show any other authorities on the team—for example, the software development manager, quality assurance manager, configuration control authority, server build teams, user directory and messaging teams, and so on. The project organization chart can be included in either the Quality Plan or Project Plan.

As well as being a reminder of who does what when carrying out the SharePoint 2010 implementation, it serves as a record of who is responsible for what component. Here's an example: SharePoint is installed in an organization where there is no record of who installed the product. Worse, a third-party component was installed through a subcontractor and there appears to be no record of this.

This example simply shows there will be significant issues going forward concerning the support and management of the platform if there is nobody accountable and there is no documentation detailing how SharePoint was installed. A project organization chart shows the authorities for the project, including all those who are responsible for a relevant section of the project. All parts of the organization chart need to show what area of the project is covered and who is covering it.

A Review Must Be Held Before Acceptance

Prior to starting the project into the Design phase, a review of the Quality Plan, Project Plan, and Risk Management and Configuration Plan needs to be carried out by the project manager, client, and technical authority. This is the last opportunity the company has to reassess whether the project can fulfill the requirements of the contract for the stated price.

Incredibly, this critical aspect of implementing SharePoint 2010 is the least looked at.

Reviewing the Quality, Project, Risk Management and Configuration plans is done to ensure that there are no major unforeseen changes between the agreed-upon delivery and the contract. For example, a statement of requirement of SharePoint 2010 at the bidding process may have changed again at SharePoint 2010 Quality Plan delivery. As with all SharePoint 2010 implementation reviews, all are organized by the project manager who involves the representatives of the teams relevant to tasks prior to the review. As the implementation project gets underway, reviews should be carried out on a regular basis throughout the Plan and Build phases of the project. I've found it best to go for a weekly review, on the last workday of the week, just before everyone goes out for a drink or for an end-of-the-workweek get-together. This is to gather updated news concerning the progress of the project, including any issues reported by the team, client, or stakeholders. These meetings should be marked on the Project Plan, and none should be canceled. If you do miss any, the timeframe for the project might increase because issues in reviews have not been resolved or communication throughout the project team will not be efficient.

Prepare the Plans During the Startup Phase

The Startup phase of a SharePoint 2010 implementation project is defined as the period from the acceptance of the contract through to the establishment of the major project plans.

Chapter 4

The SharePoint 2010 Project Plan and the SharePoint 2010 Quality Plan are two key documents that must be prepared before any detailed investigations of client and user requirements can occur.

The SharePoint 2010 Project Plan Is Used to Monitor Progress and Control All Resources

The SharePoint 2010 Project Plan defines the what, why, where, and when on a project. It should address or reference the following topics in *one* document:

- Section 1 — Project Overview

- Section 2 — Milestones/Deliverables

- Section 3 — External Dependencies

- Section 4 — Assumptions/Restrictions

- Section 5 — Work Breakdown Structure

- Section 6 — Program Schedule

- Section 7 — Resource Requirement

- Section 8 — Project Reporting

At a minimum, the SharePoint 2010 Project Plan should consist of a Gantt chart indicating the Work Breakdown Structure (WBS), project schedule, and resource requirements.

> **Note**
>
> Use a Gantt chart to plan how long a project should take. A Gantt chart lays out the order in which the tasks need to be carried out. Gantt charts show dependencies between tasks and let you see immediately what should have been achieved at any point in time. A Gantt chart lets you see how remedial action can bring the project back on course, and can easily show deadlines and highlight significant events. Microsoft Project 2010 includes this capability. More information about that product and Gantt charts can be found at: *http://www.microsoft.com/project/en/us/tips-tricks.aspx*. SharePoint 2010 also includes Gantt chart views on any SharePoint repository that includes a start and end date.

Throughout the project, the Project Plan should be used as a key document to monitor progress toward delivering the requirements.

Tasks Must Be Planned to Meet the Delivery Schedule

The SharePoint 2010 project needs to have a WBS, dividing the work into constituent tasks, that is appropriate to the nature, size, and complexity of the activities involved.

> **Note**
>
> A complex project is made manageable by first breaking it down into individual components in a hierarchical structure, known as the Work Breakdown Structure (WBS). Such a structure defines tasks that can be completed independently of other tasks, facilitating resource allocation, assignment of responsibilities, and measurement and control of the project. In a SharePoint project, you might have a set of tasks relevant to installing SharePoint—for example, obtain hardware, define prerequisities, install software, configure software, create site collections, define security, and so on.

An initial WBS should be created during the initial phases of the project and is fundamental to the planning exercise. It provides the basis for the control of resource and, budgets and the recognition of milestone achievements.

Once the contract or task has been authorized, the WBS might need to be enhanced to provide greater detail of the task structure. The WBS must reflect sufficient detail to show clearly the activities necessary to achieve each deliverable. Major tasks within the WBS must have clearly identified *milestones* that allow the progress of the project to be monitored.

All projects should use Microsoft Project (the recommended version is Project 2010) to generate and maintain the schedule. Additionally, a SharePoint 2010 site should be created as a central project management office for the SharePoint implementation project.

> **Note**
>
> Project Standard 2010 can only save files to SharePoint—all the other functionality requires Project Professional 2010. See *http://download.microsoft.com/download/F/6/E/F6E62DAD-91FE-4B5C-839E-E50BDF6B90B2/version_comparison_desktop.pdf* for more information.

If you do not have Project 2010, you can use SharePoint to define a basic project schedule using the Gantt View option.

> **Note**
>
> One more point: in my experience in implementing SharePoint, I have always defined an external SharePoint instance running my SharePoint implementation explicitly for the project. Then later, as the Plan and Build phases come in, shift that into a Share-Point One-Stop Shop so that all those who need access to the data can get to it.

> **Note**
>
> To provide a basis of education and learning to users concerning SharePoint, your implementation of the new platform needs to include a central point where users can go concerning SharePoint. This is called a *SharePoint One-Stop Shop*. In time, as the business grows with SharePoint and Power Users emerge, roles can be expanded so that the business takes more control of the One-Stop Shop and therefore is even closer to managing SharePoint users. For more information concerning the SharePoint One-Stop Shop, see Chapter 13, "Planning and Implementing the SharePoint One-Stop Shop."

Discuss with the technical authority the options for having a SharePoint instance for the project team in the early stages. This is a good way to go because you have the ability to showcase the project to the client, and later on you can provide it as a historical audit of the project within a SharePoint site when the production version is available and your SharePoint One-Stop Shop is available.

Management of Resources Is the Key to Success

The project manager is responsible for obtaining and monitoring the resources necessary to undertake work. Resource planning should be undertaken in parallel with the preparation of the WBS. Resource levels can then be monitored against requirements throughout the life of the project. In the event of changes to requirements, these should be re-estimated to ensure the work can be completed within the agreed-upon deadlines.

If there is either a deficiency or excess in available resources, the project manager needs to notify the client.

One role of the client is to resolve resource issues across project boundaries (with the aid of its technical authority). With SharePoint, because many teams are involved with the project team, you might need a method of monitoring and controlling these resources. One method is the consolidated "Contract in Progress" form.

Resources shall be formally tasked, by means of written instructions, against authorized plans and budgets relating to the WBS. Examples of acceptable tasking documents are as follows:

- Work Instruction Form (recommended)

- Expansion in number of members of the team's TOR

- Memo

- A record in the Project Plan

- Observation reports

- Entry in a day book for tasks of less than five days in duration

The Standard Filing Structure Ensures Good Document Access

As well as using a SharePoint 2010 site for the centralization and collaboration of SharePoint project content, you need to control and plan the site's format and the structure of its content. Therefore, a project filing system must be established to ensure the correct maintenance of project records. The project manager is responsible for defining the referencing system for the project. The location of such files should be recorded in the SharePoint Quality Plan.

The recommended structure for such a filing system and the associated numbering scheme, collectively referred to as the file referencing system, is described in the online article "SharePoint Projects Document and Data Control" found at: *http://spsdocdatcontrol.geoffevelyn.com*.

The SharePoint 2010 Quality Plan Will Define Who Does What and How

Each SharePoint 2010 project must have a SharePoint 2010 Quality Plan. The SharePoint 2010 Quality Plan must detail what is required for work on the project to be conducted in an effective and efficient manner while meeting the client's goals and expectations (and also remaining consistent with the client's quality system, if one exists).

The SharePoint 2010 Quality Plan has two sections: Project and Processes. The first section (Project) addresses project-specific issues, such as staff roles and responsibilities, deliverables, external standards, and design review or audit programs. The second section (Processes) deals with processes and procedures required to describe the way in which the work will be executed.

Important topics in the Processes section that shall also be addressed are risk management and management of subcontracts. The SharePoint Quality Plan must list the key, top-level documents and plans to be created on the SharePoint 2010 project. This list will provide the individual team members with the knowledge of where vital information on the SharePoint 2010 project is held.

The SharePoint Quality Plan must be signed off by the client.

Key Procedures for SharePoint 2010 Design Development

The following subsections identify the top-level procedures that should be considered in the development of SharePoint 2010 and its implementation into the client's organization. These procedures are intended to be applicable to a wide range of activities, from hardware and software design to further technical studies, disaster recovery, and maintenance and configuration management.

> **Note**
> All the relevant procedures and forms that might be employed are listed in the SharePoint 2010 Project Planning and Control Life Cycle diagram, in shown in Chapter 3, Figure 3-1.

Do You Understand the Customer Requirements?

The project manager needs to ensure the work is fully defined and understood by all parties involved; the process, procedures, and guidance are all specified in the key project documents; the SharePoint 2010 Quality Plan and the SharePoint 2010 Project Plan. Customer requirements gathering describe in detail what features of SharePoint 2010 will be deployed and in what context, which leads to defining when and how they will be deployed. Customer requirements gathering creates two further documents: User Requirements, which states what features of SharePoint will be used to meet user objectives, and System Specifications, that identifies the components, services, and configuration that build the SharePoint instance(s). User and System Requirements are covered in Chapter 11, "Making Sure SharePoint Meets User Requirements" and Chapter 12, "Producing the System Specification," accordingly.

Amazingly, in some SharePoint projects I've seen, there have been no customer requirements and/or no system specification. All SharePoint 2010 implementation projects need to have a User Requirements document and System Specification document.

All Client Loan Items Must Be Controlled

Any item received from the client for use on a project must be controlled. This includes documents (for example, reports or drawings), hardware, and software. Documents loaned to the project should be recorded in a Client Loan register. The client typically will provide you with test data to use for implementing your SharePoint 2010 environment. They may also provide you with infrastructure diagrams, technical specifications, and other documentation that will support the SharePoint 2010 implementation. It is very important that you make a log of these so that you can identify what items have been provided, how they have been used, and when they should be passed back to the client.

Create a Record of All Technical Work

When implementing any aspect of SharePoint 2010 as part of your implementation project, you need to ensure that any technical activity is recorded and traceable. Input requirements, including any assumptions made, must be recorded and reviewed. The resulting technical documentation should also be reviewed.

An appropriate method of bringing the design records together, including a review process, is described in Chapter 10, "SharePoint Configuration Management."

One of the key documentation sets used in the implementation process is the step-by-step documentation the project manager creates in a test environment for the installation of SharePoint 2010. You might hear the client say things like, "The environment I have is not the same as the environment I installed in last time; therefore, the installation process is different." This is not the case and is never a good argument.

To produce a repeatable set of instructions to install SharePoint 2010, you create a test lab environment in accordance with the client requirements and carry out a normal installation of SharePoint 2010 to that environment, documenting the process as you go. Interestingly, I have found that the process I created for installing SharePoint 2010 is pretty much standard, meaning that the documentation I produce detailing that installation is also standard. With a little more work in terms of guidance and troubleshooting steps, you can easily create a repeatable set of templates, which when followed produce a basic system. Some sets of instructions can be scripted; however, it is always best to document every step of the process and include screen shots wherever necessary. As these steps are repeated, these instructions are reviewed, which results in a cleaner process each time SharePoint is installed, and updates to the process are recorded via configuration management (which is discussed in Chapter 9, "SharePoint Governance").

Chapter 4

Hence, when approaching any SharePoint implementation work, here is a list of tasks to complete:

- Get a test environment.

- Build SharePoint 2010 (basic) in that environment.

- Document the process, and record the technical work.

- Enhance that environment according to the technical client requirements.

- Get the technical authority to sign off.

- Detail this as a system specification.

- Get the client to sign off.

Therefore, it is important that you keep track of your deployment, because it serves as a historical, traceable record and is vital to proving to the connected technical teams what SharePoint 2010 does and how it does it based on its technical configuration.

All Technical Work Requires at Least One Review!

It is a best practice to test, test, and test again when the SharePoint 2010 configuration has been carried out, even if you are testing via a script. There is no point in simply stating, "Hey, it worked in the test lab. I documented it there, so it will definitely work without needing to test it again in my production environment or my staging environment." The reviews that need to be done are set to provide a level of comfort and confidence that the SharePoint 2010 environment will operate as planned. Another reason to have at least one review for technical work, is that you can confirm your SharePoint 2010 implementation works not just in the way you expect it to, but also in the way the technical authority does. The technical authority in this instance does not need to be just the client; it can include your peers or another SharePoint consultant who can validate your installation. In fact, Microsoft can provide such a service (called a *health check*), which allows you to further validate your installation against Microsoft best practices. The point is that all subsystems need to be tested thoroughly and validated. The database server in particular needs to be reviewed because this is where virtually all of your SharePoint configuration and data is stored. And because you might have multiple environments—Test, Stage, and Production—you need to carry out full reviews of each of these. Chapter 11 is devoted to this.

Of course, all reviews must be documented. Do not assume that a client will accept your installation as valid unless you are able to back it up with hard facts. Additionally, documenting the reviews will show any shortfalls in the implementation so that if you need aid you can provide the necessary documentation to the person helping you.

Prove the Product Meets the Customer Requirements

The process of planning the SharePoint 2010 verification and validation for any of its technical implementation is described in Chapter 14, "Releasing SharePoint 2010 to the Client." This procedure describes the requirement to generate the Verification and Validation Plan, which addresses how to prove SharePoint 2010 meets the client requirements. It also describes the planning for acceptance testing where there is a contractual requirement to undertake such activity. Verification and validation involve conducting a number of activities. However, the procedure focuses on two main activities: conducting technical reviews and SharePoint 2010 testing.

Manage the Configuration of SharePoint 2010

It is absolutely critical that the items that comprise the SharePoint 2010 deliverable (documents, drawings, software, and hardware) be subject to configuration management. This procedure is described in Chapter 10. The SharePoint architect and the project manager need to identify the configuration items on a hierarchical basis with the top-level item identifying the complete product.

Configuration management of SharePoint isn't exactly new. People have called this other things, such as technical documentation, the SharePoint product pack, change management sheets, and so on. Configuration management is clear for SharePoint 2010: it requires a record to be kept of all work carried out to configure SharePoint 2010. During the installation of SharePoint 2010, there are many tasks to do. Here are some examples:

- Prepare the server environment (Internet Information Services, SMTP, .NET Framework).

- Prepare the database environment (SQL Server, service accounts, and so on).

- Prepare the software installation.

- Carry out the software installation.

- Configure the SharePoint installation.

Chapter 4

In providing SharePoint 2010 to an organization (even as a pilot), no one in their right mind would stick a DVD into a server DVD drive; click Next, Next, and Next again; enter some configuration details without recording anything; and then say to the client, "Eureka! I've provided you with SharePoint," and declare that it has been successfully implemented. Without documentation or historical information concerning the makeup of the environment, that SharePoint implementation will be a disaster.

Additionally, if you modify a SharePoint environment that is already in place, you would do so with the assumption that configuration management information was available. This information details the original environment, including any changes made to it so that the individual applying the latest change could do so with as complete an understanding of the environment as possible. If there was no configuration management carried out at the time of implementation, any future modifications, enhancements, or changes would be difficult, if not risky, to make.

To see a summary of why configuration management in SharePoint 2010 is very important, look at Table 4-1. It lists the subsections in a SharePoint 2010 implementation related to configuration that you should record along the way. These items need to be recorded because it's likely that the implementation's configuration at some point will be changed, referred to, added to—in short, reviewed or revisited in the life cycle of the product. Note that this list is not exhaustive; however, you'll find it useful when you want to know what needs to be documented and to what level in SharePoint 2010. In Chapter 11, I go into even more detail on the types of data that should be captured and how. Table 4-1 can be used as a guide indicating the breadth of what you need to record in terms of configuration management. The first column shows the high-level section related to the implementation, and the second column shows the heading under which you need to gather information.

Chapters 10, 11, and 12 contain more information to help you with configuration management.

Table 4-1 **SharePoint 2010 Implementation**

Section	Detail
Governance and Culture	Web folder client usage
	Users' self-site creation
	Users' site management
	Metadata definitions
	Training
	Policies, assignments, creating and publishing, customization

Section	Detail
Naming Conventions	Database names
	URLs (host headers)
	Site-collection URLs
	Managed path names
	Document Library names
	Active Directory SharePoint accounts
	Content source names
	Scope names
	Server names
	Web application name
	Web application folder name
	E-mail-enabled list names and aliases
Security	Password and account support for nonemployees (extranet)
	Web App groups deny
	Unique permissions definition
	Authenticate methods
	Services associations
Search and Indexing	Location of information
	What information
	Content sources
	Scheduling
	Hardware specifications
	Bandwidth (interserver in farm)
	Rules
	Administration
	Evaluation of content sources
	Thesaurus
	Scope
	iFilters and protocol handlers
	File types, Icons, and Optical Character Recognition (OCR)
	Accounts
	Best Bets
	Server name mappings
	Hardware configuration
	Relevance and tagging
	Optimization

Chapter 4

Section	Detail
Disaster Recovery	Single site
	Server recovery
	Farm recovery
	Datacenter failover
Staffing	SharePoint architect
	SharePoint developer
	Training provider
	Search and indexing
	Taxonomy (information analyst)
	Content types
Personalization	Active Directory attributes
	Profile attributes
	Profile import schedule
	Audience
	Social networking
Document Library Planning	No libraries in a new site (for example, no default Shared Documents library)
	Enable the required document checkout for editing
	"Documents in a view" totals
SharePoint 2010 Capacity Planning, Reporting, and Monitoring	Baseline performance counters
	Web applications and application pools
	Managed paths
	Data requirements and sizing
	Monitoring requirements
	Downtime periods
	Server redundancy
	Site quota templates
	Auditing reports
	Storage usage reports
	Activity reports
	Performance and service-level agreements (SLAs)
Branding and Consistency	Site definition features
	Workflow processes
	Master page development
	Content types development
	Rollup features

Section	Detail
Web Applications	Security needs
	Information consumption needs
	Taxonomy needs
	Collaboration needs
	Site-collection management
	Political issues
	Service Requirements

Summary

Every SharePoint 2010 implementation project requires two things to be successful: planning and control. Planning ensures that individuals who are tasked with investigating the requirements from the client do so knowing when it needs to be done and why. Control ensures that adequate methods exist for capturing all the requirements.

There are several outputs for these processes—for example, SharePoint 2010 specification documents, logical and physical releases showing the layout of the services, documents that reflect a clear understanding of who is accountable for various tasks. These outputs are crucial because they lead into the build and deployment of SharePoint 2010 from an infrastructure perspective (servers, software, and so on) and from a business perspective (education, training, acceptance, governance, and ongoing support).

Without planning and control in place, there is no governance. And without governance, there is chaos. This chapter described the meaning and format of SharePoint 2010 project planning to help you avoid chaos in your SharePoint 2010 implementation. It emphasized the need to engage the right people and use the best processes to ensure your planning efforts lead to a successful SharePoint implementation. And when those processes are in place, you must ensure they are structured, standardized, and understood by all parties in the SharePoint 2010 team.

Chapter 4

Building Your SharePoint 2010 Team

To implement SharePoint 2010 in an organization, you need to involve a number of resources:

- Project manager

- Coordinator

- SharePoint consultant

- SharePoint 2010 One-Stop Shop

- Interfacing teams

- Third-party resources—for example, those supplying special features that SharePoint 2010 cannot provide out of the box

- Business analyst—responsible for gathering client requirements and mapping these to SharePoint solutions

- Information architect—responsible for organizing and labeling Web sites, intranets, online communities, and software to support usability and searchability

- Communications, testers, education, and training

I'll describe these various positions so that you can see what kind of people serve as these resources and to determine the relevant skill sets they should have. After you've read the preceding list, you might be tempted to ask, "Hey, what about a developer?" I dedicate a few of the upcoming sections to reasons why you *don't* need a developer for putting Share-Point 2010 into an organization.

What Is the Terms of Reference Document, and Who Creates It?

The Terms of Reference (TOR) document is created by the project manager using information from the SharePoint 2010 Quality Plan and Project Plan. The items within the TOR are used to specify who has the authority and responsibility for the various areas of work. These items should always be reviewed to ensure they reflect the size and scope of the SharePoint 2010 implementation. The TOR is written before you assemble the team, meaning that you don't attempt to create it until you know what needs to be done, who is going to do it, and in what context it will be done.

> **Note**
> You need to create a TOR for each member of the team because each will have different responsibilities. All TORs are to be entered into one document, and you should make a reference to the TOR document from the SharePoint 2010 Quality Plan in the section "Project Organization and Responsibilities." Changes to a TOR need to be updated in the TOR document.

What you don't want is a situation where the client has given you resources because they assume your team will be just like any other IT project out there. SharePoint 2010 should not be treated that way because it is a *content management system*. This means the storage, sharing, auditing, security, tagging, and categorization of project information requires the business to be an integral part of the project. If you think of SharePoint 2010 as just another software product and that installing it simply involves a click here, a click there, and a brief installation exercise, you'll find that it will not solve many business issues. Also, by taking such an approach, you are failing to use your team's skills to the extent required by the product. This flawed approach at the start ultimately leads to the failure of the SharePoint 2010 implementation.

So, you start by creating a TOR, which the client or the client's technical authority then signs off on. This document gives you and your team focus and helps you put in place your SharePoint 2010 project mantra. In the following sections, I'll discuss who the key people are on a typical SharePoint 2010 implementation team.

When building the TOR for your SharePoint delivery team, make sure you write each one in a standardized way. Table 5-1 provides an example for project managers.

Table 5-1 Terms of Reference List for Project Manager Role

Job Title	Project Manager for "SharePoint 2010 Project Name"
Line of Business	Content Management Systems "SharePoint 2010 Delivery"
Job Holder	"NAME"
Commencement Date	"DATE"
Reporting To	"CLIENT OR BUSINESS GROUP MANAGER," "BUSINESS AREA"
Purpose	Your job, as manager of the "SharePoint 2010 Delivery" project, is to ensure that your team achieves the contracted deliverables to the satisfaction of your customer in the time frame required and within the approved budgets.

Project Manager

The project manager has a single, overarching responsibility: to deliver the successful completion of the project within the guidelines of the budget, resourcing, and scope. The delivery effort requires planning, control, and technical judgment—the project manager's responsibilities are primarily related to planning and control.

Project Manager Role

For the project manager to carry out his responsibilities, he requires the full support of the client's business group; therefore, the authority to plan and implement the SharePoint project is granted by the client through the TOR for the project manager role. The project manager, then, has the ability to recruit the team and set the TOR for each team member. It is absolutely critical that the project manager has final say on this, and any alterations to any individual's TOR must be agreed to by the technical authority or client and the project manager.

To support the project manager in larger SharePoint implementations, you should include a project coordinator, who will help gather and organize documentation. Essentially, in larger projects, the project manager requests support from the project coordinator for things such as document and data control. This support role is useful in SharePoint 2010 because the coordinator can manage the project site within the SharePoint 2010 One-Stop Shop (which is discussed in more detail in the section "The SharePoint 2010 One-Stop Shop" on page 93).

Terms of Reference

The SharePoint project manager is responsible for the following:

- To plan and control the activities of the SharePoint 2010 project by maintaining an up-to-date program and cost-to-completion tracking, monitoring project progress, and initiating corrective action where required

- To ensure that all staff allocated to the project are gainfully employed, minimizing contract effort

- To liaise with other managers in the business group and line of business (LOB) when planning staff allocations to ensure that the project's requirements for staff are met; that vacancies are identified in good time where they exist; and staff, whose allocation to the SharePoint 2010 project is ending, are reassigned as quickly as possible after their assignment is complete

- To ensure current and planned expenditure is contained within approved budgets, and to ensure that no work is undertaken without authorized financial cover

- To ensure that the team adheres to the SharePoint 2010 Quality Plan

- To provide technical guidance to project staff, or to delegate such guidance to a nominated member of the team

- To delegate the management of tasks and subtasks where appropriate, and to ensure that the management of those subprojects conform to the SharePoint 2010 Project Plan and SharePoint 2010 Quality Plan

- To manage project risks using, where appropriate, a formal risk register within the SharePoint 2010 Project Plan

- To ensure that technical reviews are held and recorded and that follow-up actions are discharged and closed down

- To provide monthly reports or, as otherwise directed, record the status of and outlook for the project

- To check, in conjunction with the designer technical authority, that staff members allocated to the project have sufficient qualifications and experience to do the work they are being tasked to undertake

- To contribute to staff performance reviews as part of the appraisal process

- To manage the equipment and facilities under your control in accordance with company policies and procedures

- To communicate matters of company, divisional, and local issues to staff, and to represent their concerns to your client manager

The SharePoint project manager has the following authority:

- Tasking of staff assigned to the project

- Authorization of all formal project documentation

- Financial authority, within the limits set

- Authorization of time sheets for project staff

SharePoint Architect

The SharePoint architect is a key resource for the SharePoint implementation. This person is knowledgeable of the platform from the operating system through dependent technologies such as DNS/WINS, firewalls, infrastructure design, capacity, growth, performance, and resiliency. This person also must have a strong understanding of what it takes to fulfill a SharePoint 2010 business requirement.

In summary, this person will be very knowledgeable about SharePoint 2010 Foundation and SharePoint 2010 Server.

SharePoint Architect Role

Because this role is central to the provision of a SharePoint platform, the project manager and the client's technical authority must work together to recruit this individual (because this is a client-facing role). This person will interface with the SharePoint project team, the client's technical teams, and the business (for example, information analysts) on a daily basis. It is the SharePoint technical authority's design, the communication of that design, and the output of that design to the configuration of SharePoint 2010 that maps to the client's vision, so this person does need to be highly skilled.

Terms of Reference

The SharePoint architect will be responsible for the following tasks:

- Advising on the design and analysis techniques, as well as on procedures that should be used in the SharePoint project

- Detailing disaster-recovery specifications

Chapter 5

- Detailing capacity plans

- Detailing network security

- Providing support to the project manager in reviewing the customer requirement; helping to produce the requirement specification

- Endorsing the verification and validation of the SharePoint 2010 implementation, including the following tasks:

  - The number, level, and timing of technical reviews

  - The approval of the technical review records produced

  - Approval of all technical documentation produced

  - Signing of design certificates (particularly if there are third-party products assigned to the SharePoint implementation)

SharePoint 2010 Administrator

The SharePoint 2010 administrator is responsible for the initial configuration of the platform and follows the rules stated by the SharePoint architect and technical authority. She provides the groundwork for SharePoint monitoring and diagnostics.

There are a number of excellent tools within the central administrator function in SharePoint 2010, including a SharePoint Best Practices Analyzer and Health monitor, which will help administrators solve problems. Additionally, the ability to manage the SharePoint 2010 environment—in terms of disaster recovery, backups, and reporting—is much improved.

SharePoint Administrator Role

It is important to have a SharePoint administrator in the early days of the SharePoint 2010 implementation because the administrator becomes a third line of support after SharePoint 2010 is live.

Terms of Reference

The SharePoint administrator is responsible for planning, operating, maintaining, and optimizing the SharePoint 2010 environment. On a day-to-day basis, this person is expected to work with other internal teams defining services, hosting, and maintaining security authentication and data mirroring. This person also works through central administration monitoring quotas, throttling, reporting, and carrying out system maintenance.

The SharePoint 2010 One-Stop Shop

SharePoint 2010 is an awesome tool for project management document control and planning. It provides all the relevant features and benefits, allowing you to build a successful and repeatable project management office. This project management office will include and become the SharePoint One-Stop Shop for the organization, functioning as a crucial resource.

One-Stop Shop Role

This SharePoint 2010 site will house everything related to the SharePoint 2010 implementation. This includes policies, statement of operations, FAQs, "How Do I" files, performance and resiliency information, backup information, requests for sites, keywords, and even an Admin section for SharePoint 2010 administrators to use.

Terms of Reference

The SharePoint One-Stop Shop is responsible for the following:

- Serving as the central repository for all project-related material related to the implementation of SharePoint 2010

- Provisioning of collaborative features that allows information to be shared among project members and project visitors

- Providing a home for any organizational topics related to SharePoint 2010.

More information about the SharePoint One-Stop Shop is detailed in Chapter 13, "Planning and Implementing the SharePoint One-Stop Shop."

Interfaces: Teams in the Organization

A significant number of components and platform technologies are connected to any installation of SharePoint 2010. What makes SharePoint 2010 really special is that you can add further components to it with ease. Of course, you would never connect all of this yourself, because you are not Superman! You need various teams to work with you. Also, by bringing in these teams, you increase their knowledge of the platform and ensure they have an understanding of it from a technical and support perspective.

Chapter 5

Here are a few of the technologies required to enable SharePoint 2010 to operate:

- Active Directory

- Microsoft Office Exchange

- Microsoft SQL Server

- Microsoft Windows Server

Some people might argue that they can easily install SharePoint by themselves in a single-server environment. While this is achievable, it's not really advisable. If you install SharePoint, Active Directory, Exchange, and SQL Server on a single server, you'll end up with not having an easily scaled solution or a supportable platform. Some SharePoint projects start that way and then fall into trouble because the person installing SharePoint has not factored in at the start of the implementation where the client wants to go with SharePoint. And that person has not identified what the user requirements are and worked out how SharePoint will grow with the organization.

Here is an analogy. Say you have a car with a steering wheel, wheels, an engine, and lights. You need to change the oil. So that means looking at the engine—it doesn't mean that you start removing the steering wheel, unscrewing the lights, and so on. It doesn't mean that you have dozens of people doing all sorts of things when the only thing that needs to be done is the oil change.

In a small SharePoint 2010 implementation, you could easily have Active Directory, Exchange, and SQL Server all running on the *one* Windows Server with SharePoint 2010 running on top. But in a multisupport-driven organization with disconnected services, it would be unwise to do that. In fact, that would be virtually impossible to manage. For example, connecting to a local SQL instance when you have a SQL team managing a SQL cluster for the organization is not making SharePoint robust. Surely, SharePoint would be pushed into the SQL cluster environment so that it can be supported. The same goes for Exchange and Active Directory. Imagine that you connect SharePoint into a locally installed Active Directory on the server in a multisupported environment where there is an Active Directory team in place. Doing that creates support issues for the Active Directory team. Finally, imagine the performance and support issues that arise from running all technologies on one server.

If there is no multisupported environment and all support is provided by one person, you still do not necessarily have to install all technologies on one machine. Remember that you need to be able to validate the installation and provide an effective support service.

If you are that person and are reading this book, I strongly recommend that you speak to the client and identify the shortfalls of taking on SharePoint with limited human resources to support the technology.

Most often, you should assume Active Directory, Exchange, and SQL Server should be run by separate teams. You need to have a list of these teams in your SharePoint 2010 Quality Plan. The project manager and technical authority should negotiate who from those teams will tie into the SharePoint 2010 project, and they need to draw up TORs for those teams so that each team member understands what will be required of them and when.

> **Note**
>
> **You, as project manager (along with your SharePoint architect), can conduct further workshops and meetings to gather more information about how the current infrastructure operates.**

Role of the Teams

The roles of these teams are multidimensional, and I will not go into details in this book. However, providing the right kind of information to them (as shown in the following list) is crucial in ensuring that the installation of SharePoint 2010 goes well:

- **Active Directory**   Service account creation procedures, format of the accounts

- **SQL Services**   Database-creation procedures, account-creation procedures

- **Exchange**   SMTP connectivity information, domain connectivity, e-mail creation procedures, security issues

You might have noticed that I added security issues to information needed by the Exchange team. Providing the Exchange team with security information is extremely important for any SharePoint installation. All teams have procedures concerning the provision of their services to SharePoint. Each will have security procedures detailing how relevant services will be provided. For example, let's consider service accounts.

In SharePoint, you have to install Exchange using a number of service accounts. You could easily make up these service accounts and then ask your Active Directory team to create them for you.

Chapter 5

However, the Active Directory team might have some security procedures concerning the creation of these accounts. They might ask for the accounts to be formatted in a certain way (for example, to have *as_* in front of each service account), for the password to be *complex*, and for the accounts to sit in a certain organizational unit (OU) in Active Directory. All of this is acceptable for SharePoint 2010 of course, but the key thing is to ensure that you and they are aware of these security procedures up front and that they are enforced on your SharePoint 2010 installation. However, it should also be pointed out here that the Active Directory team would like for certain things to be defined for SharePoint service accounts concerning account expiration, failed logon attempts, group policies, and so on—some of which might cause support and operational issues for SharePoint. For example, employing account expiration settings results in the service settings for SharePoint to be reconfigured for new passwords every so often, meaning there can be disruption to services.

Remember, it is not your place as either the project manager or the SharePoint architect to question the procedures the client teams have. However, it is your responsibility to adhere to their procedures and ensure they adhere to yours. And you'll find some organizations where none of these procedures exist. It is therefore best practice that you form the SharePoint 2010 configuration management procedures for your environment quickly.

Let's take SQL as an example. A significant portion of a SharePoint 2010 implementation is SQL centric. Therefore, it is absolutely critical that the security provision between SQL and SharePoint is agreed to by the SharePoint architect and the SQL team.

A good example is in the installation of SharePoint 2010 and determining what rights the farm account requires in SQL land. SQL DBAs might come back to you complaining that the security permissions required for this account are far too high. (In SharePoint 2010, the farm account could have dbcreator and securityadmin rights.) They would be right if they were talking about SQL, but this is *not* SQL—it is a SharePoint installation. I've even seen a SQL team set the permissions of the farm account to a lower level privilege and then wonder why the SharePoint administrators are jumping up and down at errors related to creating sites. Clearly, the rules about setting permissions on accounts must be established at an early stage, and the SQL teams need to understand the rules concerning SharePoint user accounts.

> **Note**
>
> I've found that the best way to manage a SharePoint 2010 implementation is to ensure that the SQL instance for SharePoint 2010 implementation is *contained*, meaning that SharePoint 2010 has its own dedicated SQL that is not mixed with other databases that are not SharePoint 2010 specific. The reasons for this are quite obvious when you find that organizations using other SQL databases have a different take on how often maintenance (for example, backup and disaster recovery) can be carried out on SharePoint 2010; you can see how that might affect their access to SQL databases that are not SharePoint 2010 borne.
>
> Before approaching the SQL technical teams within the organization, you need to have an idea of what your SharePoint 2010 disaster recovery model will be. This means you need to determine the ability for SharePoint to continue if something happens to its environment that forces you to fail over to a backup environment. Because these sites are 90 percent SQL, you know that SQL has to be fault tolerant for SharePoint. So a sample solution for this scenario is to ensure that if there is such an event, the databases are mirrored to a second SQL instance. And yes, that would definitely be easier to do if all the databases to be mirrored come from one SQL instance dedicated to SharePoint.

Terms of Reference

SharePoint teams have the following responsibilities:

- Providing Best Practice governance and procedures—for example, service accounts, naming conventions, monitoring plans, escalation paths, and service-level agreements (SLAs)

- Providing technical aid—for example, provisioning of Active Directory, Exchange, SQL Server, and so on

- Providing support for knowledge transfer—including keeping teams abreast of information concerning SharePoint 2010, such as information related to monitoring, troubleshooting, and so on

Business Analysts

When implementing SharePoint 2010, there are two levels of research required: technical and business.

For the technical research, the SharePoint architect and technical authority (through the teams selected) get an understanding of what technical resources will be required to physically place a system and how they will be implemented.

For the business research, the business analysts step in. These people are tasked with guiding and documenting the client's requirements in detail, and they communicate that information back to the SharePoint architect and technical authorities (through the project manager).

Interestingly, the business analyst post is often downplayed or eliminated by those who want to quickly push out SharePoint and those who are more focused on the technology instead of the information and collaboration challenges faced by the organization, which determines how the technology can be placed to meet those challenges.

Remember the client vision? Those are the statements made back in the SharePoint 2010 Quality Plan. The client's vision is not a technical vision; it is focused on how SharePoint 2010 will be used to deliver improvements to productivity. To ascertain how to improve productivity, you need to investigate the businesses' current use of technology so that the features of SharePoint 2010 that meet those requirements are exposed.

Without a picture of the client's *current use* of technology and what they might want to achieve, you cannot possibly ensure that whatever is provided will meet client expectations, be resilient, perform, and be supportable in the client's environment.

Business Analyst Role

So the business analyst position is *extremely* important. Their output is pushed back to the project manager, who then echoes the requirements to the SharePoint architect and also to the business stakeholders.

In some cases, people might argue that the business analyst and SharePoint architect should be the same person. This happens when the business analyst, who needs to interface with the business and record user requirements, is also the person who has a deep understanding of SharePoint. Combining the roles ensures that the information captured is valid and the goals outlined are achievable.

This approach has shortcomings and isn't appropriate for all types of implementations. It assumes the only information captured in the analysis is what is going to be achieved according to the guidance of a SharePoint architect, not a recording of the client requirements (whether they can be achieved in SharePoint or not). Additionally, in a large implementation, you'll wind up with an overcommitted SharePoint architect, who will be attempting to investigate, design, and help implement the wishes of both the technical and business sides of the SharePoint 2010 project.

There is also an argument that, in keeping the team small and compact, the roles of business analyst and SharePoint architect can be rolled into one. However, this assumes the SharePoint architect is directly interfacing with the business and not indirectly responsible for defining the raw SharePoint implementation requirements (such as additional technical information like server specification, capacity plans, network security, and so on, which the client might not have the sufficient knowledge to quantify or detail).

Therefore, if this is a large installation, the business analyst is separate from the SharePoint architect because the business analyst has a single responsibility: to gather the user (business) information requirements and seek an accord between the technology and the business within the guidelines of the project scope.

> **Note**
>
> Business analysts who stay with the organization after the completion of a SharePoint 2010 implementation tend to become a combination of SharePoint administrator and SharePoint champion. (A SharePoint champion is an individual in the organization who is seen among peers to have a good working knowledge of SharePoint but is not a member of the SharePoint support team.) This is in part because of their knowledge of SharePoint and the knowledge of how it has been implemented in the organization. If this takes place, the business analysts would be wise to impart further information to the business so that true SharePoint champions can emerge.

Terms of Reference

Business analysts have the following TOR:

- Help build business and functional requirements by describing what a particular SharePoint feature, process, product, or service must do to fulfill the business requirements, working closely with the SharePoint architect and information analysts.

- Help build user requirements reflecting how SharePoint will be designed and developed, and define how user test cases must be formulated.

- Help build quality-of-service (QoS) requirements. These are requirements that do not perform a specific function for the business but are needed to support the functionality. Examples of QoS requirements are SharePoint performance, scalability, security, and usability. These are often included within the system requirements, where applicable and through working with the SharePoint architect.

For more information about delivering responses in formal, well-written documents using the SharePoint 2010 Business Requirements template, see Chapter 11, "Making Sure SharePoint Meets User Requirements."

Information Analysts

An information analyst provides information about how data in the organization is created, stored, archived, and retained. In essence, they define and manage the nature of metadata management in the client's organization.

In large organizations, you might see a team responsible for this area. If you do, your SharePoint 2010 implementation needs to bring in this team as quickly as possible. If you don't, depending on the nature and size of the SharePoint 2010 implementation, you'll need to carry out further investigation using your business analyst or SharePoint architect, or you'll need to bring in an information analyst.

In SharePoint 2010, information architecture is a huge area. Here I'll mention only some of the things in SharePoint 2010 related to metadata and taxonomy.

Information Analyst Role

Information analysts are used in the early days of the SharePoint implementation (in the Plan phase). They provide information about document metadata, organizational structure, and information flows between business units. This is invaluable information for the design of sites in terms of their document libraries, data hierarchy in SharePoint 2010 (content type mapping), and SharePoint 2010 site inheritance. This information also leads to business workflow provisions and links to the work carried out by the business analyst.

The information analyst works with technical material and translates the material into lay person's terms. In terms of SharePoint 2010 being implemented, information analysts examine the process of document management in that platform and document for the users how document management should be applied in the context of their work. This means that while users need not have complete knowledge of SharePoint 2010, they need to be able to understand how the user interface works (for example, how to upload, download, create content, assign keywords, and work with metadata).

With regard to metadata and taxonomy, SharePoint 2010 provides the following:

- Social personal classifications

- Taxonomy and metadata to improve navigation and browsing

- Taxonomy and metadata to improve search and discovery

- Shared content types across site collections

- Life-cycle content management

- Centralized taxonomy administration and import metadata functionality

- Content enrichment through controlled vocabulary

It is therefore vital that taxonomy, metadata, and an information architecture be established, and that the client agree to the taxonomy management and governance that is put into place. This task area is significant, and it has a life cycle of its own. The outputs of the information analyst provide taxonomy design, standard processes, and (if it's properly implemented) well-trained users. This means that even after the SharePoint implementation is completed, the processes related to taxonomy, metadata, and the implemented architecture continues. There needs to be separate resources applied to these areas outside of the project, and the client needs to understand this from the outset—right at the point of defining the SharePoint 2010 Quality Plan.

Information analysts categorize the data so that it is easy to locate. Hence, in terms of the SharePoint 2010 feature set in search and enterprise metadata management, they should be right at home. SharePoint 2010 metadata management includes working with terms, managed terms, and managed keywords, as shown in Figure 5-1. Search capabilities include tagging, as shown in Figure 5-2.

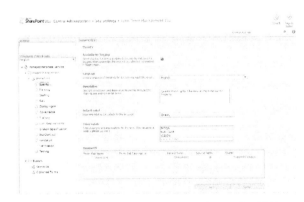

Figure 5-1 Metadata management in SharePoint 2010.

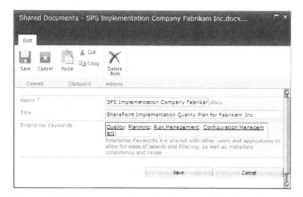

Figure 5-2 Tagging interface for keywords in SharePoint 2010.

Terms of Reference

SharePoint 2010 information analysts have the following responsibilities:

- Supporting the SharePoint architect and business analysts by providing blueprints of data flows in the organization, including taxonomy and metadata structures

- Organizing and labeling SharePoint 2010 online communities to support usability and findability

- Designing and constructing the structure of the information in the organization, or if it has already been done, helping to refine this for SharePoint 2010

Interfaces: Consultants from Outside the Organization

So far, I have been assuming that all the roles of the SharePoint implementation team are brought in—meaning that roles such as SharePoint architect, business analyst, information analyst, and even the project manager are recruited. I have also assumed that you have sourced these roles individually, and not from a SharePoint job list.

Before continuing, so far I have also assumed that the reader is, or is going to be, the SharePoint project manager.

Let's now look at two examples where you might need an external consultancy:

1. Assume for a moment that you are the client, and you want to implement SharePoint but do not have any project managers or in-house SharePoint expertise available. In this circumstance, it is possible for SharePoint to be implemented by an external company (for example, a subcontracted *consultancy* like a Microsoft Gold Partner with SharePoint expertise).

You can go to the following link for a more detailed explanation: *http://www.microsoft. com/uk/experts/explained/default.mspx.*

2. For this step, I'll jump back to assuming you are the project manager, but you need some functionality to be added to the SharePoint implementation that can only be provided by an external consultancy—for example, backup tools, document management tools, and so on. Therefore, this tool must be delivered by the external consultancy. The relevant functionality is assumed to be delivered as part of a SharePoint implementation where you already have brought in the SharePoint project team.

In Example 1, a benefit of using an external consultancy for a SharePoint 2010 implementation is knowledge transfer to the organization. When using an external consultancy to implement SharePoint they most likely will have their own project manager who will then be responsible for implementing SharePoint. A project manager hired as a consultant—that is, one who is not part of the client organization—will require more time to prepare than an internal project manager, because the internal project manager will already be in tune with the relevant project management procedures and policies. However, it is distinctly possible that an externally provided project manager from a SharePoint consultancy will have more experience and not be tied to any political issues; however, they may have to take longer to ensure full cooperation with staff in the organization.

External consultancies, while adding cost, do provide excellent service if they are knowledgeable about the product, have dealt with implementing SharePoint 2010 before, and follow repeatable processes and procedures (like the ones I am covering in this book). Keep in mind, though, that at the end of the process of implementing SharePoint 2010, the external consultants should not just step away, because every implementation must be supported in some way by the consultancy.

The process of having the outside consultants hand over their duties to internal teams and individuals is important and is covered in more detail in Chapter 14, "Releasing SharePoint to the Client."

> **Note**
> The client might request the use of an outside organization to provide SharePoint if they believe the outside consultants will not be hampered by the internal politics of the organization; or they might believe that there is no skill set available in the organization based on their requirements. (For the latter, this would have to be proven to the client; the client won't simply assume this.) Also, the client might regard the use of an internal project management office as too closely aligned with one portion of the business or another, or they might conclude that the processes of the organization concerning technology releases are not mature enough.

Terms of Reference

Remember, you only need an external consultancy if you are a client who does not have access to project management resources and no SharePoint knowledge resources are available.

If you are as project manager going to engage the services of an external consultancy, then you must create a TOR so that the consultancy is clear on who it reports to, and the scope of the work it is going to carry out. I have provided an online article explaining the procedures you could apply to the management of subcontractors. To view the procedures, go to: *http://www.sharepointgeoff.com/sharepoint/spssubcontractor.aspx.*

You must identify the scope whether it's to help implement a specific element (like Records Management Taxonomy), or an external product that interfaces to SharePoint.

Developers: Are They Needed in a SharePoint Implementation Project?

Some organizations faced with wanting to implement SharePoint have done so by recruiting a SharePoint developer contractor who then installs SharePoint, carries out customization, and then leaves the organization. This approach, as you can imagine, leaves the client with a virtually unsupported platform, resulting in it being completely rebuilt at some point because it either becomes impossible to upgrade or there is a lack of configuration management information available. Other companies find that they are locked into attempting to keep the SharePoint developer, who then becomes a kind of a SharePoint administrator and developer—remember, no one is a SharePoint Superman!

As you'll see from reading this chapter, a SharePoint project team is much more than someone getting a copy of SharePoint 2010, dropping it into a server DVD drive, and after a couple of clicks tells the customer, "Here's SharePoint! Have fun!"

Developers in SharePoint are not planners, neither are they architects, business-focused analysts, or information architects. Their task is to take SharePoint and add functionality relevant to a specific client requirement that is not in SharePoint, or it is to customize the look and feel of the platform—again, to a specific client requirement. SharePoint 2010 provides power to users to customize their Web sites more than SharePoint 2007 allowed them to; hence, the requirement for branding is lessened (to a degree) in SharePoint 2010. However, in a SharePoint 2010 implementation you do not need a developer to install SharePoint 2010, because there is no specific client requirement that requires customizing SharePoint 2010 in the planning, deployment, or release stage. Development in SharePoint 2010 is a completely separate project because that carries its own quality planning, delivery, configuration, and deployment phases.

I've seen and implemented environments where there have been heavy customization requirements, and where there have been absolutely no requirements or need to modify SharePoint out of the box. In neither case is a developer required from the outset, because the client wants SharePoint. It's what needs to be done with SharePoint post implementation that warrants further development.

So let me be clear here. Development means programming. Programming means coding. That requires separate tools, processes, and management. It is not the same as implementing SharePoint to a client's infrastructure. I am not saying developers are not required—they are *definitely* required. But their involvement in the configuration of a SharePoint implementation is minimal, unless the user requirements are such that a SharePoint developer is needed to build in the extra functionality needed.

This means that when the initial build is completed, and there needs to be development, that is when you bring in the developer to add customization, branding, coding, automation, Web parts, or whatever the user requirement is. As part of the implementation of SharePoint, you'll need to prepare for the developer by providing a working environment.

In Chapter 7, "The Business of SharePoint Architecture," I discuss how development environments should be introduced as part of the SharePoint 2010 implementation.

The role of the SharePoint developer is to create solutions to meet user requirements that cannot be provided out-of-the-box. These solutions can include more than those I just mentioned in situations where the SharePoint architect has agreed with the project manager that a client or user requirement can only be fulfilled by a developer. If a developer is required, there needs to be a Work Breakdown Schedule (WBS) for each of the development tasks, and these must be wrapped into the deploy and build stage so that the project manager can reach an agreement with the client on the timing, the work required, and all additional costs. All work carried out by the developer is subject to configuration management.

A SharePoint developer is an ASP .NET developer who is comfortable in Microsoft Visual Studio and has SharePoint development skills on top of this ASP .NET base. Yes, the developer could just use SharePoint Designer and do a load of custom development without ever touching Visual Studio or .NET code. But they need to have knowledge of SharePoint Designer and Visual Studio to be a complete SharePoint developer. The developer's skill set should span the following possible project tasks:

- Customize functionality of specific Web parts—for example, the DataView Web part

- Assemble workflows

- Establish branding and style—for example, master pages, styles for Web parts, and so on

Chapter 5

- Develop Web parts

- Develop features (including list definitions, site definitions, and so on)

- Develop list event handlers

- Develop a workflow

Communications, Testers, Education, and Training

To ensure successful implementation of SharePoint 2010, you must address issues and resources related to communications, testing, education, and training.

Communications

The communications team is responsible for updating staff on the developments of the SharePoint 2010 implementation. During a SharePoint implementation, there will be lots of news for staff concerning Training, Support, Demonstrations, Question and Answer sessions, and opportunities to engage with the project team. Utilizing this role is vital as it helps staff properly engage with SharePoint and helps them feel as if they are part of the implementation.

Testers—Quality Assurance

During the gathering of user requirements, individuals will be assigned the role of *tester* of a particular feature or service that has been requested, or be designated as a quality assurance resource to confirm that the feature or service works effectively. These individuals are assigned their roles by the business in the context of what is to be tested, with the agreement of the project manager. For example, if there is a requirement for a SharePoint site, people who will act as testers and quality assurance personnel are identified during the gathering of user requirements. These resources carry out acceptance testing. Acceptance Testing of SharePoint is extremely important. The goals that SharePoint must meet in terms of the client vision, and the requirements set out by the users need to checked as being delivered to their satisfaction.

Education and Training

Education and training continues throughout the project, and every member of the core team has a responsibility to educate the client and staff about SharePoint 2010. However, education and training should be classified as a project in its own right, because as new users get on stream, a strategy is needed for how they will be trained and what the training model will be. The SharePoint 2010 One-Stop Shop is useful in this area because you can use FAQs and "How Do I" files within the site to provide guidance information. However, the training strategy needs to include workshops, face-to-face training, and one-on-one training, as well as supporting end user and development training. Education and testing go hand in hand. There is no point in providing the client with a new platform its users do not fully understand unless the client can run validated tests on it first to ensure they can confirm that what they requested is in place (or not) and they understand how to use the platform.

Building the Team

When you have your team together, you need to ensure they are all clear on what needs to be done. Therefore, you create the TORs for them in a TOR document, reference the TOR in the SharePoint 2010 Quality Plan, and post the TORs to your SharePoint One-Stop Shop. (The SharePoint One-Stop Shop is a central site to store project information and is further discussed in Chapter 13.)

There are four types of sessions you need to include as part of the project:

- Strategy Brief Session

- Architectural Design Session

- Engagement Summary Session

- Demonstrations and Presentation Session or Sessions

The purpose of these sessions is explained in the following sections. It is important that these sessions are given priority and that you include every one of them. For demonstrations and presentations, you need to repeat sessions as the project unfolds. For example, you might find that you want to demonstrate the test environment to a technical team, demonstrate an intranet site to a team, or describe the features of SharePoint 2010.

Strategy Brief

If building materials are randomly dropped from the sky, there is a chance that they might land and form a building—but the odds are pretty small. Creating a high-quality building requires detailed plans and skilled implementation of those plans.

Chapter 5

SharePoint includes a vast number of building blocks (tactics) that can be employed to maximize return on investment (ROI). To use them effectively, it's important to develop a blueprint (a strategy) in advance that does the following:

- Defines specific goals

- Establishes a baseline

- Defines specific tactics

- Defines budget allocation

- Defines metrics, measurements, and milestones

Therefore, your Strategy Brief to the client must cover the following:

- Describe business goals

- Describe SharePoint 2010 features and benefits

- Describe Office 2010 features and benefits

- Describe any infrastructure related to optimization and benefits of SharePoint 2010

The output of this session is a record used to help create the SharePoint 2010 Quality Plan.

Architectural Design

The Architectural Design Session (ADS) enables the client to focus their vision, productivity objectives, principles, and standards. It helps create a SharePoint roadmap to guide the selection, deployment, operations, and adoption of SharePoint.

The ADS moves through three phases, loosely described as Discovery, Envisioning, and Planning:

- **Discovery**   Description of the business and context

- **Envisioning**   Extract business scenarios that can be described and built, and consider the technology and approach for those scenarios

- **Planning**   Critical to describing the features of the technology, mapping these features to the business needs of the customer, and then describing the physical design that is required to support the business requirements

The ADS is used as a starting point to gather user requirements and create the System Specification document. User requirements are covered in Chapter 11, "Making Sure Share-Point Meets User Requirements," and the System Specification document is covered in Chapter 12, "Producing the System Specification."

ADS requires the description of design decisions meeting the client's requirements, including requirements related to the following topics:

- Enterprise content management

- Enterprise search

- Social collaboration

- Portal collaboration

- Taxonomy metadata

- Work processes business intelligence

- Infrastructure design

- Capacity design

- Governance and SharePoint management top-level decisions

- Risk discussion

- Tools and resources required

- Deployment strategy

- Cost model

This session follows from the Plan phase, where information is gathered. It's a session hosted by the SharePoint architect, business analyst, and information analysts and provided to the client technical teams as set by the technical authority.

Engagement Summary

Review, finalize, and document the SharePoint 2010 high-level solution. In this, you consolidate the SharePoint 2010 Quality Plan and summarize how SharePoint 2010 could integrate with the client's environment and meet SharePoint 2010 drivers and requirements. This is the final meeting with the team and client before the build of the SharePoint 2010 environment is undertaken and allows the client to pose any final questions before signoff.

Presentations and Demo Sites

It is very important that, as the project takes off, you have break-out sessions for staff and the client to see SharePoint 2010, allowing them to try out features of SharePoint 2010, thus getting more engaged with the product. A good way to provide areas for the staff and client is to use the SharePoint test environment (one of the environments that would be created), which houses a number of SharePoint test sites.

> **Note**
> You can also demonstrate SharePoint 2010 by using the 2010 Information Worker Demonstration and Evaluation Virtual Machine. This is a download that contains a set of two Windows Server 2008 R2 Hyper-V Virtual Machines (VMs) for evaluating and demonstrating Office 2010, SharePoint 2010, and Project Server 2010. You can download it from the following site: *http://www.microsoft.com/downloads/details. aspx?FamilyID=751fa0d1-356c-4002-9c60-d539896c66ce&displaylang=en.*

Using demo sites is useful when user requirements are being collected by the business analyst. If you show SharePoint sites in a workshop designed to capture user requirements, the attendees can be shown areas of SharePoint sites and then asked questions. This enables the attendees to become further engaged with the product and learn more about its features and benefits.

> **Note**
> As users move onto test sites, be aware that you should provide any test site with full visibility of another test site (so the whole organization can play together if necessary). Training should be provided to those requesting test sites; this will create SharePoint champions who can then communicate positive things about the platform to other users and cascade trained knowledge. Test sites, of course, are fully "test" sites, so no backup or retention plans are available for them. Users should be made aware of this so that if, for example, they want to use the sites for real, the relevant sites can be migrated to stage for full testing and then onto production as soon as the stage testing has been signed off on by the business.

Summary

All implementation technical teams are similar, but SharePoint 2010 projects are not a pure technical effort. A SharePoint 2010 implementation requires people with business skills, technical skills, project skills, information analysis skills, training skills, and so on.

A SharePoint 2010 project implementation team also requires a clear set of tasks. These tasks, related through project WBSs right back to the SharePoint 2010 Quality Plan, are tied into the TOR for each of the team members. The project manager builds these TORs because that person is accountable to the project. The first section in this chapter gives headings for a TOR that you can use as a guide.

In any SharePoint 2010 implementation project, there are many technical tasks, business tasks, and key people that are required:

- **Design**   SharePoint architect, SharePoint administrator, business analyst, internal teams, and external teams

- **Taxonomy and Metadata**   Information architect

- **Governance**   SharePoint architect and information architect

- **Build**   Internal and external teams, SharePoint architect, and SharePoint administrator

- **Configuration**   SharePoint administrator, SharePoint architect, and internal teams

- **Deploy**   SharePoint administrator, SharePoint architect, SharePoint developer, and internal teams

- **Test Quality Assurance**   Client business elected, and technical authority

- **Support**   SharePoint administrator

- **Maintenance**   SharePoint architect, SharePoint administrator, governance (business)

While it is possible that the people in the preceding list can be drafted into the project as a mixture of consultants and internal staff, it is vital that a budget is available to outsource the expertise if it is not available in the organization where SharePoint 2010 is to be implemented. Good examples of outsourcing are the SharePoint architect, SharePoint developer, and SharePoint administrator because these roles require deep SharePoint knowledge that might not be available in the client organization. You might have to bring in further expertise if in-house experience is not sufficient (for example, SQL teams, Exchange consultants, Active Directory consultants).

Chapter 5

All of these teams are identified by the project manager, who consults with the technical authority when negotiating the availability of internal technical team resources.

Under no circumstances should someone be randomly elected "The SharePoint Techie" and be made responsible for the design of SharePoint 2010 if they don't know the product deeply. Making your Windows Server administrator the SharePoint architect and administrator, for example, is courting disaster.

SharePoint 2010 features such as enterprise content management requires a combination of SharePoint architect, business analysts, and information architects, to ensure client and user requirements are fully investigated in a large organization. The business analysts glean the current business process and map this so that the work processes can be streamlined to SharePoint 2010. Information architects ensure metadata and taxonomy are applied to these processes—and that these are implemented into enterprise content management using the skills of a SharePoint architect. If the user requirements require further work on features that are not directly available in SharePoint, a SharePoint developer will be required as well.

A proper and successful SharePoint 2010 implementation is achieved through a combination of dedicated, skilled staff that has been given clear goals. Those goals must not only be achievable, but they must have detailed output through configuration management (the output from your team in implementing SharePoint 2010).

CHAPTER 6

Gathering the Resources for SharePoint Implementation

Building SharePoint 2010 Resources

In the Plan phase for the SharePoint 2010 implementation, tasks are focused on gathering software and hardware resources. The information related to these resources includes user and technical data, provided against a backdrop of the client's current system performance, resilience, disaster recovery plan, and business continuity plan.

During the resource information-gathering phase, reviews compare what has been made available to what the client needs are, and they are adjusted against the timeframe and funds available in the project budget. The reviews also take into account the client's vision of the predicted budget as defined earlier in the SharePoint 2010 Quality Plan.

There are many SharePoint 2010 software and hardware resources. They are detailed, complex, and often need to be recorded and quantified with care. You'll need to strike a balance between providing a system that can be scaled for growth in a carefully managed way, and one that is scaled for growth by having everything switched on just because you think the client might need it.

For example, I was called by a client who had a problem with their SharePoint implementation. It had seemed like a good implementation when it was set up—the scope of the delivery matched up with the client's support and resiliency arrangements. However, a problem developed with a service that automatically took information from a database and posted the outcomes into a SharePoint list. The client had over 300,000 items in one list, and the list was still growing. They noticed their search function starting to slow. They also noticed that the search index was growing out of control. They were running out of disk capacity. From a quick check of the list configuration, I noticed that it had Include In Search switched on, meaning that all items would be included in the search index. Another check identified that the Business Data Connection (BDC) included the indexing of all the fields, which meant that they were also included in the search scope.

Although that example might be a little too detailed, it makes the following points:

- There is little point in switching everything on unless there is a direct requirement to do so.

- You need to review and justify exactly what is required to deliver SharePoint to the client.

Additionally, some implementations of SharePoint 2010 fail to recognize that features need to be balanced. This means you must follow a program of events to get all features required from SharePoint and that risk management needs to be carried out at every stage of implementing SharePoint 2010.

For example, apply these considerations to a car. You want to buy a bigger engine for the car to make it go faster. But if you don't research whether the brakes are sufficient at higher speeds, you could be heading for an accident!

Therefore, make sure you compile a complete list of assets, and then set out a configuration management plan to deploy them.

Chapter 5, "Building Your SharePoint 2010 Team," covers the important topics of setting out the human resources, including the SharePoint architect, interfacing teams, and so on.

SharePoint 2010 technical resources are split between hardware and software expertise, so the individuals responsible for identifying the physical nature of the SharePoint 2010 technical configuration must be skilled in the platform. Put another way, they need to know not just the engine but the entire car. They must have system analyst skills so that they can be relied upon to collate, record, and design according to standard procedures and practices. They also need to be able to follow rules about how the data will be captured and where the data will be stored because that data needs to be accessed by interfacing technical teams.

What Procedures Detail Rules Concerning SharePoint Project Resource Data?

If you want details about document records and control procedures beyond what is given in this section, please see the online article "Data and Document Control" at: *http:// www.sharepointgeoff.com/sharepoint/docdatacontrol.aspx*. Also, Chapter 10, "SharePoint Configuration Management," suggests rules to implement regarding how recorded data should be altered as part of a formal change control process. And Chapter 13, "Planning and Implementing the SharePoint One-Stop Shop," contains information about the SharePoint One-Stop Shop.

> **Note**
>
> The SharePoint 2010 One-Stop Shop centralizes the documentation related to the document control process and configuration management for other interfacing teams to access.

Think carefully about your document control and records retention strategies. Going down the route of assuming, "I could easily get a record of all SharePoint 2010 resources by making a couple of phone calls and then enter that straight into my notepad," is probably not going to make you many friends within the interfacing teams—especially if they have processes that ensure the data is recorded in a format they are happy with. However, one of the best ways to capture the data is using SharePoint 2010, because you can ensure that the data captures meet the format the interfacing teams are happy with, that it is standard-ized, that its far easier to collate, and—most importantly—it's a *repeatable* exercise.

Using SharePoint 2010 Sites for Project Recording

SharePoint 2010 has excellent project-management recording capabilities. A starting point for taking advantage of these capabilities is to create a Project site within the SharePoint One-Stop Shop specifically targeted at being the database for the SharePoint 2010 imple-mentation. In Chapter 5, "Building Your Sharepoint 2010 Plan," I mention that you should approach a SharePoint 2010 implementation by already having a Project site (for example, a proof-of-concept environment) for the SharePoint project team. You maintain this team site until you have a SharePoint production environment, and then you migrate the team's SharePoint 2010 Project site into that environment as part of the SharePoint One-Stop Shop. SharePoint 2010 includes a *site template* that allows you to create a Project site as I just described. Using the Projects Web Database template (which you can access from the Create screen), from the home page, click Site Actions then click New Site as shown in Fig-ure 6-1.

Figure 6-1 SharePoint 2010 Projects Web Database template.

From the Projects Web Database site you can create interfaces completely with Microsoft Access 2010. This enables you to design a fully functional Project Management site to manage resource gathering for the SharePoint 2010 implementation using Microsoft Access 2010 features. You can also take advantage of further customization using the data repositories (as tables) and fine-tuning the functionality of the forms.

The SharePoint 2010 implementation project is split into three phases: the Plan phase, Build phase, and Deploy phase. You can easily transpose this approach into three subprojects and use all the processes and procedures in this book.

Chapter 3, "Content of Your SharePoint 2010 Project Plan," details the three phases of a SharePoint implementation project.

Figure 6-2 shows an example of the three phases injected into the Open Projects tab of a SharePoint 2010 Implementation Projects Database site.

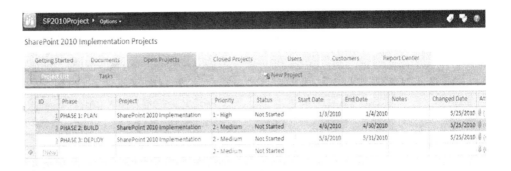

Figure 6-2 The Open Projects tab on the SharePoint 2010 Implementation Projects Database site.

The Projects Web Database template includes Open Projects and Closed Projects sections. These sections can be used to determine what phase has been completed. Each of the phases are linked to a project. Because of this, you can define tasks for each of the phases. Figure 6-3 shows a few of the typical tasks that would be included in the PHASE 1: PLAN phase.

Figure 6-3 Tasks that appear as part of PHASE 1: PLAN.

The tasks listed in the relevant sections are assigned to contacts who are listed on the Users tab.

Building SharePoint 2010 Resources: The Tasks Ahead

As mentioned earlier, various tasks must be completed to ensure you have all the information needed to move into the next phase (Build). To make it easier to understand, tasks must be completed at each stage. Table 6-1 lists the relevant tasks along with a description of each and a suggested resource you can use to help you build the resource documentation.

Complete each of these tasks, and use the resources in Chapter 11, "Making Sure SharePoint Meets User Requirements," and Chapter 12, "Producing the System Specification."

> **Note**
>
> These tasks do not run back to back, and depending on the environment being created not every task requires all the resources noted. These are given as a guide so that when you develop your SharePoint 2010 Project Plan, you are aware of the work to be carried out in a particular phase (and as such the resources you'll need). Additionally, and as a reminder, this book will not describe the details of how you build the resources; it describes what is required. To aid you, I've added TechNet links and other useful Microsoft resources where appropriate. A significant amount of resources and support are also available on the Microsoft SharePoint site, which is located at *http://technet.microsoft.com/en-us/sharepoint/default.aspx*.

> **Note**
>
> "Task" is the Work Breakdown Structure Task heading, and "Description" and "Resource" refer to what must be done for the task and who is responsible for completing that task, respectively. You'll need either Microsoft Project 2010 to enter these tasks, or you'll need a Gantt list from SharePoint to store these tasks and map them against the documentation gathered.

Table 6-1 Relevant Tasks Needed for Building Resource Documentation

Task	Description and Resource
Define Vision Statement	The project manager agrees with the client and technical authority as to what SharePoint will do for the organization.
Success Criteria	This item is a statement about what constitutes a success when SharePoint has been released to the client.
	Resource: Project manager

Task	Description and Resource
Assemble Project Teams and Define Roles	Related tasks for this item include the following: • Recruit team members. • Create a Terms of Reference (TOR) for each member. • Assign roles and resonsibilities in the TORs. (Review Chapter 5, "Building Your SharePoint 2010 Team," for more information on these tasks.) Resource: Project manager and technical authority
Gather Technical Requirements	Related tasks for this item include the following: • Detail SharePoint 2010 requirements. • Detail technology architecture. • Create SharePoint Server hardware and software inventory. • Create client hardware and software inventory. • Detail computing environment (communications rooms and so on). • Create client service delivery model. • Detail content and audit activities. • List client and server licenses. Resource: SharePoint architect, administrator, interfacing teams (for example, Desktop, SQL, Active Director, Exchange), technical authority
Gather Business Requirements	Related tasks for this item include the following: • List audience requirements. • List user productivity requirements. • List access and permissions. • List content management requirements. • List migration requirements. • List taxonomy/metadata requirements. Resource: Business analyst, end users, project manager, SharePoint architect
Design Objectives	Related tasks for this item include the following: • Map SharePoint 2010 against current computing environment. • Confirm integrated software strategy (for example, using Microsoft Office 2010). • Investigate storage requirements. • Determine strategy for communicating project details to staff. • Determine information architecture approach. • Determine branding requirements. • Review with client and achieve signoff. Resource: Project manager, SharePoint architect, technical authority, client

Chapter 6

Task	Description and Resource
Identify Coexistence	Investigate and resolve company and external partner operating systems, protocols, topology, and service delivery models. Resource: Project manager, SharePoint architect, technical authority
Create a Test Lab	Related tasks for this item include the following: • Select locations. • Confirm space, environment, power, and network requirements. • Design logical and physical configuration. • Determine access, roles, and permissions to the lab (including the change control process, such as configuration management). • Sign off. Link (server requirements): *http://technet.microsoft.com/en-us/library/cc262485.aspx*. Resource: Project manager, SharePoint architect, SharePoint administrator
Risk Assessment	Related tasks for this item include the following: • Identify and analyze risks. • Investigate and detail escalation. • Evaluate quantity impact. • Document risks. (For more information on the SharePoint risk-management procedure and how to use it, see the online article titled "SharePoint Risk Management: at: *http://www.sharepointgeoff.com/spsprjmgmt/riskmanagement.aspx*). Resource: Project manager, technical authority, client
Project Communications	Related tasks for this item include the following: • Plan, build, and deploy a communications strategy. • Define who should be informed, how the communications should be delivered, and the timeframe and standards to be followed. • Document and sign off on the strategy. Resource: Project manager, client, technical authority
Define Education and Training Strategy	Related tasks for this item include the following: • Define requirements. • Define education strategy and delivery for end users. • Define education strategy and delivery for interfacing teams. • Document and sign off on the strategy. Resource: Project manager, SharePoint architect, interfacing team (using an external trainer is a possibility)

Task	Description and Resource
Review Software and Hardware	Related tasks for this item include the following: • Investigate client hardware and software, compare them to SharePoint 2010 hardware requirements, and document the differences. • Investigate the current desktop applications and determine if an upgrade to Microsoft Office 2010 is beneficial. • Upgrade hardware/software if needed. (Note that this could end up being another subproject!) • Document and sign off on this task. Resource: Interfacing teams, technical authority, SharePoint architect
Plan Security	Related tasks for this item include the following: • Define the framework of SharePoint 2010 service accounts. • Define the framework of logical content. • Investigate internal security (for example, Active Directory, infrastructure connectivity), including connectivity to Internet. Resource: Interfacing teams, SharePoint architect
Performance Planning	Related tasks for this item include the following: • Investigate, document, and confirm connectivity and bandwidth, both current and required. • Investigate, document, and confirm network performance levels, and diagram network topology to meet requirements. • Document and sign off on the plan. • Upgrade the network as required. (Note that this could end up being another subproject!) Resource: SharePoint architect, interfacing teams
Disaster Recovery and Continuity	Related tasks for this item include the following: • Document the current disaster recovery plan (at the SQL Server level and server level). • Document, confirm, and produce a plan for SharePoint 2010 failover, and list disaster recovery requirements. • Confirm Recycle Bin and site recovery planning. • Document and sign off on the plan. Resource: SharePoint architect, interfacing teams
Localization (Language)	Related tasks for this items include the following: • Determine and install the languages required on the test platform. • Review the settings using SharePoint 2010 Multilingual User Interface (MUI). You can find more information about this at: *http://technet.microsoft.com/en-us/library/cc262108.aspx*. • Document and sign off on this task. Resource: SharePoint architect, SharePoint administrator

Chapter 6

Task	Description and Resource
Integration	Related tasks for this items include the following: • Confirm the SharePoint 2010 version required (Foundation, Standard, or Enterprise). • Confirm the SharePoint client tools required (for example, SharePoint 2010 Workspace, Microsoft Office Communicator). • Confirm ForeFront Protection 2010 for SharePoint. You can find out more information about this at: *http://technet.microsoft.com/en-us/forefront/ff521619.aspx.* • Determine the need for each of the following services. If they are required, install and configure them on a test platform. Document and sign off on the following services: Search Service Application, Profile Service Application, Access Services, Business Data Catalog, Excel Services, Managed Metadata Service, Secure Store Service, Usage and Health, Visio Graphics Services, Reporting Services. Service applications in SharePoint 2010 are a huge improvement to the product, addressing many of the scalability compromises inherent in the SSP model in SharePoint 2007. Service applications can now be built by third parties and are available in both SharePoint Foundation and SharePoint Server. Service applications significantly impact farm topologies; therefore, it is more important than ever to understand the core concepts. Resource: SharePoint architect, SharePoint administrator
Maintenance	Related tasks for this item include the following: • Plan the farm backup and restore strategies. • Plan granular backup strategies. • Plan routine maintenance. • Determine quotas. • Configure zones and alternate access mappings (AAM). • Plan site use and deletion. • Document and sign off on the strategies. Resource: SharePoint architect, SharePoint administrator

What Is the Output of the Resource Gathering?

After you have documented all the tasks listed in Table 6-1, you can create a *SharePoint 2010 Requirement and System Specification* document. Once you have completed your document, you can put it through a *verification* exercise, which is required prior to seeking signoff. The signoff is crucial—it marks the start of the next and final stage of SharePoint 2010 implementation: the Deploy phase.

The SharePoint 2010 Requirement and System Specification document is described in Chapter 12.

Gathering Business Requirements

To begin this phase, you need to identify the business requirements and the people who will be needed for the implementation.

SharePoint Business Analyst

The responsibility of the business analyst is to collate and clearly record the client's requirements so that they can be mapped to SharePoint. Before the business analyst can collate the recorded data, a number of resources are required:

- A location to store the collected data

- A list of all the key data users and those who have a stake in managing data in the organization

- A list of coordinated events to ensure the data is recorded in each area

- A standard set of questions that can be asked of each group

So, what is the connection between capturing client usage of content and the technical and software requirements? Let me give you a few examples.

Example #1

Client A is using a software tool to record the state of items in a product life cycle. This tool is known to the technical staff only from the perspective that they have to support it; however, they don't use it on a daily basis (because they are not the end-users). Hence, they are concerned only with the inner workings of the software (the engine) and not directly concerned with making it work (driving it).

The data gathering by the business analyst captures how the product life cycle works and what the client does with the tool to make that happen. This data is crucial because it allows the SharePoint architect to ensure that the life cycle of the product is mapped to the features of SharePoint.

> **Example #2**
>
> Client B creates content that is output in Adobe Acrobat format. The client is keen to be able to search the output based on keywords injected into the PDF file.

A number of things need to take place. First, the business analyst records the process of file generation and where and how the keywords are defined and injected into the PDF. Information analysts might be required (if available) to provide a higher level perspective on how these "keywords" are defined for the organization. SharePoint architects and administrators are then needed to ensure the search functionality as well as the SharePoint 2010 Managed Metadata Service is configured and enabled correctly.

Therefore, there is a direct relationship between the data provided by the business analyst and the data provided from the SharePoint architect. The business analyst provides user requirements defined by the business. The SharePoint Architect provides design and system specifications to meet those user requirements. There needs to be a coordinated effort within the project team to ensure that data is defined, prioritized, and scheduled as tasks so that SharePoint 2010 receives the configuration it needs to get the requirements as detailed in the data.

SharePoint Architect and Technical Authority

The technical authority works closely with the SharePoint architect by providing the necessary experts needed in the field for all the interfacing teams (for example, SQL, Active Directory, Exchange). These experts provide information that helps ensure SharePoint 2010 fits into the client's environment. They are also important in helping to procure equipment (software and hardware), and manage access to the locations where SharePoint 2010 is to be delivered (for example, server communication rooms and data centers). It is during this phase that the equipment required is identified and procured and the SharePoint 2010 test environment is created.

The SharePoint architect creates a SharePoint 2010 physical topology based on the client requirements concerning resiliency, performance, connectivity, and disaster recovery. The server model exposed in that physical topology can be a distributed environment.

Let's look at an example where you provision a small SharePoint 2010 topology based on a three-tier small farm comprising the following:

- Two Web front-end servers

- One application server

- One SQL cluster

Gathering Business Requirements

It sounds straightforward. However, this presents an operational challenge. Let's say the two Web front-end servers and the application server are to be supported by SharePoint personnel. The SQL cluster, however, is already supported by a dedicated team of SQL database administrators (DBAs). This means there must be cooperation between the SharePoint personnel and the DBAs. The teams must aid one another, and the SharePoint personnel must investigate the DBAs' rules concerning connectivity to SQL—for example, in the generation of service accounts, their permissions, disaster recovery, backup, and so on. This also means that the agreed-upon physical topology for SharePoint will require another level to be added to the resource matrix, called support of the SharePoint 2010 platform. Support of SharePoint 2010 is described as the nature of who will look after the platform and how. If support for the topology is not agreed on, there will be difficulty for SharePoint 2010 to scale up beyond the physical topology, because the topology is what defines the level of support that needs to be applied to SharePoint.

Taking the preceding model further, you also need to list the specifications of the servers— memory, CPU, hard-disk capacity, network connectivity, and so on. As part of the architecture, you factor in resiliency. So, for example, you might indicate that the hard disk drives are set up as a Storage Area Network (SAN). SAN is an architecture used to attach remote computer storage devices such as disk arrays, tape libraries, and so on, in such a way that they appear to be locally attached to the operating system on the relevant servers. Therefore, it is possible to to attach or unattach drives to SharePoint servers for disaster recovery reasons.

Thus, the information the SharePoint architect needs to gather is significant. Knowing what to gather is one thing, but there has to be a road map to the installation detailing what relates to what. I suggest the creation of the following seven documents:

- A Hardware Architecture document that deals with the topology, Web front end, application, SQL connectivity, and connected technologies and systems.

- A Variables and SharePoint 2010 Configuration document that takes into account software configuration, service accounts, IP addresses, host names, and the service application topology.

- A Software and Related Components list that lists software needed (for example, Windows Server 2008, SQL Server 2008, Office 2010, Visio 2010, Project 2010 and so on) and other components (for example, dotNET, IIS, ASP, and other prerequisites).

- An installation guide that includes information about server builds (for the operating system, disk configuration, and so on).

- An installation guide dealing with prerequistes related to installation and configuration.

- An installation guide that uses all of the preceding documents to install SharePoint 2010 according to the topology defined in the first document listed. It should also cover the actual steps from start to finish; from basic server SharePoint 2010 installation through site collection and service application configuration.

- Testing documents to verify and validate the installation completed.

These seven documents are also used in the creation of the SharePoint 2010 Requirements and System Specification document.

Chapter 12 provides more information on this topic.

Summary

The key success factor for recording the resource data for SharePoint 2010 is to standardize the approach. Resource gathering for SharePoint 2010 starts in the Plan phase of the implementation project. Configuration management also comes into play during the Plan phase and allows you to standardize how data is gathered.

As discussed in this chapter, the problem is not just building the resources; it is making sure those resources are defined, prioritized, and scheduled correctly. Therefore, this chapter provided a task list that states the jobs required to gather the requirements and indicates who the key people are who need to be responsible for doing that. As each of the Work Breakdown Structure (WBS) tasks are collated, the relevant project managers and leads need to sign off on them.

When you have completed defining the vision statement and the success criteria, only then can you assemble your project teams. To gather your technical requirements, you need your project teams. To design the environment, you need to know what hardware and software is available, what the licenses look like, and so on. It's vital, therefore, that you get a handle on this so that your project goes smoothly and you meet all the project requirements. Each of these tasks can and should be signed off on as completed and all should have reviews.

There will be many instances where the requirements of the client cannot be fulfilled on day one of SharePoint 2010 being released to the client. This can happen for any number of reasons: budget, timeframe, lack of resources, and so on. Configuration management provides procedures to use to ensure that the client is aware of what to expect from the final product. These procedures capture information about the project history: how the product was created, what data was made available from the end users, how it was tested, and so on. It's a key facet of the SharePoint 2010 Quality Plan.

Configuration management covers the management of all assets in the project. The data gathered is the most important asset. SharePoint implementation assets are a combination of business and technical data—any additions, alterations, or deletions of that data needs to be controlled.

In this chapter, I described the importance of SharePoint 2010 planning and the tasks that need to be done. It is vital that the project team has a full understanding of what is in place, what the pain points are for the end users, what end user requirements are related to SharePoint, what needs to be done, and what resources need to be sought to deploy SharePoint 2010 (which is the next phase). This means gathering and building resources, both business and technical.

I also described where best to get online information (by using resources such as TechNet and Microsoft sites). However, what is clear is that you need the skilled human resources (critically, the SharePoint architect and business analyst) to ensure data has been gathered correctly and relates to SharePoint 2010.

What follows is the Deploy phase. This is discussed further in Chapter 14, "Releasing Share-Point to the Client." Before that, we need to concern ourselves with more areas related to planning: customization, governance, configuration management, user requirements, system specification, and making sure there is somewhere to store planned data.

More information on this topic can be found in Chapter 11, "Making Sure SharePoint Meets User Requirements."

The Business of SharePoint Architecture

Describing SharePoint Business Architecture

ARCHITECTURE refers to the art of building. The word "architecture" has many meanings. Probably, the most understood meaning is "the art of constructing structures such as homes and buildings." The architect designs the blueprints of the home or building, taking into account factors such as design, space, light, materials, stability, load, and future needs.

Architecture is important because it accounts for the functional and nonfunctional requirements early on. Microsoft Office SharePoint Products and Technologies are powerful tools that increase collaboration and sharing of content. If implemented correctly, SharePoint can store and serve a vast quantity of information very well. However, without proper architecture and governance, a SharePoint deployment can become a disorganized collection of sites, links, users, and documents that hamper productivity, which makes it harder to find information.

Good architecture and governance plans (discussed in Chapter 9, "SharePoint Governance") lay down guidelines for deploying SharePoint as a solution to common business challenges. The architecture of SharePoint includes:

- Designing and allocating the hardware infrastructure needed to support the site

- Listing out the sites and site hierarchies that will serve the needs of the business

- Establishing users and roles that will be given permissions to the sites

- Establishing the relationships between sites

- Planning for the needed site features, site customizations, and site and list relationships (which include how data will be rolled up and aggregated from sites and lists to provide an overview of information)

A good governance plan outlines the administration, maintenance, and support of the SharePoint environment. The governance strategy seeks to ensure that SharePoint is used in accordance with the designed goal and that the best practices are followed to keep the portal manageable and usable. Best practices include processes for operation in the portal for tasks such as creating sites and lists, assigning permissions to users, using consistent naming conventions, and generally enforcing the guidelines.

Information architecture, which is discussed in Chapter 9, provides an important input to SharePoint governance.

When creating a building, architectural concerns include data gathering, planning, and the design of that building. The SharePoint architect must design the SharePoint building to withstand the test of time (meaning the architect must *future-proof* the implementation by building in robustness and resiliency) and, based on future client requirements, be able to expand easily (in other words, scalability with an eye on future upgradeability of SharePoint installation based on factors such as business need, hardware, software resources, and so on).

For SharePoint, there are three levels of architecture: hardware, software, and information.

Hardware Architecture

To deliver a robust SharePoint 2010 environment, it is necessary to carry out technical design, which looks at all areas of SharePoint 2010 concerning the equipment it will run on or be connected to and systems and processes it will interface with. The following is a list of planning requirements:

- **System requirements**   Determining what is required to deploy SharePoint 2010.

  You can read more about the minimum hardware and software requirements for installing and running SharePoint Server 2010 at *http://technet.microsoft.com/en-us/library/cc262485.aspx*. To read more about deploying SharePoint Foundation 2010, go to *http://technet.microsoft.com/en-us/library/cc287737.aspx*.

- **Services architecture**   Determine what service applications are defined and how they are structured. For further discussion, see the sections titled, "Concept" and "Topology" in Chapter 12, "Producing the SharePoint Specification."

- **Logical architecture**   Presents the design in terms of isolation. This planning task looks at farms, service applications, Web applications, content databases, site collections, sites, zones, MySites, and so on.

- **Authentication**   Examines authentication methods, such as claims-based authentication topologies.

- **Server hardening**   This task focuses on server snapshots, ports, protocols, and the Web Server, Application Server, and Database Server roles.

- **Business continuity**   Examines the business decisions, processes, and tools put in place to handle a crisis. A crisis can affect the organization or be part of a local, regional, or national event. Business continuity and disaster recovery are huge areas in SharePoint and planning for them is an important part of ensuring a resilient and robust platform.

  Find out how to apply business continuity to SharePoint at *http://sharepointbcp .geoffevelyn.com* and how to apply disaster recovery planning to SharePoint at *http://sharepointdr.geoffevelyn.com*.

- **Performance and capacity**   Determines the process of mapping the design for SharePoint 2010 to a farm size and the hardware needed to support the business goals.

  Performance and capacity are discussed further in the section "Performance Requirements," on page 199, in Chapter 12.

- **Virtualization**   SharePoint 2010 is fully supported when deployed in a Windows Server 2008 Hyper-V environment. This task examines the licensing and topology. This topic is further explained in Chapter 8, "SharePoint Customization."

Software Architecture

The software architecture of SharePoint is the structure or structures of the system, which comprise software elements, the externally visible properties of those elements, and the relationships among them. So decisions to be made include determining what components of SharePoint are needed, what will be visible, and the structure of SharePoint. For example, is SharePoint going to be treated as an out-of-the-box solution, slightly modified with internal applications, or will it include third-party additions? Will it simply need just team site components (for example, the free SharePoint Foundation version), or do you need more service application, enterprise content management, or metadata features, such as those provided through SharePoint 2010 Enterprise?

Software architecture examines SharePoint from a site and solution planning perspective, taking into consideration site components, security, governance, enterprise content management, Web content management, managed metadata, business intelligence, data and processes, access services, quota management, and social computing.

As an example, suppose that you're going to implement SharePoint in an organization that already has SharePoint but needs to expand. They have a third-party tool providing some functionality that the client finds useful. From scoping the information architecture, you found how much usage it gets, how the data is used, how it flows, and so on. From further investigation of the software architecture, you find that the relevant tool cannot grow with the service. This means revisiting the functionality in terms of the information architecture and finding an alternative, which then drives the software architecture.

Information Architecture

Information architecture involves studying the type and amount of information used within an organization, organizational structure, information flow, process flow, and more. This is an extremely important aspect of the Plan phase. Without it, SharePoint is not defined to meet the client requirements, because information architecture leads to SharePoint user strategy in terms of content management. Identifying the organizational information and management information goals combines the work of information analysts and business analysts, coordinated by the project manager and feeding back to the SharePoint architect.

Large organizations have documentation plans and methods of managing their data across the organization (for example, retention plans and archive plans), and some use information analysts to manage, coordinate, and categorize how members in the organization deal with information. Additionally, organizations face legal and regulatory compliance requirements that directly influence how data is retained long term. In the United States, for example, the Sarbanes-Oxley (SOX) Act established record-retention rules in July 2002. It is highly recommended that companies have a records-retention policy that complies with regional and national laws.

> **Note**
>
> If you keep too much data and are sued, the plaintiffs have the right to go through all data retained. However, if you have a policy that adheres to both regional and national retention policies under SOX, you are only liable to retain the information within those guidelines, and that information is all that can be used in a lawsuit.

Another benefit of a good records-retention policy is a decrease in storage costs. The information analyst details from the ground level the organizational data concerning information standards and policies set out by the business. (The information analyst is described in Chapter 5, "Building Your SharePoint 2010 Team.") Information architecture establishes information control and compliance policies so that accumulating information is done in a well-managed way and does not create data chaos.

SharePoint 2010 provides enterprise content management tools that can help lower costs associated with the control and storage of information, decrease complexity, and increase user participation relating to content control. Combining SharePoint 2010 with Office 2010 takes information management to a higher level by extending information control from the desktop environment to SharePoint 2010 sites and content.

The aim of information architecture in SharePoint is to reduce the manual end user actions related to metadata, to scale policies and processes across all types of content in an organization, and to increase compliance and transparency. To meet this goal, there must be an examination leading to the creation of an organizational taxonomy. During the design phase of the SharePoint project, the information analyst (working with the SharePoint architect) creates an organization taxonomy by examining metadata and information policies.

The business analyst can provide, through the collection of user requirements, an understanding of what the typical content life cycle is in the business. This shows how end user content becomes managed content. Typically, managed content begins its life as temporary information created by the individuals in the organization, leading to work in progress (and this means multiple individuals working on the same content) and in the backdrop of retention and disposition (business teams or individuals deciding on whether documents should be archived and what their state is, either approved, published, or other). SharePoint 2010 provides tools to ensure the content life cycle can be designed and adhered to. Enterprise content types, document sets, information management policies, metadata, term sets, and content organizers can be established using SharePoint 2010 document management features.

How Is Information Architecture Defined?

Here are some basic steps for setting the information architecture for SharePoint 2010:

- Carry out an investigation and inventory of existing content.

- Classify the content by performing the following tasks:

    ○ Look for definitions of structure, policy, and defaults.

    ○ Identify organizational-level content by enterprise, department, and team.

    ○ Define what "general use" content is.

- Organize content into enterprise content types and document sets, keeping the following factors in mind:

    ○ Content types contain definitions of structure, policy, and defaults.

    ○ Content types can inherit from other content types.

    ○ Document sets exist when work spans multiple documents.

- Decide where information management policies apply. When doing this, be sure to consider access permissions, auditing, user restrictions (for example, no printing), retention, and deletion.

- Decide on applicable metadata by performing the following tasks:

  - Define customized columns, and associate them with documents and lists.

  - Define any cases where the system or user might take different actions based on the characteristics of an item. Note that the characteristics of the item are metadata.

  - Find out what common things users will want to sort or filter items on.

  - Find out what words or phrases users are likely to tag items with.

  - Use Choice or Lookup columns in SharePoint 2010 sites.

  - Use the existing taxonomy if the organization has one.

- Map the physical flow of the document, including the sites, lists, and libraries where the content will be physically located throughout the document's life cycle.

Further Reading

SharePoint 2010 architecture is a massive topic, and this chapter covers the basics of three areas. I suggest you pursue further understanding of this topic because to address it will result in a successful SharePoint 2010 platform.

You can read more information about information architecture in a governance overview on TechNet at *http://technet.microsoft.com/en-us/library/cc263356.aspx*. You can also find a general perspective on planning and architecture at *http://technet.microsoft.com/en-us/library/cc261834.aspx*.

Summary

This chapter described the three types of SharePoint 2010 architecture as applied to the implementation of SharePoint in an organization: information, software, and hardware. Information architecture is known as *SharePoint business architecture* because it is the content that drives SharePoint. The data to be captured in this architecture requires investigation, process mapping, metadata (data about data), and categorization.

Once information architecture requirements are agreed upon, the project team can focus on ensuring the technical components required to meet user requirements and flow are mapped to the SharePoint 2010 Requirements and System Specification document. The content of this document comes from an examination of hardware and software (for example, hardware and software architecture). The SharePoint architect, among others (such as business analysts and information analysts), works closely with the interfacing team to detail the three architectural levels.

Hardware architecture is a physical topology and a road map indicating the structure of the equipment needed to deliver SharePoint and connectivity to internal and external services, such as e-mail, user directory services, and external file shares. It takes into consideration performance, resiliency, and security.

Software architecture relates not solely to the structure of SharePoint applications. It can include internally developed or externally provided applications or systems to provide further functionality not present in the SharePoint 2010 implementation.

SharePoint Customization

When to Customize SharePoint 2010 and Some Reasons for Doing It

When implementing Microsoft SharePoint 2010, the key to success is to keep things simple. In my experience, the business representatives on the team, who are excited about SharePoint from your demonstrations and SharePoint project mantra, are likely to go for looks as the top priority when developing an internal SharePoint presence.

There are many references and lots of information online and in paperback concerning branding, customization, programming, and automation. Coding enhancements in SharePoint are also a major plus because they show the level of modifications that can be applied to this technology, but they can also bring countless disadvantages if not carefully controlled and prioritized.

Implementation of SharePoint invariably includes customization, additions, modifications, and enhancements. You must be sure to prioritize these as part of user requirements, client requirements, or both. Your SharePoint 2010 Project Plan needs to package this SharePoint customization work into Work Breakdown Structures (WBSs) and apply them as part of the Design and Build phases of the project.

Even if you are not going to customize SharePoint to the point that it requires a developer to add functionality, you must make certain the client understands what is required in terms of technical and human resources to customize SharePoint. Acquiring the right amount of equipment and the correct personnel to carry out the relevant tasks is absolutely vital for success.

When faced with implementing SharePoint, I am usually gifted with a horde of development requirements from the customer. Sometimes, the customer is familiar with SharePoint in detail and has seen demonstrations. The Web developers in the company have also seen it and already want to modify, customize, and enhance it (usually with comments such as,

"SharePoint doesn't do X. I don't think that's right, so let's make it do X, Y, and Z."). These comments might reflect some good considerations, but to customize SharePoint to carry out some developed functionality means its application programming interface (API) must be fully understood.

As a good example of how a customization process can go wrong if it's not properly controlled, I'd like to share a story. I received a call from a client who wanted his company's SharePoint system re-evaluated. Apparently, SharePoint had been implemented by a Windows Server administrator, and the implementation strategy was "Just use it." When I arrived on the scene, I was greeted by a Web developer, who said something like the following:

"I am a Web developer and know CSS and Java. I'm going to change how SharePoint looks because it does not look pretty. It's a Web site, so it should not be difficult to brand it and make it look different and work better."

I suggested it might be a better idea to learn SharePoint development and understand the models under which SharePoint can be customized. He disagreed, stating that he could have branding done in no time at all.

So, the following day, I came across the same Web developer, and he says to me, "I can't do it. SharePoint is rubbish." I replied, "No, you have not understood the platform. Web development and SharePoint Web development are not the same."

The developer learned the hard way that SharePoint Web development is much more than using your understanding of HTML and cascading style sheets (CSS). It requires you to have an understanding of ASP and the SharePoint API. (Web developer skills are discussed in Chapter 5, "Building Your SharePoint 2010 Team.") In this instance, I suggested to the developer's boss that the developer be sent through training, ending with taking the Microsoft Certification test to prove he can handle SharePoint development.

Good SharePoint developers really know their stuff. Typically, they possess Microsoft Certification in Application Development in SharePoint. For more information about what this entails, you can read an overview of "Exam 70-573, Microsoft SharePoint 2010, Application Development," at *http://www.microsoft.com/learning/en/us/exam.aspx?ID=70-573* **and "Exam 70-576, Designing and Developing Microsoft SharePoint 2010 Applications," at** *http://www.microsoft.com/learning/en/us/exam.aspx?ID=70-576*.

The key is that SharePoint development needs to be controlled and managed with a great deal of care. SharePoint 2010 is feature rich, with an extremely detailed object model that covers all facets of the platform.

Let's begin with a bold statement:

A SharePoint developer is not a high-priority requirement of a new SharePoint implementation if the SharePoint implementation does not include modification through programming.

Take a look at Chapter 5 to see the kind of people required to make SharePoint become a successful reality in an organization that has never used SharePoint.

The need to "brand," for example, will come from user requirements, which are part of the Plan phase of the project. In the Plan phase, you define the user requirements, which might include branding. If that is the case, the tasks related to branding are packaged so that they are carried out after implementation of SharePoint, because you must first ensure that SharePoint is available.

In the Build phase, you create the SharePoint platform. If you have a user requirement to customize SharePoint, the Build phase is where the development tasks take place.

In the Deploy phase, the client signs off on the SharePoint implementation. Again, if the user requirements demand customization of SharePoint, you must have separate sign-offs for whatever customization takes place per user requirements.

Branding (for example) must go through user acceptance testing, but it is not the key requirement in getting users educated and trained in working with SharePoint if they have not used the platform before. Making SharePoint functional is all about meeting the users' information and management challenges. That does not include the immediate customization or modification of SharePoint core features. In short, yes, customization is required and the customization requests must be prioritized before that work can take place—but customization is not 100 percent vital to making SharePoint a success.

That said, as part of the SharePoint implementation, you must devise a development platform or logical approach to providing customization when a timeframe is given for customization work to be done. This chapter describes a design for a SharePoint 2010 development environment and how it could operate. This model assumes a development platform is built in-house—in other words, that there is a distinct possibility that SharePoint 2010 development will take place within the organization.

If there is a SharePoint test environment, a SharePoint user acceptance environment, and a SharePoint production environment, that is a good level of SharePoint resources for providing a development environment as well, which equates to a fourth environment.

In the past, development environments were restricted because, to build components, an increased level of resources would be required by the developer. SharePoint 2007 could be installed only in a Windows Server environment and not to the desktop. Developers were given either virtual environments (using Virtual PC or VMWare, for example) or in some cases a separate desktop to build SharePoint tools on. This arrangement could be difficult to manage and control because, generally, it was considered time consuming and sometimes problematic to connect local resources to the SharePoint virtual instance (for example, mapping local drives, USB drivers, external CD ROMs, shared drives, and so on).

Development Environment Options

A development environment is a sandboxed environment. The term *sandbox* is commonly used in the development of Web services to refer to a mirrored production environment for use by external developers. Typically, a developer creates an application that uses a Web service from the sandbox, which enables developers to validate their code before migrating it to a staging environment so that it can be tested by users before being published to the production environment. Sandboxing is used by Microsoft, Google, Amazon.com, PayPal, eBay, and Yahoo, among others.

In SharePoint 2007, there are three development environment options. (They are listed in the following section titled, "SharePoint 2007 Development Environment Options.") In SharePoint 2010, four options are available. (They are listed in the section titled, "SharePoint 2010 Development Environment Options," on page 141.)

If you are keen on finding out more information about running a SharePoint 2010 development environment on Windows Vista, Windows 7, and Windows Server 2008, go to *http://msdn.microsoft.com/en-us/library/ee554869.aspx*.

SharePoint 2007 Development Environment Options

The three options available in SharePoint 2007 are as follows:

- **Remote access to a shared SharePoint development server**   You can use this option if your project includes people who do not need their own SharePoint server—for example, designers and technical testers (those who work with the developers and test their code).

> **Note**
> There are logon restrictions to bear in mind. Specifically, a maximum of two administrators can be logged on to the server at any one time—either two logged on remotely, or one local and one remote administrator. And this assumes that different accounts are being used to log on. This means the same user cannot simultaneously log on locally and remotely.

- **Run a local virtual machine (VM) and use Boot to VHD (Virtual Hard Disk)**   This is a recommended approach. It causes the most hassle, but it provides the best performance. (Note that this will work only if Windows 7 is the host.)

- **Give every developer their own physical SharePoint server**   There are many reasons why this is not a good idea; clearly cost is a big drawback. SharePoint 2007 can be installed only on Windows Server and most developer machines do not run Windows Server as the host operating system. Tweaks to install SharePoint to Windows Vista were available, but they were considered risky because your development environment does not fully reflect the production server.

SharePoint 2010 Development Environment Options

Here are the four options available in SharePoint 2010:

- **Remote access to a shared SharePoint development server**   You can use this option if your project includes people who do not need their own SharePoint server. The disadvantages of this approach are the same as described in the section titled, "SharePoint 2007 Development Environment Options," on page 141.

- **Run your own local virtual machine:**

  - **Use either Hyper-V or VMWare/VirtualBox.**   Create a virtualized version of SharePoint 2010 running Hyper-V or VMWare within the desktop environment. The 64-bit requirement means that you cannot use Microsoft Virtual PC, so you have to use either Hyper-V (which requires a Windows Server host) or VMWare/VirtualBox.

  - **Use Boot to VHD (Virtual Hard Disk)**   This approach works only if Windows 7 is the host. Install SharePoint 2010 on your Windows 7 PC. (This is not recommended unless you are a competent developer who knows that the environment needs to be similar to or the same as the production environment.) In this case, you are not fully representing the production server because you are running Windows 7 and SharePoint 2010 is running on Windows Server 2008.

Examining the Development Options

Because custom functionality will be requested to build on the out-of-the-box features that SharePoint provides, a development environment will be required to satisfy the standard .NET development process. This development environment will likely be used to validate SharePoint components developed either by internal development staff or external consultants.

The standard approach entails development to be carried out in each developer's Share-Point 2010 environment. Each developer's solution would then be deployed to an internal SharePoint 2010 developer server environment to test the integration of these components before proceeding to the user acceptance stage.

You need to mirror the setup of the production environment in the developer server environment. A good approach is for the SharePoint developer server environment to be a standalone virtual environment in the same domain. This arrangement makes it easier to perform the user acceptance testing, and it allows for easy mirroring to the staging and production environments.

Figure 8-1 shows an example of such a topology.

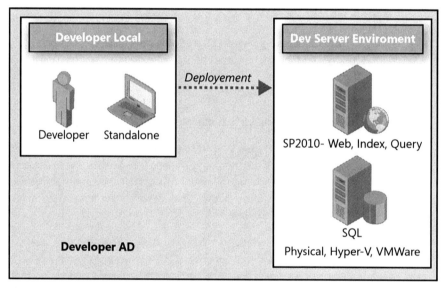

Figure 8-1 An option showing the relationship of a SharePoint 2010 developer local machine to a developer server environment running SharePoint 2010.

Figure 8-2 represents an option for a development environment using SharePoint 2010. Each developer has a local machine with another machine acting as a SharePoint 2010 development environment, and they are built to marry up (in terms of configuration) with the production environment. The test environment is scoped in terms of topology to operate like the user acceptance test environment.

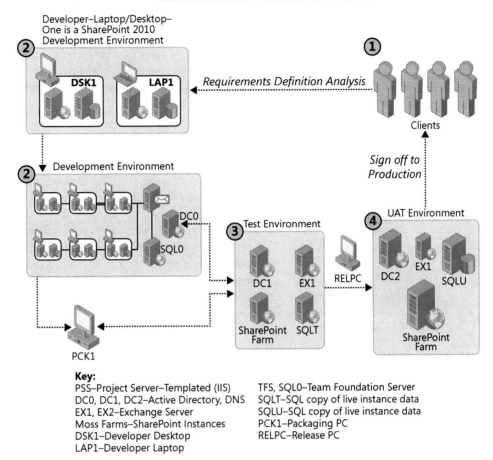

**SharePoint 2010 Development Lifecycle Model Option
Does not include Production Environment**

Key:
PSS–Project Server–Templated (IIS)
DC0, DC1, DC2–Active Directory, DNS
EX1, EX2–Exchange Server
Moss Farms–SharePoint Instances
DSK1–Developer Desktop
LAP1–Developer Laptop

TFS, SQL0–Team Foundation Server
SQLT–SQL copy of live instance data
SQLU–SQL copy of live instance data
PCK1–Packaging PC
RELPC–Release PC

Figure 8-2 A sample development environment in SharePoint 2010.

In the diagram shown in Figure 8-2, number 2 represents the SharePoint development environment, which marries up with number 3 (the test environment) and number 4 (the staging or user acceptance testing environment.

> **Note**
>
> Be aware of the content being made available to the development environment. You need to post segments of data only to the development environment, not to the entire production content databases. Back up relevant site collections, and restore them into the development environment. However, be aware of absolute links in the site collections and ensure these point to the relevant environments and not back to the production environment (where it's possible for users visiting the user acceptance testing environment to alter information in production).

The developer can build applications within their own machine space and use source control products such as Microsoft Team Foundation Server. Then they can package it up using the Packaging PC so that it can be deployed to the test environment by the SharePoint administrator. Before the applications are deployed, there is work carried out concerning preparation of the test environment. Generally, a snapshot of the environment can be taken before the deployment (if the test environment is virtual). Note that this can be difficult if the environment includes multiple servers and therefore requires multiple snapshots. Another method is to use configuration management techniques (which are discussed in Chapter 10, "SharePoint Configuration Management") and document the configuration of whatever the deployment is going to customize so that it is possible to roll back the configuration by following the documentation made before the deployment was carried out.

So, based on the *success* (meaning successful deployment and the expected results of deployment) of the test deployment and results that are measured, a decision can be made to move to the next stage and apply for user acceptance testing. This involves providing the package of the product to the Release PC, which is used to provide the package to the user acceptance and production environments. If the clients sign off, the product can then be deployed to the production environment using the Release PC.

> **Note**
>
> The processes of configuration management (the topic of Chapter 10) as well as validation and verification allow you to manage the release of SharePoint products and the timing of user acceptance testing. More information about validation and verification is available at *http://sharepointvandv.geoffevelyn.com*.

The developer's realm of control includes only the development environment. The developer does not have the ability to directly manipulate the test, user acceptance, or production environment. The developer interfaces with SharePoint administrators to ensure that adequate documentation and communication regarding the installation of the package is available. If configuration management is in place, the package will be available.

Development Governance

To properly manage a SharePoint development environment, it is important to have an enforceable SharePoint 2010 software development governance plan in place. The purpose of this governance is to describe the requirements for developing new products in the SharePoint 2010 environment and implementing them into that environment.

Once there is a SharePoint development environment in the company, the client should be made fully aware that they are fully responsible for developing, maintaining, and participating in a System Development Life Cycle (SDLC) for any future SharePoint 2010 development projects.

For more information about SDLCs, see *http://en.wikipedia.org/wiki/Systems_Development_Life_Cycle.*

Note that development efforts for SharePoint must be treated as projects because they carry the same phases as a SharePoint 2010 implementation project: Plan, Build, and Deploy.

All SharePoint 2010 software developed in-house that eventually runs SharePoint 2010 production servers should be developed according to the SDLC. At a minimum, the plan to develop (the Plan phase) should include a preliminary analysis or feasibility study; risk identification and mitigation; systems analysis; general design; detail design; development; quality assurance and acceptance testing; implementation; and post-implementation maintenance and review.

I cannot stress enough the importance of *planning* any SharePoint development, rather than just diving in, writing some code, and pushing it directly onto the SharePoint production servers. The areas of SharePoint that can be developed, enhanced, modified, and so on are vast:

- Collaboration

    - Manipulating existing out-of-the-box workflows. Note that power users can be granted access to SharePoint Designer to make modifications, although this should be ratified as part of the SharePoint Governance Plan. Will some users have access to SharePoint Designer 2007? In my experience, SharePoint Designer should be provided only to those who are qualified developers in the organization; it should not be made available to users who are not sufficiently trained in the product, because damage to sites and content can occur if users do not understand the uses of the tool.

    - Build Office SharePoint Designer 2007 workflows.

    - Build Visual Studio workflows.

    - Customize SharePoint sites.

- Enterprise Search

    o   Build a custom content source.

- Enterprise Content Management

    o   Build variations.

    o   Portal personalization.

A governance methodology ensures that developed software will be adequately documented and tested before it is used, and that designated owners and server custodians for the critical information being accessed are aware of the product.

Also, SharePoint 2010 administrators must perform periodic risk assessments of SharePoint 2010 production servers to determine whether the controls employed are adequate. All SharePoint 2010 production and user acceptance platforms should have an access control system to restrict who can access the system as well as restrict the privileges available to these users.

There should be a separation between the SharePoint 2010 production, user acceptance, development, and test environments. Where these distinctions have been established, development staff should not be permitted to have access to SharePoint 2010 test, production, or user-acceptance platforms. Likewise, all production software testing must use sanitized information on the SharePoint 2010 user-acceptance platform. All application-program-based access paths other than the formal user access paths should be deleted or disabled before software is moved into production.

When developing SharePoint tools, it is also important to designate ownership and control of those tools; this is especially important when working with an externally provided developer who has been subcontracted. Because the client owns the development platform, components such as SharePoint 2010 applications, Web Part or application source code, Web Part or application object code, documentation, and general operational data should be protected as if it were the client's property. When working with an external developer, make sure that the source code will be made available to the client in their "Statement of Works" document. If that has not been done, it is strongly recommended that the Statement of Works be corrected or that the work not be undertaken. The only time nonsource software should be implemented is when the user base requests third-party software. This request should be carried out in conjunction with a support agreement, keeping the vendor on the hook for corrections.

As for the ownership of requests and authorization for a SharePoint 2010 application, the client needs to take the appropriate steps to ensure the integrity and security of all Share-Point 2010 Web Parts and application logic, as well as data files created by (or acquired for) SharePoint 2010 applications.

Additional Resources

Creating a developer platform requires careful consideration, and there are many options available. With SharePoint 2010, there are some new client workstation development options. Using Hyper-V to host your development environment is a good choice, particularly if you're interested in replicating your production environment with multiple servers.

Hyper-V Getting Started Guide

This guide will help you get Hyper-V installed and create your first virtual machine. To access the guide, go to *http://technet.microsoft.com/en-us/library/cc732470%28WS.10%29. aspx.*

Windows Server 2008 R2 Hyper-V Virtual Machine

This download contains a set of two Windows Server 2008 R2 Hyper-V virtual machines (VMs) for evaluating and demonstrating Office 2010, SharePoint 2010m, and Project Server 2010.

> **Warning**
> You need a minimum of 8 GB of RAM to run these VMs. Also, over a broadband connection, this download can take the majority of the day to download and exceeds 100 GB in total size. To download them, go to *http://www.microsoft.com/downloads/ details.aspx?FamilyID=751fa0d1-356c-4002-9c60-d539896c66ce&displaylang=en.*

Installing a Development Environment with Microsoft SharePoint 2010 and Microsoft Visual Studio 2010

This article describes how to install a development environment with Microsoft SharePoint 2010 and Microsoft Visual Studio 2010. The development environment that you create by using these instructions will not support SharePoint farm installations, and you should not host active production sites with this configuration. To read this article, go to *http://msdn. microsoft.com/en-us/library/ee554869.aspx.*

Chapter 8

Summary

This chapter focused on SharePoint customization. It touched on the technical and human resources required, and the reasons why customization should be deemed a separated project.

When implementing SharePoint 2010 into an organization that requires development to occur on the platform, the question that I seem to get asked a lot is this:

"What environment gets created first"?

Even if the client states there is a requirement for a development environment, someone will almost always ask this:

"Do we need one at all"?

If the business analyst, while gathering user requirements, received responses requesting that SharePoint 2010 be customized to meet a specific user requirement, and that request had been sanctioned by the client, and there was an agreement to customize SharePoint 2010 to meet those requirements, then maybe there is a case for creating a developer environment. However, the real question is this:

If the client has a development team, are the team members skilled in SharePoint development?

Allowing developers who have few skills in SharePoint development to have access to SharePoint to create customizations is courting disaster. Even if there is a requirement to customize SharePoint, do not think that simply putting in a SharePoint development platform will solve the problem. Be sure to assess the human resources required to carry out the customization, and make sure the personnel selected are up to the job. If necessary, ensure that they get training.

As for the environment, developer environments are created *after* the SharePoint implementation is completed—even after resiliency and disaster recovery platforms are in place. The development environment is the last environment to create because the SharePoint implementation must be robust and resilient before any modifications are decided upon.

SharePoint Governance

What Is SharePoint Governance?

SHAREPOINT governance is not a hardware, software, or people resource solution. It is an organizational strategy and methodology for documenting and implementing business rules and controls related to your client's data. It brings cross-functional teams together to identify data issues impacting the company or organization. It works with business and technical interfacing teams to develop SharePoint solutions for data issues. And you do all of this through a Governance Committee made up of decision makers across the business. These people work with their teams to conduct research, analysis, and implementation of SharePoint.

SharePoint governance planning adds legitimacy to a SharePoint implementation. Defined governance rules, roles, and responsibilities in the Plan phase ensure the business is provided with the resources to make the SharePoint implementation a success. A SharePoint governance plan describes the business-critical nature of the SharePoint implementation and provides the evidence for requesting the necessary people and money investments.

Governance in SharePoint is crucial. Governance never works without business involvement. Your project team should not define governance procedures unless sanctioned by the business.

Before continuing to explain how to build SharePoint governance, I should point out that SharePoint governance can be made simple or complex. The bigger your SharePoint implementation and the more resources used, the more complex the governance plan should be. The Governance Committee should be formed at the start of the Plan phase of the project. The key reason for SharePoint governance is not to force users to do certain things on SharePoint but to provide communication and education. SharePoint governance provides a face to SharePoint and can be used to introduce the platform to the client, because the formation of the SharePoint Governance Committee embodies the vision (as described in the SharePoint Quality Plan—see Chapter 3, "Content of Your SharePoint 2010 Plan").

The top priority of the Governance Committee (once formed) is the creation of the Share-Point Statement of Operations. That output is the face of SharePoint and is a continually updated document.

Governance and Culture

Successfully implemented SharePoint governance planning depends on the culture of the organization, because it needs to define the rules applied to the management of Share-Point and the rules applied to content when people work with the platform. For example, company ABC might allow any user to create sites on the SharePoint production platform, whereas company DEF might request that users make a help desk call to have a site cre-ated. Some people will say, "It's better for users to create their own sites on SharePoint," and I would not wholly disagree with that. However, if that type of access to SharePoint is left unchecked, there is no way to control the growth of the SharePoint platform. There are many other areas in SharePoint related to the use of data, where it is stored, and who has access to that data.

Here is a list of areas in SharePoint where, in my view, decisions about data or site manage-ment need to be reviewed:

- Can users access information via Web Folder clients? This is the ability to see or access SharePoint via a mapped URL back to your Microsoft Office client software. For example, company ABC might allow users to *map* a drive letter to a document library on a SharePoint site and to manage files through the use of Windows Explorer.

- Can users create and manage their own Web sites?

- Is distributed administration provided through technical staff only or through a combination of business and technical staff? The geographical distribution of the company might affect the level of support supplied if the SharePoint implementation follows the regional spread of the company.

  For example, if you are considering having one administrator responsible for a regionalized SharePoint installation, something is going to slip. How are records and documents described (how is *metadata* used) to ensure descriptions are consistent across departments, divisions, and agencies?

  Metadata is the description of physical content. The grouping of metadata is car-ried out by the information architect at a global level and then regionalized into site administrators at department, office, and group levels. Collation of this material is key to defining the aspects of search and to content scoping. Metadata is also a crucial aspect of Enterprise Content Management (ECM) and lends it itself to the categoriza-tion of functional site material.

> **Tip**
> For more information on Enterprise Content Management there are lots of good articles at *http://blogs.msdn.com/b/ecm/*.

- Should end users be trained on how to administer sites before they need to manage them? Do you need to train the trainers so that a cascade of training can be provided? Check the service delivery and the support model—for example, if your support model includes end users as the first line of SharePoint technical support and administration, your training plan must include that also.

- Who will assign users and permissions in SharePoint 2010?

- Who will create and approve content for sites?

- Who will secure sensitive information?

- Who will be able to create new sites?

- Who will be able to publish content to Web sites?

- Who will be able to customize sites?

What Does SharePoint Governance Look At?

SharePoint governance typically examines the following items:

- SharePoint 2010 farm structure and quality. What level of SharePoint topology has been defined: the connectivity, resilience, and performance levels?

- Web structure and content format. What kind of sites are being provided, where are they being provided, why are they being provided, who are the owners, what are the content levels, what is the taxonomy, and what metadata will be used?

- Subarea design. What kind of data flow, content control, and site structure will be used? Who is responsible for defining that?

- Conceptual design. What framework is in place to structure sites (for example, managed paths, logical separations at the site level, and so on)?

- User group management. Is there a user group for SharePoint or an IT user group that requires SharePoint input? Or should one be formed? What are the rules concerning its operation?

- Quality management

- Risk management

- Subcontract technical management

- Development and design cycles

- Configuration management, including documentation

- Verification of the portals

- Acceptance

Governance Is Not a New Form of Government!

The SharePoint Governance Plan will focus on *what* needs to be governed and controlled and *who* is part of what team. This is not a new form of government! It needs to be kept simple, understandable and focus on what really matters. The overall success of the Share-Point implementation hinges on maintaining control while being bombarded by requests from everybody in the organization. The governance plan facilitates management of SharePoint. SharePoint governance outlines the maintenance, administration, and support for the organization's SharePoint environments, and it helps identify lines of ownership for both business and technical teams. To make the SharePoint Governance Plan understandable, you need to have a model that describes at a high level how the different site types of SharePoint fit together. You need this level of definition to address the different types of sites the organization will use.

Usage policies and procedures also need to be included that not only state inappropriate use but also provide a more consistent and usable system—for example, acceptable use, training strategy and SharePoint 2010 "Statement of Operations" guides.

The Model

Figure 9-1 shows a few of the site types that are included in a typical SharePoint implementation. Like all things hierarchical, there are a few high-level sites at the top, and the number of sites grow as you add divisional portals, team sites, project sites, and even MySites as you travel down the pyramid from the top.

The important thing to note about this model is that the site and portals at the top consist mostly of published content and usually require tight governance. As you move down the pyramid, governance becomes looser and the purposes are more related to team collaboration than corporate communication.

Also, more temporary or short-lived sites exist on the lower half, and the permanent sites are more common as you move up the pyramid.

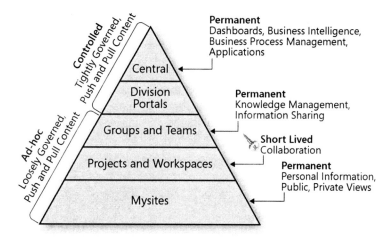

Figure 9-1 A sample SharePoint governance model.

Sites on the lower half usually need to be provisioned quickly so that people can collaborate efficiently. The sites on the top are visible to many more people and require a bit more planning.

As part of the build of the Governance Plan, you should list the key hosts within the segments of the pyramid. This gives the governance team real data to associate with each of the relevant areas.

Who Governs?

You need to assign appropriate individuals in the organization with defined responsibilities in the governance team. Individuals with the ability to make the necessary decisions—not just initially, but throughout the life of SharePoint—they should be part of or connected to the governance team for SharePoint.

The best approach I've found for building a governance team is to start with the lead steward. This individual (or more than one) should be selected by the SharePoint client (with some consultation from you). Having the client pick the lead steward ensures that the lead steward will work hard and allocate the time needed; it also means that the steward has exposure to upper management and likely has some clout within the company.

The key part of this is the *clout* or recognition the lead steward has inside the company. You'll need that lead steward to leverage that visibility to build the stewardship council.

Your lead steward is from the business side, has many connections within the business, has executive support, and likely has the leadership ability to put together the SharePoint Governance Committee. The path to follow, at a high level, can be summarized as follows:

1. Identify the lines of business involved.

2. Find a business leader from each line of business (LOB).

3. Secure five percent of the time of these leaders for the Data Governance initiative. Use executive support as leverage if needed.

4. Have one-on-one meetings with the business leaders (prior to any large meetings) to show the value of the program, and how you can help them!

5. Have a kick-off meeting to get the initial buzz going.

To balance the SharePoint Governance Committee, the committee should be composed of business and technology individuals in the organization. By combining these, you persuade them to work together to define and enforce a SharePoint governance plan. The Governance Committee is made up of two groups: the Strategy Team and the Tactical Team.

As Figure 9-2 shows, the Governance Committee brings the Strategy Team and Tactical Team together (Site Administration, Functional Owners, Portal Administration, Development Team and Operations Team—representatives of which collectively make up the Tactical Team). Although the Strategy Team will meet only on a quarterly basis after SharePoint has been implemented, the Governance Committee is an extension of the Tactical Team and meets regularly to make the necessary decisions to keep your SharePoint implementation moving.

The Governance Committee is concerned with requests for new high-level sites, requests for customization or configuration, oversight and scheduling of operational changes, and much more. This committee must have representation from all the areas of the Tactical Team (Site Administration, Data Owners, Portal Administration, Technical, and Developers), and also overlaps into the Strategy Team. This structure provides good representation and communication flow.

Strategy Team

A good Strategy Team includes a balance of business owners and technology leaders. This team has active involvement from the SharePoint client, executive and financial stakeholders, IT and business leaders, security and compliance officers, development leaders, and information workers.

Figure 9-2 Strategy Team and Tactical Team for SharePoint governance.

This team is charged with finding the right balance between technology and the business, *and* between centralized control and decentralized empowerment. They drive the deployment from a strategic perspective and provide the overall insight and direction needed by the tactical teams. They are constantly looking for synergies where SharePoint can help the organization operate more effectively or efficiently.

They understand how the business is growing, and where it could be growing. In the end, their role is about leveraging SharePoint to improve on business processes.

Tactical Team

The Tactical Team, as its name suggests, is focused on operations, portal and site administration, functional ownership of specific sites, and building the framework and features of the portal. The tactical team builds the infrastructure (hardware, operating system, and so on), provides database support and network connectivity, provides security, and supports all of SharePoint's features. This team is also responsible for global SharePoint configuration, site provisioning, site administration, and SharePoint maintenance.

Statement of Operations

A SharePoint Statement of Operations is the core resource for the Governance Committee and is a key output of the group. The Statement of Operations is continually updated. It is a framework that describes the nature of SharePoint to the organization. It describes the basic outline of SharePoint in the organization, support responsibilities, key policies defined, escalation of SharePoint issues and outages, service availability, and the makeup of the service.

Segments of the Statement of Operations are as follows:

- **Description of the SharePoint hosts on the production farm**   This is a list of all the SharePoint hosts, including a description of the host objective and who the owner or owners of the host are.

- **A description of the SharePoint platforms**   This is a list of the SharePoint platforms (for example, the test, user acceptance, and production platforms). The list should be split by type. For example, you might have a mixture of SharePoint 2010 and SharePoint 2007 platforms.

- **Support**   How SharePoint is supported—including the location of FAQs and training material—and the different levels of support available to SharePoint, as well as a description of the support model (how SharePoint is maintained). For example, some organizations have their technical support teams split into three lines:

  - First line: those who first receive user calls, log the calls, and escalate the response if necessary

  - Second line: those who deal with the escalated issues and maintain SharePoint sites

  - Third line: SharePoint administrators, as well as architects who maintain and design SharePoint in the organization

- **Responsibilities**   Describe who is responsible for technical site administration (typically, the SharePoint administrator), maintenance, and configuration. Also describe who is responsible for business site administration (typically, site owners) and the escalation paths based on certain parts of SharePoint. Business administration specifies the different levels of SharePoint permissions (Owner, Contributor, Reader, and so on) and defines who is responsible for what on a SharePoint site.

Governance

Project and quality management includes the management of the system structure and how the Web applications, site collections, sites, and data interrelate. It ensures that sharing of information is kept at an optimum level and that SharePoint can evolve through a controlled process.

For example, in one organization where governance was defined, sites were configured in such a way as to disallow the creation, renaming, and deletion of team sites within subareas. This forces the following of the business process to manage the sites within the portals. Specific members will be granted rights to create sites within the site collections, but this will be managed by second-line and coordinated from third-line design activities.

In the Statement of Operations, you also need to indicate statements for the following areas—all of which relate directly to SharePoint governance:

- **Training**   Describe the SharePoint training strategy, including where the users should get their training, how the training is requested, and what scope of training is provided (for example, contributor, owner, administrator training, and so on). For more information about defining SharePoint training, see the section titled, "Training Users When Production is Ready" on page 232 of Chapter 14, "Releasing SharePoint to the Client."

- **Policies**   Management of SharePoint requires the production of policies that educate users on best practice and organizational rules. The SharePoint Governance Committee should draft these initially as statements in the SharePoint Governance Plan, and then turn them into separate documents. These documents are listed in the Service of Operations so that users can locate them easily. Note that the SharePoint Governance Committee does not have to immediately write every policy in the following list because these are examples and some of them might not apply to the SharePoint implementation being carried out:

    - General Web policy and security awareness

    - Site creation

    - Content management

    - Publishing policy

    - Personal information publication policy

    - Version control policy

- ○ Auditing policy

- ○ Team sites policies

- ○ Image use policy

- ○ Contact list use policy

- ○ Alert policies

- ○ Discussion board policy

- ○ SharePoint Site Storage Size (Quota)—Policy

> **Note**
>
> The following is taken from an MSDN blog article about site quota management:
>
> Set quotas at a level that balances the need to manage storage with increasing numbers of support calls from site owners who are being told their site is out of space. Do the math in your organization by understanding the current and anticipated storage needs for sites and determining how many calls you want to get. Don't set your quota at the expected average site collection size, or you will get support calls for quota increases for half of your sites. Instead, set quota size toward the top end of the acceptable level of storage and consider how much the storage costs versus the support call or the cost of time involved in increasing the quota. Although storage has become very cheap, quotas will encourage users to be responsible with their data. If, for example, you anticipate having 1,000 site collections supporting team collaboration, and you anticipate that site collections will require between 100 MB and 600 MB of storage, evenly distributed across that 500 MB range, then by setting a quota of 550 MB, you can anticipate that 10 percent of the site collections will end up over quota. That means you can expect, over time, approximately 100 support calls requesting "exception" from the policy.

- ○ Server hardening policy

- ○ SharePoint 2010 Branding and Design policy

- ○ Data storage policy

- ○ Workflow Services policy

- ○ Search index policy

○ Metadata and categorization policy

○ MySite content update policy

○ Site information policy

- **Setting Access Rights**   Description of who is responsible for setting site permissions and what the procedure is for setting permissions.

- **Key Links**   Links to key processes, procedures, and related documentation.

- **Customization**   Description of what SharePoint customization is, and what the policy and procedures are concerning SharePoint modification, including the process for external SharePoint developers working with an internal SharePoint platform (for example).

- **Availability**   A description of the nature of the SharePoint platform and how available it is, including any planned outage days of the week, month, and year. It also specifies open hours of operation, backup times, and any related procedures for service outages.

  Availability is discussed in greater detail in Chapter 12, "Producing the System Specification."

- **Inputs**   Description of connected services to SharePoint, including the names of the owners of those connected technologies—for example, Microsoft Active Directory, Exchange, SQL, Microsoft Office Communicator, and so on.

- **Escalation**   Description of the procedures concerning escalation of SharePoint reported issues and who is in the chain of escalation, starting from first line through third line.

> **Note**
>
> People who are set at SharePoint Site Owner are given this permission because it is assumed they know how to set user permissions in a SharePoint team site—that makes them fully responsible for managing the integrity of the site content. Site Owners set the permissions, and they approve access to a site. The help desk should never set the rights from a request unless it is absolutely necessary—for example, a SharePoint site where there is no defined Site Owner manager.

Chapter 9

Summary

In SharePoint, you can have governance, or you can have chaos. If you are not prepared to have governance in your SharePoint implementation, don't start a SharePoint implementation project.

The aims of SharePoint governance are as follows:

- Create the people infrastructure to govern and support the SharePoint environments.

- Document the initial governing policies and procedures of the SharePoint environments.

- Communicate the need for the business to provide the ability to apply governance to the areas of SharePoint that matter to the business.

So, be prepared to educate the user base and show how important SharePoint 2010 governance can be. Be evangelistic when talking about the relevant procedures and policies. Set up awareness sessions and restate the reasons and benefits of implementing SharePoint 2010.

Don't be afraid to meet all kinds of representatives from the business and describe how governance can be implemented and be successful. Provide encouragement and show appreciation. Some client environments will not have SharePoint governance; in order for them to implement it, you will need their participation and consent for adoption. Consider the client population, and create a program that continuously provides encouragement and support.

CHAPTER 10

SharePoint Configuration Management

S HAREPOINT configuration management (CM) involves controlling specifications, draw-ings, software assets, and related documentation that define the functional and physi-cal characteristics of a SharePoint implementation, down to the lowest level required to assure standardization. The CM process also provides a documented, traceable history of the development life cycle of SharePoint in an organization, including any modifications, upgrades, or variants.

On many small SharePoint projects, the only deliverable is a single report that needs to be controlled rather that configured, without the full weight of CM policies being applied to it. A *controlled* document is produced in accordance with document and data control policies. (For more information, you can read my blog post, "Document and Data Control," at *http://spsdocdatcontrol.geoffevelyn.com*.)

When implemented, SharePoint is defined by identifying configurable items based on its technical, administrative, and maintainability criticality. The selection process is one of sepa-rating the elements of SharePoint on a hierarchical basis for the purpose of managing their baseline characteristics.

For an implementation, your Build phase tasks show what is to be implemented in Share-Point, and each of these items falls under CM—meaning this procedure relates to how to control any work carried out in the installation of SharePoint. All features associated with the SharePoint implementation, the installation and the configuration of those fea-tures, and all associated assets (for example, documentation) are subject to configuration management.

Here are the Build phase tasks:

- Deploy a pilot system.

- Deploy a staging system.

- Deploy a production system.

Within each of these tasks, there are subtasks concerning the installation of hardware, software, and key components. There are also major decision gates from stakeholders in these tasks (sign offs, for example) from the completion of the SharePoint pilot to staging to production. CM is critical in ensuring that changes to these environments are controlled.

In SharePoint, a *configurable item* is any entity that requires control. You could therefore apply configuration management processes to any data content types in SharePoint. This is further discussed in the paragraphs that follow.

Figure 10-1 illustrates the degrees of control, which are applied to a configurable item during its implementation life cycle.

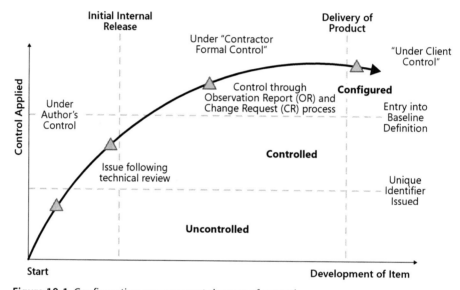

Figure 10-1 Configuration management degrees of control.

Initially, an item is uncontrolled while under development by the author. The author is the creator of the item (for example, the SharePoint administrator, architect, interfacing team member, or perhaps even the person uploading a document into a document library). The item becomes controlled after a *unique identifier* has been allocated and the item is subject to review. After the development of an identified configurable item is sufficiently stable to declare a baseline standard, it will be subject to configuration control processes.

To control an item under development, use an Observation Report (OR) and Change Request (CR) process. An Observation Report is used to capture, describe and provide evidence of the required change that needs to be applied. The Change Request backs up the Observation Report. The Change Request details the impact the change will have, related components, and schedule. The change request needs to be reviewed and an agreement reached with those affected by the change request.

Documents that are not identified as configured items (for example, the SharePoint 2010 Quality Plan and SharePoint 2010 Project Implementation Plan) will still be controlled in accordance with document and data control. (For more information, you can read my blog post, "Document and Data Control," at *http://spsdocdatcontrol.geoffevelyn.com*.)

On small projects, CM techniques can be applied by the project staff using a simple Share-Point list to control baselines as well as to record the version or issue status of the identified configurable items.

On larger projects, particularly where a large number of hardware drawings or modules of SharePoint features have been produced, CM can be delegated to specialist staff. The advantage of a central site CM facility, with its own specialized staff and archive, is that it provides for the long-term maintenance of project configuration records. However, the production of SharePoint add-on features (for example, Web parts, automation, branding, site definitions, and so on) is particularly well suited to the use of CM and tools, remaining under project control.

> **Note**
> The complexity of the SharePoint implementation might also define what product you use to manage CM. For example, if you have a development team working in the SharePoint project, you might want to use Microsoft Team Foundation Server. (A video that describes how Microsoft uses this product can be seen at *http://channel9.msdn.com/pdc2008/TL04/*) or at the Subversion Web site (*http://subversion.apache.org*.) However, a SharePoint 2010 Team site can also be configured to hold an issue tracking list to carry out basic CM tracking and product life-cycle control.

Chapter 10

Configuration Management Applies to SharePoint

CM is mandatory for all SharePoint projects, not just during the SharePoint implementation. You cannot have a controlled SharePoint environment without records concerning its makeup and traceability concerning changes made. As a project manager, you cannot hand over SharePoint just with a document stating, "I've finished implementing SharePoint for you; off you go." You are conducting a system handover, meaning that you are handing over everything the project implementation can be audited on and everything that the project has assets for (and that includes all documentation, technical specifications, software assets, and so on).

CM is needed for any deliverable of hardware or software or when there is a change to either of those in the production arena. CM applies to configured items that are used in the development of a SharePoint product but are not a deliverable in their own right. Typical configuration items include the following:

- SharePoint 2010 specification (design, topology, network connectivity)

- Test plans

- Drawings (overall and detailed)

- SharePoint software assets, and any additional development applied to SharePoint, including any code, program listings, and associated documentation

- Service or user manuals

Other items that CM applies to must be identified by the project staff during the SharePoint implementation and are subject to review by the project manager or a nominated configuration authority.

SharePoint CM defines processes that describe the following:

- Makeup of infrastructure

- Software and hardware assets

- Modification and procurement

- Tracking and auditing

Understanding the Components

Even before building a SharePoint instance—and even before someone mentions, "Hey, what kind of server do you want?"—you need to create a report based on the schema required for your SharePoint sites. To do this, you document through analysis the capacity and performance levels your SharePoint farm needs.

Assuming that you have accomplished these steps and have defined the specification, you then need to ensure that you have the level of documentation required to install SharePoint from start to finish.

> **Note**
> It is vital that you have people running SharePoint CM who follow the process and can engage others to follow it. When CM personnel leave a SharePoint project without qualified replacements, the relationship between a well-implemented CM program and maintaining basic project integrity can become painfully clear.

Item Identifications

The basic or lowest level of configuration items for SharePoint under which CM will apply is the software under which SharePoint operates.

If the initial design of a site is not under strict control, the site does not need to come under formal configuration policies, but in some circumstances it is really important. For example, imagine that a SharePoint Team site starts as a small Project Management Office (PMO) site in a company where the culture isn't strict in terms of Web site control and where they did not document the PMO site design. Without company buy-in to CM, there is a risk of SharePoint 2010 implementation failure—because quality cannot be inspected in Share-Point use.

Failure to introduce CM and to introduce it without full support and understanding from the client leaves SharePoint 2010 implementation projects open to issues of credibility and a loss of customer confidence, as well as additional unplanned costs in time and resources required to perform rework.

When to Apply Configuration Management in SharePoint

You can use CM in SharePoint for just about anything that needs to be controlled, from an item going into a site, to a process concerning document management, to a workflow tied to an issue tracking list, to administration of a site. Because CM is a methodology that can be applied, all you need to do is follow the procedures laid out in this chapter. This book, which focuses on the implementation of SharePoint, is concerned with the three phases of implementation and how that maps to CM. Those phases are Plan, Build, and Deploy.

SharePoint CM ties well into managing SharePoint through issues related to outages and failures that result in users being unable to carry out their work.

For example, let's say an element of SharePoint implementation has failed. Users are unable to save new work to their sites. Upon initial investigation, it appears that the SQL server has no capacity remaining after an upload of data from a file server. It also appears that there was little monitoring or measurement of growth rates on the SQL server. Because you have a Configuration Change Board (CCB)—or your SharePoint Governance Committee if you don't have a CCB—you can count on them to plan and manage this situation so that the client is comfortable that the resolution will result in a more effective platform.

The CCB, coordinating with the technical authority and interfacing teams, can do the following:

- Ensure that investigations are performed into the cause of failures and that suggested changes to the SQL platform are evaluated.

- Allocate resources to such investigations (for example, the interfacing teams, whether they be the SQL teams, infrastructure teams, or others).

- Determine the faults and their underlying causes. As an example, the "fault" would be that there was not enough space on the SQL server, while the "cause" would be insufficient planning, lack of monitoring, lack of governance, or all three.

- Authorize the investigation of design changes and any necessary corrective action and monitor the effectiveness of such actions (such as altering the disk type, altering disk capacity, or strengthening the monitoring process).

- Monitor the progress of these investigations.

- Identify reliability and significant failures.

- Identify maintenance problems.

The Project Manager Specifies the Configuration Management Policy

The project manager is responsible for defining the CM policy and the techniques to be applied on the project. If the policy deviates from that stated in the CM procedures, those deviations must be defined in the SharePoint 2010 Quality Plan.

Additional issues that also need to be recorded in the SharePoint 2010 Quality Plan are as follows:

- The designated CM authorities for the project. Who is responsible for managing the process, making decisions, and owning SharePoint 2010 (business and technical)? (For more information on this topic, see Chapter 9, "SharePoint Governance.")

- The identity of the root document or source from which all configuration status records can be traced. (Normally, this is the SharePoint 2010 Quality Plan.)

- The project manager should appoint a configuration authority who will control the CM activities on behalf of the project manager.

Table 10-1 lists common configuration terms used in a SharePoint 2010 implementation project.

Table 10-1 Configuration Management Terms

Term	Definition
Configuration Item	An item selected for CM. Configuration items are established on a hierarchical basis, with one item comprising the complete product (hardware and software). This is then broken down into its lower level constituent items or parts, each with its own reference number.
Configuration Baseline	A specification or product that has been reviewed and agreed on that therefore serves as a basis for further development. A baseline can be modified only through formal change control processes.
Controlled Item	An item that is not identified as a configured item but still requires controlling in a formal manner (for example, the SharePoint 2010 Quality Plan or SharePoint 2010 Project Plan).
Configuration Control	The systematic evaluation, coordination, approval, and dissemination of proposed changes and the implementation of all approved changes in a configured item.
Master Record Index	The index or indexes to the master set of drawings and specifications that define the configuration item. This term is used generally to refer to a set of indexes that provides a record of the configuration items.

How to Apply Configuration Management in SharePoint

To apply CM in SharePoint, you need to state a policy for its use and define the related procedures. You need to ensure that any deviation from this policy, together with designated CM authorities for the SharePoint 2010 implementation project, is documented in the SharePoint 2010 Quality Plan. Other CM details can be contained in the SharePoint 2010 Quality Plan or in a separate CM plan, depending on any contractual arrangements or the size and complexity of the SharePoint implementation.

As the SharePoint Plan phase starts, so should CM. You must choose a set of methods, procedures, and tools to satisfy the requirements in the following lists. If the client organization does not have any CM processes in place, you need to create those processes. An excellent method of doing this is to use your project management site (as detailed in Chapter 6, "Gathering the Resources for SharePoint Implementation," which discusses SharePoint components and associated pieces in the section, "Using SharePoint 2010 Sites for Project Recording" on page 115) for CM because that is also where all the project data will be stored.

If the client does have a full CM process running, investigate it and find out if either there is connectivity between that and the Project SharePoint site or the CM process in place includes the following requirements:

- Enable unique identification and description of SharePoint 2010 and its components.

- Enable the evolution of products and their components to be controlled and traced.

- Enable identification and control of the means by which products will evolve to satisfy their requirements.

- Record securely and maintain all the information required.

- Provide validated, identical copies of products.

> ### Note
> Sites in staging and production SharePoint environments should be functionally identical. This means that the site structures should be the same; however, that does not mean they should be identical data-wise. Trying to make SharePoint sites fully synchronized between staging and production environments requires a significant amount of time and becomes more of an issue as the amount of data grows in the production environment.

To satisfy these fundamental requirements, the CM system should provide the following:

- Methods for unique identification and version control for all products and all components of a product

- Methods for receiving and acting on observations about a product and for recording and controlling changes that arise

- Methods for keeping track of all items being produced or used by a project, including items inherited or subcontracted

- Methods for defining the means by which a product can be built or rebuilt, specifically including any special requirements after delivery or after project completion

- Methods for marking, storing, and handling all required media types

- Procedures for controlling replication and distribution of products

Bring the SharePoint Item Under Control As It Develops

Figure 10-2 illustrates when a SharePoint item should be brought under control and how the process could relate to a SharePoint 2010 issue tracking list (if there are no configuration tools available).

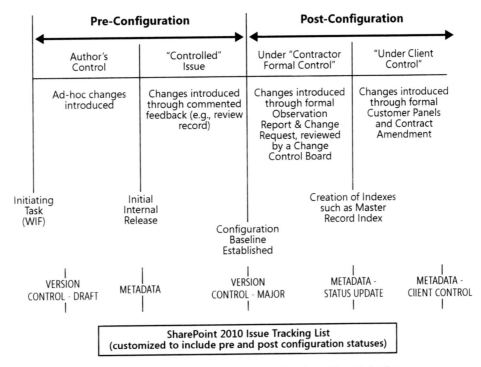

Figure 10-2 Configuration management item process related to a SharePoint list.

Figure 10-2 shows the passage of a configurable item from its generation to the point where it comes under customer control. Each of the vertical lines represents a formal stage in the development of the item. After the internal review cycle is complete, the item will be raised to version 1, or if it's being updated, to the next appropriate version number, and then it is issued for external use. From that point on, its status shall be recorded in the Configuration Baseline Index and any changes to the item must be introduced via formal configuration control procedures. (See the section, "Changes to Configured Items Must be Controlled" on page 171.) When the client takes delivery and control of the product, a formal Master Record Index needs to be generated for each configuration item.

> **Note**
> The creation of a *configuration baseline* is not a one-time only event. These baselines are often recreated over time as major, coordinated changes to the environment are approved.

Control the Item Prior to Configuration Management

While a configuration item is being developed during the preconfiguration stage, the author is free to make whatever changes might be necessary on a day-to-day basis. Understanding the development of the item is still important, and significant changes should be recorded as part of the configuration item.

For example, in SharePoint 2010, you could (as shown in Figure 10-2) construct a list with version control switched on using minor and major versions. These versions allow you to enter comments as the item moves from draft version to draft version until it becomes a configured item.

Bring the Configured Item Under Configuration Management at the Right Time

As the development of the item stabilizes, the baseline standard can be declared and the item brought under configuration control. Each configuration item must be given a unique reference number. All configurable items must be regularly reviewed. The review record might initiate further changes to the item, causing the draft number to be raised. Maintaining all the comment copies of a technical document is not necessary, provided the record or minutes are maintained to provide the traceability of the review process.

Establish a Configuration Baseline for Each Item

A configuration baseline index shall be formally maintained as a status and history record of the project's configuration items. The index must include the hierarchy and interrelationships of the items.

At appropriate points in the project development and certainly when the product is ready for delivery, it is necessary to produce an index of all configuration items. This index is often called the Master Record Index (MRI). For software products, a *build definition*, which defines the software and computing content of the release, must be prepared.

A suitable Software Build Definition template is available at: *http://sbt.geoffevelyn.com.*

A Configuration Status Account Provides History

Configuration status accounting is a mechanism for providing records of the current status of all the project's configuration items. The configuration status records provide complete traceability of what has happened to the configuration to date; these records can be centralized into the SharePoint 2010 implementation project site.

For example, you could have an item subject to version control and carrying metadata—a multichoice column called Configuration Status, for example. This Configuration Status column could have values defining the configuration level of the item. This means that not only do you have traceable history, but you can also identify when and who made alterations to the configuration status. Also, if any comments were made at the time, they would also be available.

Changes to Configured Items Must Be Controlled

Once an item comes under configuration control, changes can be introduced only by means of a formal change control process. All items in a SharePoint production environment and SharePoint user acceptance document come under CM. Figure 10-3 shows a SharePoint 2010 implementation in a processing chain.

The control process is designed to ensure the following:

- The basis of the documentation supporting the configured item is maintained to reflect the delivered version.

- The interfaces to other configured items, hardware or software, are clearly defined.

- The traceability of configured items back to contractual requirements can be demonstrated.

- Correct authorization is given to any changes.

- The traceability between changes and modified parts of configured items is maintained.

- For SharePoint software, simultaneous updating of a configured software item is prevented.

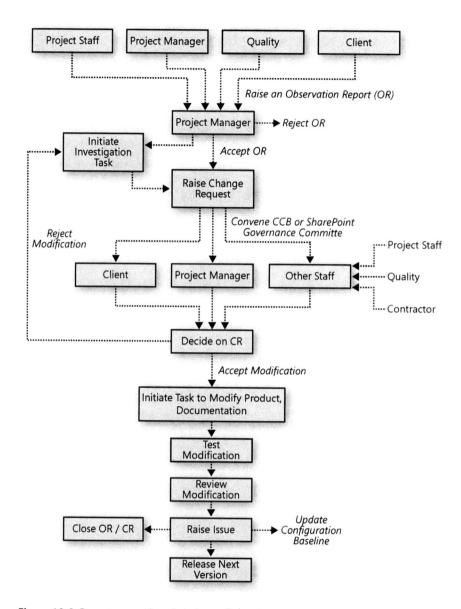

Figure 10-3 Report processing chain in configuration management.

A need for a change can be identified by any of the functions connected with the project, by a subcontractor or by the client; the reporting processing chain as depicted in Figure 10-3 identifies that the configuration board is responsible for reviewing changes.

All such requests for clarification or concessions, queries, or simply suggestions for improvement in the SharePoint item should be documented.

Summary

Every item concerning SharePoint running in a production environment is subject to CM, whose rules are bound by service management, governance, and the SharePoint 2010 Quality Plan.

There will be those who would attempt to argue that CM is overkill, because there is far too much "process" and it would hamper SharePoint creativity. My response takes the form of a question:

How do you know who created what?

If the client cannot answer what constitutes SharePoint operations, they do not have an environment under control, neither do they have an environment duly documented to show the purpose, premise, and operation of the SharePoint environment.

CM manages, records, and structures project data so that anything that takes place in delivering a product has a history from the point it was designed to the point it was implemented. For example, in the Plan phase of the SharePoint implementation, a number of investigations lead to document outputs that require signoff. These documents make up areas of the SharePoint implementation.

Chapter 10

Making Sure SharePoint Meets User Requirements

The SharePoint 2010 implementation needs to meet user requirements and the client's vision. The client's vision can be defined through the three high-level organizational goals:

- Organizational productivity

- Personal/team productivity

- Infrastructure productivity

The three goals are also described in Chapter 2, "SharePoint 2010 Project Mantra," and Chapter 3, "Content of Your SharePoint 2010 Project Plan."

The user requirements need to be obtained to ensure that you have a managed SharePoint platform, an understanding of interconnected tools and applications, and an understanding of how they will map to user requirements. Additionally, collecting these requirements allows you to better identify where data should be consolidated, reduce and improve data management, and reduce duplication.

The output of this investigation leads to the production of a framework describing the structure and features applied to SharePoint 2010.

If user requirements are not investigated, there will be *SharePoint implementation pain*, leading to a failure in *SharePoint governance*, and a failure to raise to an appropriate level the users' understanding of SharePoint 2010 and what the platform is capable of. These shortcomings will make it difficult to implement and manage the SharePoint platform and lead to the following user-related problems:

- Because there are no policies defining what SharePoint should be used for, users will be free to do what they want, when they want, with no accountability or responsibility to the content. This will result in a situation known as "SharePoint Wild West." This is one of the major reasons why SharePoint implementations fail: the lack of user requirements leads to a lack of governance because users have no idea what the product is, what premises it is based on, or what the strategy is for using it.

- Users will be able to manage security themselves without understanding it is applied in SharePoint. Another major failing in implementing SharePoint is assuming that security is a walk in the park when creating security control and access to data rules in SharePoint. Full Control permissions in a Shared Drive folder are not the same as Full Control of a SharePoint site. Neither are the responsibilities of individuals who have Full Control of a SharePoint site. The confusion related to this lack of understanding is worse if users are not trained in the use of SharePoint. User requirements, therefore, need to include security settings at the item, repository, and SharePoint 2010 site level.

SharePoint 2010 is an enterprise application, meaning that things such as backup, disaster recovery, system uptimes, and Service Level Agreements (SLAs) are vital. A key part of gathering user requirements is determining the premise and scope of user SharePoint sites. (Will they be project sites? Will they be short-term or long-term Human Resource sites? What about security, creation, archiving, retention, and so on?)

Business function priorities are vitally important to know, too. Gathering user requirements includes identifying areas of the business that will require high levels of access to SharePoint, monitoring rules, various levels of backup, and business continuity and disaster recovery features and timing.

Backup is extremely important. Users will request information concerning backups and how they will be done. As part of the user requirements, you need to establish the testing methods of those backups. For example, in organizations where SharePoint has been implemented with Production, Staging, and Testing areas, it is easy to take backups from Production and have them tested in the Testing area. Additionally, these backups can be used to refresh similarly named sites in the Staging area. This at least gives you the opportunity to test SharePoint 2010 backups.

User requirements lead to an understanding of the SharePoint scale and growth potential. For example, a Finance Web application could have a dedicated Excel Services application, while a different Excel Services application instance might be available to the rest of the SharePoint 2010 implementation.

This leads to centralization—SharePoint 2010 is designed to be a jumping-off point for all intranet access needs, and this introduces the concept of having all data sourced from one place. If user requirements are not collated as a whole, there is no way of understanding how best to set SharePoint as that jumping-off point. As a result, user adoption of Share-Point 2010 will suffer.

In the Plan phase of SharePoint implementation, there are five crucial areas that need to be fully investigated before the Build phase:

- Finding out what the users want to do with SharePoint 2010

- Data growth planning

- Content usage policies and governance

- Training and education planning

- Monitoring and maintenance planning

Investigations into these areas provide questions that the business analyst and SharePoint architect can use to find out what users want to do with SharePoint 2010. Asking users what their SharePoint needs are will help you decide what will be deployed in the SharePoint 2010 implementation—specifically, whether you are going to provide one or a combination of the following:

- Intranet portal

- Social computing

- Application

- Search

- Documents or records repository

- Workflow

- Extranet

- Intranet

- A connected Microsoft Access 2010 database or a replacement of Access 2007/2003

- Collaboration sites

- Team sites

Finding out what users want to do with SharePoint 2010 is what I'll cover in detail in this chapter. A successful SharePoint implementation requires resources whose ability is to extract user requirements and help convert those to SharePoint 2010 features. The key person is the business analyst, who works closely with the business users, SharePoint architect, and information analyst. Technical requirements are gathered by the SharePoint architect and interfacing teams through the client's technical authority.

To implement SharePoint 2010, you must make sure that the user requirements are captured in a *standard* and *repeatable* method, in a form understood by the business and technical stakeholders of your SharePoint implementation. There is no point in creating a wonderful questionnaire for business unit A and then modifying the questions for business unit B when the requirement is to gather information concerning what they do with content, how they use content, how they search it, how they process it, and so on. The questions therefore must be standard enough for business unit A and business unit B to answer without you modifying the questions.

Before going into that important section of this chapter, I'll touch on some other areas of requirements gathering that link into user requirements to create a SharePoint 2010 specification.

Data Growth Planning

When gathering user requirements, bear in mind the size of data and potential SharePoint 2010 growth by developing a Data Growth Plan. The Data Growth Plan shows the current content requirement in the organization, the expected content requirements upon SharePoint 2010 implementation, and a predicted need (typically sized for one year beyond the implementation). After the user requirements concerning data have been investigated and sized, you should post further technical questions with the interfacing teams (particularly with the teams dealing with storage and Microsoft SQL Server) and infrastructure teams if applicable (for servers that will hold your SharePoint 2010 farm).

Sizing a Site

Suppose that you want to size a particular site because users want to migrate documentation from a network file share into a document library in the site. The users have stated, "I want the file share to be at least 20 GB." How do you know what the real growth need is?

Without having a storage resource management (SRM) tool continuously scanning the customer's environment for several years, there is no 100 percent accurate method to help you answer this question. However, there are some good tools that are freely available on the Internet and commercially available that can allow you to scan file systems and determine, based on creation date, how things have grown in the past. The caveat is that these tools have no way of accounting for data that might have existed in the past but were deleted. Typically, you will see that growth in a customer environment has ramped up over the last three years, so even taking this potentially inflated number as the guideline might turn out to be a fairly accurate representation of what the next three years will look like. Also, be sure to consider any potential large projects that the customer might have coming up that would significantly skew the storage requirements.

From user requirements, the output you need to include in the Data Growth Plan is a document that indicates how many sites, documents, and pages are projected (aggregated from the users surveyed). This document should also include information concerning where the content is located, whether the content is centralized or geographically dispersed, what content will be scoped in searches, and whether there will be multiple search platforms. (In SharePoint 2010, you can have multiple search applications in different farms and on different servers to spread the load.)

Of importance to the interfacing teams will be a report on data load that indicates the required disk space usage and an administrative strategy concerning future growth (for example, site quota rules that will echo your SharePoint 2010 governance plan).

Data growth is not just about measuring the amount of data. Data growth is also concerned with infrastructure, and this means carrying out *capacity planning and performance goals*. Because SharePoint makes it easy for an organization to centralize data, some organizations fail to consider what happens when they do not coordinate the effort of sizing organizational data and determining whether the infrastructure will be able to handle the data.

Chapter 11

CAUTION

Unplanned data growth can lead to several issues. Insufficient workflow processes, disorganized content, and lack of a top-level site creation strategy can lead to difficulty in searching across sites, duplicated documents and records, or multiple copies and content versions. The only way to manage this is by applying SharePoint governance, and to apply rules concerning the location, tagging, and data growth rates in sites and across the organization. To further manage site growth, I advise you not to allow self-service site creation, and to use a process whereby new top-level site requests can be created through centralized support. Additionally, you should enable quotas on top-level sites so that you or selected individuals (site collection administrators) can be warned when a site reaches quota maximum thresholds.

There is an excellent whitepaper that describes how to develop a full understanding of the capacity needs of your SharePoint 2010 implementation. It is divided into four sections:

- Capacity management and sizing overview for SharePoint Server 2010

- Capacity planning for SharePoint Server 2010

- Performance testing for SharePoint Server 2010

- Monitoring and maintaining SharePoint Server 2010

This document is available at *http://technet.microsoft.com/en-us/library/cc261700.aspx*.

Content Usage Policies and Governance

As detailed in Chapter 9, "SharePoint Governance," creating policies (including policies regarding content usage) is part of the responsibility of the Governance Committee.

A key area in the gathering of user requirements is creating the questions related to data access. Who has access to data produced, stored, and archived by the relevant team, business unit, group, or organization? As you might recall from reading Chapter 5, "Building Your SharePoint Team," one of the information analyst tasks is to ensure that data is categorized and defined within the organization. The person assigned that task might also be aware of the security definitions of that data—in terms of what audience has access to the data on an organizational basis.

Another way of determining policies surrounding content is to analyze documents; how they are created, who creates, edits, reviews, approves, and so on.

When gathering SharePoint user requirements, it is very important to investigate and determine how content is created, stored, communicated and distributed. In the online Content section, there are example questions you can ask to help identify content policies and governance at *http://spsuserrequirements.geoffevelyn.com.*

Training and Education Planning

SharePoint training and education is vital to ensure the success of your SharePoint 2010 implementation and guarantee its continued use. Training and education is a continual process, especially because SharePoint 2010 is an evolutionary platform. As the organization changes and evolves, so does SharePoint. Changes in the organization will affect how people work with the platform, because as their roles change so do their responsibilities with regard to the data the organization creates and manages. Therefore, as people change with the organization, so do their training needs. You need to identify the kind of training that will be required to implement SharePoint 2010, and then implant a strategy for training to continue after the implementation.

It is not possible to explicitly state how to set the requirements for training on a business unit basis, as the level of SharePoint training needs to be balanced against the scope of the SharePoint implementation. For example, implementing a SharePoint 2010 environment in an organization whose staff have not used SharePoint before will be different from an implementation that is an upgrade from an earlier version of SharePoint. And the complexity of these training requirements will grow with the scope of the program's implementation (for example, if SharePoint is just one of a suite of applications and tools being deployed in Microsoft Office 2010, or so on).

Training is based on what the users will be doing with SharePoint. Therefore, it is suggested that a strategy and roadmap be outlined to cover SharePoint training. To build a strategy concerning who gets trained in SharePoint 2010, you need to examine the types of training needed and how to apply it.

There are two main types of training in SharePoint 2010 when it comes to day-to-day general use of the user interface: contributor training and owner training. Contributor training tends to be the most common because users need to know how to collaborate using SharePoint 2010. For example, they need to know how to create, modify, delete, and archive content they are responsible for in SharePoint 2010. Owner training is relevant to individuals who need to control access to content on the site, manage basic permissions, and administer their site in terms of adding, modifying, and structuring their site to best meet the requests of their users.

Chapter 11

> **Note**
>
> There are other recommendations concerning training levels. These levels can some-times be broken down into the following categories: Site Collection Owner, Content Owner (in the case of a publishing site where approvers are required), and Contribu-tor. You might also need a category for leaders from respective business groups who volunteer within the organization. Bear in mind that training in the organization can be achieved in many ways. The key is that the client gets to see and agree on how the training will be applied and that the training marries up with the client's operational productivity *vision*.

> **Note**
>
> Do not forget that you might require individuals to manage SharePoint 2010 centrally using the SharePoint 2010 Central Administration interface and manage SharePoint 2010 servers on a day-to-day basis. Training is especially critical for those who need to prepare themselves for SharePoint 2010 if they have been administrators in SharePoint 2007. Although there are many training resources for SharePoint administrators, a good place to start is with a course called "SharePoint Server 2010 Advanced IT Profes-sional Training," which you'll find at *http://technet.microsoft.com/en-gb/SharePoint/ ff420396.aspx*. The SharePoint Server 2010 Advanced IT Professional Training course is a deep technical learning series for current SharePoint Server 2007 professionals who are looking to upgrade their skills to SharePoint Server 2010.

Training is critical to the success of SharePoint 2010. The client organization is responsible for training every user to use SharePoint 2010 well enough to perform their roles at an acceptable level and to meet the expectations of the client's SharePoint 2010 vision. Train-ing is also an important method of handling change. If users are well informed and know what is happening, why it is happening, and what benefits can be gained from the train-ing, they feel reassured they will be properly and professionally trained and supported in their responsibilities regarding the SharePoint 2010 platform. This fosters the notion that the transition will be far easier for the organization. Training for SharePoint 2010 is not a one-time process and requires careful monitoring. The organization needs to provide addi-tional training, especially as users become more sophisticated in the use of collaborative techniques.

> **Note**
>
> As well as using traditional classroom training, organizations might find that blended learning and e-learning methods can be used to supplement standard IT training techniques. Microsoft provides a lot of e-learning courses on SharePoint at *http://www. microsoft.com/learning/en/us/training/sharepoint.aspx.*

For blended learning, you might find that providing an "Introduction to SharePoint 2010" class leads to an "Introduction to Collaborative Working in SharePoint 2010" class. You can then use traditional classroom training methods supplemented by multimedia presentations, demonstrations, floor-walking activities, and user guides.

> **Note**
>
> Providing online training guides, "How Do I" links, FAQs, and other online educational material related to SharePoint is very important. This material should be centrally positioned and easy to find. The best way to implement this is using SharePoint and creating a special site called the *SharePoint One-Stop Shop*. Doing this and combining the Search features of SharePoint 2010 to tag and assign Best Bets to key topics (like how to set permissions) is a major plus in the implementation of SharePoint 2010. The One-Stop Shop is further discussed in Chapter 13, "Planning and Implementing the SharePoint One-Stop Shop."

> **Tip**
>
> When you are building user requirements and discussing training, users need to understand what kind of training is available and the scope of the training. You should set out your courses from the lowest level to the highest achiever level. Table 11-1 provides an example of a user training strategy. Feel free to adopt and modify it to meet your own training strategy for SharePoint 2010.
>
> **Table 11-1 User Training Strategy**
>
> | Course | Content |
> | --- | --- |
> | Introduction to the Single Information Platform | An awareness presentation of at least 30 minutes introducing SharePoint 2010. Use this class to explain key features on a live platform. |
> | Introduction to Collaborative Working | Focuses on Microsoft Office features that relate to SharePoint, such as SharePoint 2010 team sites, working with document management (document libraries, version control, and check in check out), and so on. |

Course	Content
Intermediate Collaborative Services	Covers topics such as SharePoint 2010 one-to-one sharing, one-to-many sharing, and publishing. This class should also provide an introduction to workflows and instruction for more in-depth use of authoring and version control features.
Advanced Collaborative Services	Covers the use of Excel Services, Visio Services, Access Services, and Project Web Databases, all of which help users take advantage of the full collaborative features of SharePoint services, including temporary workspaces, workflows, acceptance, publishing, creating subsites and so on.

Roles That Need Training

The following roles will require high-level training of individuals within an organization that implements SharePoint 2010:

- **Team Site Administrator**   A user who is assigned the task of managing a collaborative environment on behalf of business peers

- **Workflow Manager**   A user who creates, approves, or rejects requests using workflows within SharePoint 2010

- **Content Administrator**   A user who publishes material and must produce, update, and manage organizational content

- **SharePoint 2010 Champion**   A user who demonstrates expertise in the use of the SharePoint 2010 feature set and has the skill set to understand the principles of SharePoint 2010 collaboration

> **Note**
> Many other roles can and will exist over time, but Table 11-1 demonstrates that although basic training in SharePoint might suffice at the outset, more advanced skills applicable to specific job functions will be required for users of SharePoint 2010.

You should set up a Training Coordination group, depending on the size of the organization and the breadth of the SharePoint 2010 platform, or seek the aid of the client's training department. This group needs to determine SharePoint 2010 training strategies at an early stage so that users will know what training they will receive and when. A point worth noting is that some users will avoid being trained or try and pick things up themselves. This is natural, but you should warn against this approach because the SharePoint 2010 environment is sophisticated and governed by policy. Policy and governance is part of training and educating users to work with SharePoint 2010 productively. Therefore, all users should attend mandatory training, which should include (at the very least) the first two sessions listed in Table 11-1. Training should not be an optional exercise for end users.

Monitoring and Maintenance Planning

User requirements will also help define Service-Level Agreements (SLAs). SLAs underpin SharePoint support and enable maintenance planning. SLAs also link to SharePoint governance and configuration management (CM) policies. Maintenance planning includes backup procedures, disaster recovery procedures, and contingency planning. Monitoring planning relates to the makeup of the technical aspects of the SharePoint environment—the software, hardware, operating system, networking, and tools used to set performance (*reliability*) levels and define *availability*. (Availability, reliability, and maintenance are important areas of a SharePoint System Specification. For more information, see Chapter 12, "Producing the System Specification," specifically, the "Availability, Reliability, and Maintenance" section on page 202.)

CAUTION

SLAs are a double-edged sword. IT benefits from them by having an expectation of how long a site or function can be down, which allows for planning and potential equipment acquisition and implementation. The business benefits from them because there is a clear demarcation of functionality within the farm and a clear indication of what the expected service restoration time will be after an event has affected the farm. Different SLAs apply to different functions. Hardly anyone would agree that a personal site (MySite) has nearly the service footprint of a core portal site failure, yet they are both site collections; therefore, using the same SLA for each does not make sense.

Monitoring and maintenance requirements should also include a list of personnel from the interfacing teams who are responsible for providing maintenance to connected technologies if the SharePoint administrator is not involved in supporting those technologies (for example, SQL Server, Microsoft Exchange, Active Directory, and so on).

SharePoint administrators will in time have to create customized monitoring of the components and many services of SharePoint 2010 once it is deployed. Additionally, they will need increased alerting capability—meaning, that if certain issues arise with the SharePoint 2010 platform, administrators can be informed of them promptly. With regard to monitoring tools, it is strongly suggested that wherever possible, you use Microsoft-provided ones. SharePoint has some extremely good monitoring tools and uses Windows PowerShell to aid in scripting; however, SharePoint administrators might argue that it's not possible to fine-tune SharePoint and hence would rather go down the third-party route to fulfill a certain requirement, or even create their own tools using, say, Microsoft Visual Studio. Whether administrators use third-party tools or create their own, the use of these kinds of tools must be justified, and the tools must be rigorously tested in your test environment before they are applied to your production environment using the configuration management process.

> **Note**
>
> SharePoint Server 2010 includes an integrated health analysis tool called SharePoint Health Analyzer that enables SharePoint Server to automatically check for potential configuration, performance, and usage problems. This means the monitoring features in SharePoint 2010 can help you to understand how the SharePoint Server 2010 system is running, analyze and repair problems, and view metrics for the sites. For more information, see the TechNet article at *http://technet.microsoft.com/en-gb/library/ee748636.aspx*.

> **Note**
>
> Microsoft System Center Operations Manager 2007 (SCOM) is a product designed for enterprise health monitoring; it integrates closely with SharePoint 2010 and provides the most comprehensive and flexible solution for monitoring the health of SharePoint farms. With SCOM, the level of reporting and alerting is more granular and easily managed than with SharePoint's standard health monitoring.
>
> SharePoint 2010 ships a management pack for System Center Operations Manager, which includes the following items and capabilities:
>
> - Improved Knowledge articles
>
> - More relevant events and monitors
>
> - Surfaces SharePoint Health Analyzer (SPHA) rules
>
> - Integrated with Unified Logging System (ULS)
>
> The SCOM 2007 Management Pack for SharePoint 2010 contains more documentation for using these products together, which you'll find in the Management Pack Guide for SharePoint Foundation 2010, and one for SharePoint Server 2010. Be sure to reference both guides for managing the server product. You can download them from *http://www.microsoft.com/downloads/details.aspx?displaylang=en&FamilyID=c8a9d749-b7a8-412a-b2db-f3e464ed3fcf*.
>
> You'll find more information on SCOM at *http://technet.microsoft.com/en-us/systemcenter/om*.

Finding Out What Users Want To Do with SharePoint 2010

User requirements are a very important aspect of the SharePoint 2010 implementation. Finding out what users want to do with SharePoint 2010 requires the development of user requirements. When user requirements are correctly delineated, they can facilitate a successful SharePoint 2010 implementation.

Users are king when it comes to creating and managing electronic content; their usage patterns shape what features of SharePoint should be provided. Without their input into what areas of productivity gains they want to see and an understanding of how the client's vision links to that, SharePoint 2010 will become nothing more than another Web site implemented by a technical team without any connection to the business.

It's difficult to describe all the facets of user requirements in detail in this book because it is an area of great complexity; therefore, I have provided a full article and a downloadable document, which is available at *http://spsuserrequirements.geoffevelyn.com*.

Please read this document if you need to understand what user requirements need to be captured, how they should be captured, and who should capture them.

Summary

User requirements are vital to ensure that your SharePoint 2010 implementation covers what the user will get, when they will get it, and how they will get it. There are two sets of requirements. The top-level business requirements, which come from the client, and the user requirements. The business requirements are high-level requirements you determine by asking questions such as the following:

- Can the users understand and learn to use SharePoint 2010 effectively? Can they build their own sites and distribute their content easily?

- Can the users learn the product very quickly and re-apply things they know about using the tools in the current version of SharePoint?

- Is SharePoint 2010 going to help automate work processes?

- Is SharePoint 2010 going to secure content?

- Can the organization control SharePoint or at least be advised how to?

The user requirements are more detailed than the business requirements and go down to the Site and Repository level in SharePoint. They define the objective, content, categorization, and features that need to be in place in SharePoint 2010. More importantly, these requirements provide a complete picture of what users are currently doing with their data. Remember that SharePoint 2010, when measured against user requirements, must map to or exceed those requirements to satisfy the client and users. When mapped, these requirements state what is achievable and what will be in place when SharePoint 2010 is implemented, and they allow you to prioritize future work.

You gather requirements by eliciting responses from users to key questions, analyzing user responses to your questions, validating user comments, and documenting user responses. Eliciting responses by using standard questions allows you to build a matrix of responses and process diagrams. I've given some examples of these questions in this chapter. Data you obtain through gathering information in this way is then analyzed and validated against what SharePoint 2010 can offer to meet those requirements. Finally, documentation is done so that implementation of these requirements can be applied to SharePoint 2010.

User requirements data, when gathered correctly, is in a form that allows the client to understand how SharePoint fits in. It also enables the SharePoint architect to map the structure to the design of SharePoint. Hence, it is crucial that the correct personnel resources be used to gather this data—a key role is the SharePoint business analyst because that person understands analysis methods such as profiling users, creating models, gap analysis, identifying the real requirements. In Chapter 5, I describe this role and why the post is so important to gathering user requirements.

This chapter has given you some tips on what it takes to obtain key user requirements. These are used to build the SharePoint 2010 System Specification (a list of technical requirements leading to the Build phase of the SharePoint environment and features). A discussion of this can be found in Chapter 12.

Producing the System Specification

T he preceding chapters concentrated on investigating the user requirements, client requirements, and which project team member gathers, collates, and records those requirements. This chapter concentrates on the SharePoint System Specification document, which is a list of technical requirements leading to the Build phase of the SharePoint environments and features.

The SharePoint System Specification documentation establishes consensus among stakeholders regarding system-level requirements of their SharePoint implementation. Having a well-specified set of requirements in document format reduces risks and prevents poorly analyzed, specified, and managed requirements from being included. The requirements specified in the System Specification includes information that sets the scope, size, and complexity of the SharePoint implementation. Additionally, requirements included in such documentation are able to drive the system architecture, testing activities, implementation, and overall design.

This specification should produce a complete and unambiguous set of documentation that describes the intended system in terms of its function, performance, interfaces, and design constraints.

Note that SharePoint 2010 might be just part of a larger program of providing technology to the client. For example, the client might require not just SharePoint 2010 but also client tools such as Microsoft Office 2010 and associated tools such as Microsoft Office Communicator (which is an extremely useful tool that allows for messaging and shows presence information within SharePoint 2010). If that is the case, the System Specification must include references that detail how SharePoint 2010 will interface with those products.

The System Specification for SharePoint should not be complex. The System Specification is a roadmap for SharePoint and shows connections to other technologies through those references. The System Specification document for SharePoint must be written explicitly for SharePoint 2010 and reference only other system specification documentation for any connected products.

A number of important benefits can be realized from the development of a good Share-Point System Specification:

- Improved visibility and understanding of the system enables enhanced communication with users and the project team (in particular, the SharePoint architect).

- The Build phase becomes a firm foundation.

- Verification and validation planning for SharePoint can be defined because there are metrics within the System Specification that can be mapped.

- A baseline of acceptance is set.

Formal topics included in a System Specification are as follows (we'll apply the items in this standard list to SharePoint in the "System Specifications" section later in the chapter):

- System Overview

- Functional Requirements

- Performance Requirements

- Human Requirements

- System Management Requirements

- Availability, Reliability, and Maintenance

- Interface Requirements

- Test Requirements

- Integration Testing

- Design Constraints

Before creating the System Specification for your SharePoint 2010 implementation, you must understand the following key considerations for defining the SharePoint infrastructure: SharePoint 2010 concepts, 64-bit vs. 32-bit architecture (if upgrading from SharePoint 2007), and topologies. The following sections discuss these key considerations.

SharePoint 2010 Concepts

In a SharePoint farm, servers have the following roles: Web, Query, Index, Calculation, Application, and Database. Farms have relationships such as Authoring, Publishing, Development, Test, Staging, and Production, as well as Service Applications covering Search,

Profile, Access, Business Data Catalog, Excel, Managed Metadata, Secure Store, Usage/
Health, and Visio. In a SharePoint farm, SharePoint comprises servers, Web applications,
databases, site collections, sites, lists, and items Figure 12-1 illustrates this hierarchy.

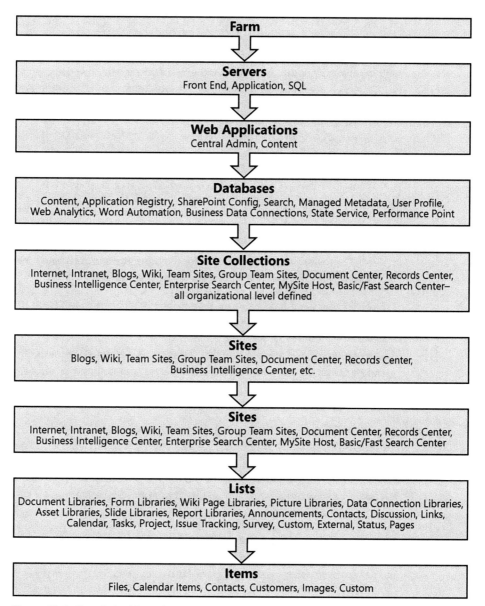

Figure 12-1 SharePoint hierarchy.

SharePoint 2010 can be deployed to a single server or many servers, thus forming a Share-Point *farm*. There are three roles that constitute tiers: the Web Server role, Application Server role, and Database Server role. In a small farm, these roles can be combined onto one or more servers. This is done to achieve redundancy, better performance, and service resilience. For example, the organization might require that the SharePoint 2010 implementation has a high level of uptime—meaning that users are not immediately disrupted when access to a SharePoint farm is lost and that the SharePoint farm needs to be robust. One method of achieving this is to add another Web server and have both servers *load balanced* (so that the servers balance the requests between them, which results in greater response time on SharePoint). Because another Web server has been added, robustness and resilience are increased and outages are reduced or eliminated; if one Web server is not available, the other will take the load.

In Figure 12-1, you can see that the servers in SharePoint are referred to as *front ends*—commonly known as Web front ends, (WFEs or Web servers)—application servers and SQL servers.

> **Note**
>
> The WFE provides the Web interfaces for the users, hosting Web pages, Web services, and Web parts that are used to process requests served by the farm.
>
> The WFE role is required for farms that include other SharePoint Server 2010 capabilities. In dedicated search service farms, this role is not required because WFEs at remote farms contact query servers directly. In small farms, this role can be shared with the Query role, which is a server role that responds to user search requests. The Query role can be placed on its own servers, and there is no hard limit to the number of servers in a SharePoint farm.

The application server is associated with services that can be deployed to a physical computer. Each service represents a separate application service that can reside on a dedicated application server, if required. Services with similar performance and usage properties can be grouped on a server or can be scaled out onto multiple servers if specific services require better performance.

Client-related services can be combined into a *service group*. These service groups can be created based on the types and level of SharePoint farms provided. For example, Query and Crawl are search roles that are cross-farm roles, meaning their services can be shared by another SharePoint 2010 farm. Other cross-farm roles include User Profile, Business Data Connectivity, Web Analytics, Managed Metadata, and Secure Store. Services that are client related are single-farm roles, meaning their services can be used only in one SharePoint farm. For example, Excel Calculation, Access, Word, PowerPoint, Visio, and Word services are single-farm roles. Other single-farm roles include Usage and Health, Performance Point, State, and Foundation Subscription.

> **Tip**
>
> After you have deployed SharePoint 2010, look for services that consume a high amount of resources and consider placing those services on dedicated hardware.

The database server is where all SharePoint services and user-related content gets stored. Search, content, and service databases are located on the database server. Search databases can include search admin, property, and crawl databases, and depending on the size of the farm, you can have more than these four types. Content databases cover all SharePoint user content related to the site collections and so on. You can have multiple content databases, depending on the volume of the content and sizing goals for the environment. The service databases include the following: BCD, managed metadata, state, secure store, usage and health, profile, social tagging, and profile sync (user profile databases), including the subscription settings databases.

64-Bit vs. 32-Bit Architecture

You should not consider SharePoint 2010 to be a single application; it comprises several components and relies heavily on other Microsoft technologies, such as Internet Explorer, Office, SharePoint Services, and Foundation Services, including SQL Server, Active Directory, and Exchange.

SharePoint 2010 is completely a 64-bit application. In previous versions of SharePoint, you could use the 32-bit version, but that raised several issues for engineers, which were primarily related to memory resource shortages. For example, workflows needed more resources, load-balanced configuration was problematic, scaling out had to be achieved, and the number of features that could be turned on was limited because that affected performance.

Although these performance issues were resolved by making SharePoint 2010 a 64-bit application, you still need to be careful to factor in the cost of migrating from a 32-bit SharePoint 2007 environment on 32-bit hardware, because the hardware will have to be replaced. Additional build tasks will be required to prepare the hardware necessary for this migration.

> **Note**
>
> If you are planning a migration from SharePoint 2007, a best practice is to have 64-bit resources (server hardware) available so that your deploy strategy uses a parallel run system. You deploy SharePoint 2010 in the 64-bit environment and then attach your content databases from your SharePoint 2007 environment. Setting up a test environment in this way enables you to confirm whether all features from your SharePoint 2007 environment continue to work in SharePoint 2010.
>
> You might encounter obstacles to overcome related to branding (if your 2007 environment is customized), features (if you have third-party or customized code applied to SharePoint 2007), and more. As you work through these issues, continue to repeat runs of the migration exercise until you and the client are satisfied that the SharePoint 2010 environment meets requirements. Doing this strengthens your configuration management plan, project planning, and user requirements planning, and it gives the client confidence that the current SharePoint platform will not be affected as the switchover build gets underway.

Topology

SharePoint 2010 can scale from one farm, two farms, or multipurpose farms to medium farms to large farms, depending on the requirement. Table 12-1 lists the deployments that are available and describes how you might define a particular deployment.

There is a good online deployment guide providing information about SharePoint 2010 deployment scenarios, step-by-step installation instructions, and post-installation configuration steps. This guide also describes how to upgrade to SharePoint Server 2010. The deployment guide is located at *http://technet.microsoft.com/en-us/library/cc262957.aspx*.

Table 12-1 Available Deployments

Deployment	Basic Description
One Server Farm—All roles on one server, including the SQL Server role	When properly prepared, such an environment can scale to thousands of users. Deciding whether to use this type of environment is mostly determined by SQL bandwidth and the amount of RAM available to SharePoint and associated services.
Two-Tier Farm—All Web and Application Server roles and databases are on separate SQL servers	This type of farm provides high availability; two clustered or mirrored database servers are recommended.

Deployment	Basic Description
Two-Tier Small Farm—1 x Web server/query server, 1 x Web server/Query server including all services and the database on a separate SQL server	This type of farm has two Web servers that can be expected to serve 10,000 to 20,000 users.
Three-Tier Small Farm—Two Web query servers, one application server, and the databases on separate SQL servers	This type of farm adds a dedicated application server for environments with moderate service usage.
Three-Tier Small Farm Optimized for Search—Two Web query servers, one application server, one search database server, and other databases on separate SQL servers	With hardware dedicated to search databases, this topology is optimized for search to work well in environments with up to ten million items.

For medium farms, scaling out (adding more servers, for example) depends on what services you want to make more resilient and available by pushing them onto their own servers. The decision to position specific services on their own servers within the farm could be based on the utilization of those services to balance and provide good performance of the Share-Point farm. Another decision to scale out servers could be based on the volume of content the farm will host and that you want more resiliency or you want to balance out performance on the database SQL servers. Decisions like this needs to be taken very carefully as you would see a potential increase in the number of Web servers, application servers, or database servers. That in turn could increase the level of support required to look after the increased server count.

> **Note**
>
> The number of users will have an effect on the number of Web servers required. Factor 10,000 users per Web server as a starting point. Adjust the number based on how heavily the servers are being used. Heavy use of client services will increase the load on Web servers.
>
> Additionally, you should start with all application server roles installed on one server (except search roles). Then, based on utilization, consider either adding more servers with all the non-search roles installed, or add more servers to dedicate resources to specific services. For example, if performance data indicates that Excel Services is using a disproportionate amount of resources, offload this service to a dedicated server.

For large farms, the strategy is to group services or databases with similar performance characteristics onto dedicated servers and then scale out the servers as a group. For example, you can create multiple Web Server Groups—one group responsible for incoming requests and another for crawling and administration. You can create multiple Application

Chapter 12

Server Groups and have each group cover a specific area, such as crawl, query, sandboxed code, or services. Finally, database servers can be grouped into search, content, and other SharePoint databases.

Note that with each topology the more you scale, the more effort you need to administer, test, support, and maintain the SharePoint implementation. The key is always to start with the essentials required to provide the initial service level and then through benchmark testing, performance testing, and user requirements analysis, scale out the environment as required.

> **Note**
> To further understand what is technically required, you should read the following TechNet article, which describes the minimum hardware and software needed to install and run SharePoint 2010. Go to *http://technet.microsoft.com/en-us/library/cc262485. aspx*. For information about SharePoint Foundation, go to *http://technet.microsoft.com/ en-us/library/cc287737.aspx*.

Before You Begin Documentation

You need a standard approach to recording your SharePoint 2010 System Specification. This is a top-level document that will refer to a number of planning documents that define the details of the SharePoint configuration.

This document should be in a format that can be understood not just by the technical team, but also by the client and anyone in the business concerned with the SharePoint implementation. This information is also used to show those who will need to know the high-level configuration of SharePoint 2010 in the future. For example, recruits hired to provide SharePoint support, SharePoint consultants and developers, and even future project managers will need access to the System Specification.

To start, you need one top-level document called "SharePoint 2010 System Specification" that describes the topologies suggested, alternative topologies, risks, and the planning documents for each of the design areas. This document then has a list of referenced worksheets covering the following areas:

- Functional, Performance

- Human, System Management

- Interface Requirements

- Test Requirements

- Design Constraints

- Availability

- Reliability and Maintenance

Tip

The SharePoint architect should read the following article to aid in determining the planning and architecture for SharePoint 2010: *http://technet.microsoft.com/en-us/library/cc261834.aspx*.

There are good whitepapers describing the performance and capacity impact of specific feature sets included in SharePoint Server 2010. These whitepapers include information about the performance and capacity characteristics of the feature and how a particular feature was tested by Microsoft. Features covered include the following: test farm characteristics, test results, recommendations for troubleshooting performance, and scalability. To view these whitepapers, go to *http://www.microsoft.com/downloads/details.aspx?FamilyID=FD1EAC86-AD47-4865-9378-80040D08AC55&displayLang=en#filelist*.

In my blog (*http://www.sharepointgeoff.com/scblogspace/Lists/Posts/Post.aspx?ID=91*), I have listed links to worksheets that you can use to record information that you gather and decisions you make to help you build your SharePoint 2010 System Specification. Note that just as you need to capture user requirements and the business analyst needs to capture data, the SharePoint architect and developers (if necessary) also need to capture data. To enable the architect and developers to do this, the project manager needs to go through that list and build the responses to team members using the user requirements document as a guide so that the decisions they make link back to specific user requirements.

Important

Make sure that as you work through the worksheets, you reference the related user requirement so that the client can see that a particular user requirement will be met. By doing this, you will identify exactly what user requirements are achievable, which will require more work, which will require more funding, and which are simply not practical and will need an alternative to be created.

System Specifications

This section provides an introduction to and a detailed overview of the required characteristics of a delivered system. To start a project properly though, you need to provide a current perspective of the client system infrastructure. Descriptions of the client network, geographical connectivity, directory services, number of staff, and support provisions you must include in your overview are listed in Table 12-2.

Table 12-2 System Specifications

Section	Description
Project Name	Written as statements. Specify the title of the project, whether there are related process documents (such as a SharePoint Quality Plan, Project Plan, or associated material), where the related documents are located, and the relevant reference numbers.
SharePoint Goals	Written as statements. Describe the purpose of the implementation and the objective of the SharePoint deployment. For example, is it a test, staged, or production deployment? If necessary, tie these statements to the client vision, and include statements giving a high-level description of how SharePoint will be used. For example, if you're performing a global deployment of SharePoint, describe briefly the user environments (for example, an intranet or Internet deployment).
Who Are the Intended Audiences?	Written as a list. Specify who needs to get access to this document and how they will consume this document.
Analysis Summary	A statement that confirms how the analysis was carried out, either at the organizational, departmental, business unit, or individual level.

Functional Requirements

Functional requirements define the behavior of the system, and they come from the user requirements. The user requirements set out what the users need in terms of data growth, governance, training, maintenance, content, applications, search capabilities, audience, taxonomy, metadata, and more. Hence, for each class of user requirements, the functional requirements must list the software specification required to match each of those classes of user requirements.

Functional requirements include the following:

- Sites and Site Collection

- Managed Metadata

- Records Management

- Document Management

Functional requirements need to describe a high-level framework for each of the site collections, as well as describe how the sites are mapped within those site collections. The
metadata and taxonomy are described here, including details about what levels will be
implemented, a list of what site collections they will be implemented in, and a high-level
description of what policies will be put in place for managing data. Any detailed documentation (and there will be detailed information here) must be referred to in terms of
where the functional region is defined. For example, you can define a site collection split
by organizational metadata, which will allow users to create sites within a framework of
the organization—for example, by function. So a site created as "Global Communications"
could sit in a "Communications" space defined by organizational metadata (making it easier
to tag, for example).

Performance Requirements

One of the nonfunctional requirements that is very important is SharePoint performance.
This performance estimates are often overly optimistic.

Performance can be a problem because it is difficult to predict, especially performance of
SharePoint, and the cost of adding extra performance into software or hardware designs
can be prohibitive because estimates are not accurate or measured completely. This problem is exacerbated by the fact that accurate estimates of performance can be made only
when the architectural design is completed. That said, it is vital that the hardware and
farm topology of SharePoint deliver the required performance. Two areas that must be
addressed are SharePoint capacity and SharePoint response.

SharePoint capacity can be divided into static and dynamic requirements:

- Static:
    - Maximum volumes of data to be stored
    - Number of users connected
    - Total number of messages input and output
    - Minimum allowance for storage
    - Minimum allowable RAM
- Dynamic, for normal and peak loading:
    - Number of transactions to be processed in a specified time
    - Maximum number of users to be connected at any given time
    - Access times and response times

- Throughout—for example, x per hour, x/2 every 20 minutes, and x/10 every 2 minutes

- Maximum percentage CPU utilization for Web front-end servers, application server, and SQL servers

- Maximum percentage of storage utilization

SharePoint response is related to the ability to express response times to hardware, to users, or to specific events in a precise manner. Response times should be stated as overall system response times under specified conditions. For SharePoint, you need to specify mission-performance criteria and express responses as absolute times or statistically. For example, you could use the following statement as a statistical response measure: "The Web front-end servers under peak operating load of 90 percent of responses shall be less than .5 seconds." Another example is an average response measurement—for example, "The Web front-end servers under peak operating load of 90 percent of responses shall be on average .5 seconds, with no response being less than .25 seconds or greater than .75 seconds."

For each response, you should consider how performance will be measured and whether specific applications or tools will be required to carry out the measurement. Performance figures must be quantifiable and achievable in SharePoint.

SharePoint 2010 includes the following features to aid in performance management:

- An improved user interface that assists administrators in understanding SharePoint 2010 more quickly. SharePoint 2010 Central Administration is laid out in a more logical way. The new UI is similar to Windows Server 2008, and it is security trimmed.

- Health monitoring. SharePoint 2010 includes a health analyzer that runs timer-based checks according to rules in various categories, security, and performance. You can create your own rules, and more rules can be added to future SharePoint 2010 service packs.

- Large-list throttling. You can now control how users can query and view data. You can set throttle controls on the number of items returned, which forces end users to create more efficient views, and you can set "happy hour" times during which you expect heavier loads to occur.

- A Developer Dashboard, which can be accessed on demand in SharePoint 2010 to show which components in SharePoint 2010 are slowing down performance. This is useful, for example, for an intranet environment because it can make it much easier to see on the fly how certain sites are performing.

- The Logging Database, which is now a central repository for usage and health information. This database enables administrators to get more information by selecting options such as Slowest Pages, Top Active Users, and many more.

Tip

To help you further in this area, you should read "Plan for caching and performance" at *http://technet.microsoft.com/en-us/library/ee424404.aspx* and "SharePoint 2010 performance and capacity technical case studies" at *http://www.microsoft.com/downloads/details.aspx?displaylang=en&FamilyID=9cf4fa6b-4c9c-4fca-b9c9-4a4f724df448*.

Human Requirements

SharePoint 2010 is provided to users and will be seen as the *enterprise collaborative* platform, which enables individuals in an organization to create and manage their own online sites, content, and more. The performance of SharePoint is therefore critically dependent on ensuring a good match between the hardware and the people who access the services on them. The work carried out by the business analyst, SharePoint architect, and information analyst while gathering user requirements provides significant information for this section of the System Specification.

Make sure you use the data gathered in the "Finding Out What Users Want To Do with SharePoint 2010" section on page 187, from Chapter 11, "Making Sure SharePoint Meets User Requirements."

You need to make sure you obtain the following information:

- **SharePoint user characteristics and style** This identifies the characteristics necessary to support the proper operation of SharePoint from the user perspective, the use of the Ribbon bar, modifying pages, carrying out administration, and so forth.

- **Identification of each component of the user interface** This section should identify each display, menu, and form. However, keep in mind that this is very difficult to do correctly, and it's a good example of post-bid requirements work. It emphasizes the importance of producing a sound framework of SharePoint components and detailing ways to use them.

- **Criteria for acceptance** Under this section, you need to understand and define the extent to which and the manner in which the SharePoint sites should be accepted. For example, you specify whether there will be real user trials, a full feature check, performance checks, and so forth. Criteria for usability can include the following:

- o **Learnability** The number of training hours needed to pass a standard Share-Point skill test

- o **Productivity**   Percentage of error-free operations per day, logged automatically after one month's experience

- o **Likeability**   Percentage of users who, after training, prefer this to the old system

System Management Requirements

System management deals with how SharePoint is operated, administered, and controlled. Overall, SharePoint operational requirements are expressed in terms of normal and abnormal operation modes. These requirements are borne from mapping out all interfaced component connections to SharePoint 2010 and identifying who is responsible for each of these.

The management requirements for SQL Server (if it is run by a SQL DBA team) will not be the same as the management requirements for SharePoint administrators. SQL DBAs will have rules detailing how their environment will be configured, rules for service accounts, rules for database growth rates, and rules for compression technologies. The SharePoint team must identify the level of access to SQL that service accounts should have, the size of content databases, and how these items should be structured. Both teams should have connection rules describing the procedure for restoring a content database onto the same server or onto other servers, including disaster recovery procedures.

It is vital that these requirements are documented as part of the SharePoint "Statement of Operations" guide, and the top-level requirements for each major interfaced component documented in the "System Management Requirements" section. The Statement of Operations is detailed in Chapter 9, "SharePoint Governance." At the highest level, recording system management requirements in the System Specification document means the client, interfacing teams, and users are aware of what governs SharePoint—that is, governance and management requirements.

Availability, Reliability, and Maintenance

Other important components of nonfunctional requirements are availability, reliability, and maintainability. These factors are interrelated but independent. SharePoint 2010, when implemented, might have very high resilience but poor availability.

For example, let's assume for a moment that the SharePoint 2010 implementation has multiple, load-balanced servers as well as good disaster recovery processes. Add into that the security applied to sites is based on an attitude of "Speak to the help desk, and log a ticket for the SharePoint administrator to assign your site permissions." Now scale this to multiple site collections with hundreds of sites that have only one administrator to set those permissions. You now have high resilience but poor availability to sites. (Imagine how long you would have to wait in line to have a permission changed if all requests had to go through one person!)

For SharePoint implementation projects, you should define availability as part of your disaster recovery plan because disaster recovery is the process by which you resume business after a disruptive event (which you also need to define). Based on that, the following three components need to be defined:

- **Reliability**   Refers to the probability of correct operation, and is measured by the elapsed time and failure rate. The more practical measures are mean time between failures (MTBF) and its reciprocal failure rate. MTBF is usually expressed in hours, and failure rate is expressed as failures per 1,000 hours.

- **Availability**   Refers to the proportion of time SharePoint is available for operation and therefore takes into account both the failure rate and the time taken to restore normal operation. For example, if you are running SharePoint backups and want to use a daily backup of a large site collection, you need to be aware that if the site requires restoration in the future the time taken to restore will have an impact on availability. If the failure rate is high and the time taken to restore is long, that is not a very good state of affairs for a disaster recovery plan on that site.

- **Maintainability**   Is both a measure of continuous improper service delivered and a measure of the time taken to restore the system from the last experienced failure.

Resilience in SharePoint is a vital goal. Resilience is measured by fault prevention, fault removal, and fault forecasting. Here are two points to keep in mind:

- Use the Health Analyzer and Logging features in SharePoint to ensure good logging capabilities exist for the key services you are supplying to the client. By doing this, you can identify the sequences indicating there are issues to resolve before the issues become serious, which is where fault forecasting comes in. Fault removal needs to be documented as part of a change control process under configuration management so that any SharePoint faults are traceable. If these faults are repeated, documentation can ensure the process to correct them and the time required to correct them are known (meaning availability is known) and that there is a standard in place.

- With regard to availability, if high numbers are shown for the rate and time, you might need to examine the resources assigned to the issue and address the configuration applied. If an important service application—for example, Excel Services—is continually failing, the failure needs to be addressed by either looking at where the resources are being drained, increasing the available resources, or moving the service to its own server.

Chapter 12

This section of the document needs to record the key SharePoint site collections, services, and components that need to have a high level of availability and a statement about each describing what will be done to meet the availability requirement. If the client requires the uptime of all site collections to be 99 percent, agreement needs to be reached regarding what constitutes 99 percent operation and who is responsible for ensuring it remains at 99 percent.

> **Note**
>
> Because most uptime guarantees are given on a monthly basis, if SharePoint was down 10 percent of the time, that translates to about three days of downtime. If this Share-Point instance was visited regularly, 10 percent downtime costs the organization (in lost sales, lost productivity, etc.) far more than the monthly cost of supporting SharePoint. Now consider the most often used uptime guarantees and see what they really mean. A 99.5 percent uptime guarantee means that SharePoint can be down for as much as 216 minutes in a month; a 99.8 percent uptime guarantee predicts there will be no more than 86.4 minutes of downtime; a 99.9 percent uptime guarantee predicts there will be no more than 43.2 minutes of downtime; a 99.99 percent uptime guarantee predicts there will be no more than 4.32 minutes of downtime; and a 99.999 percent uptime guarantee predicts there will be no more than 0.432 minutes (26 seconds) of downtime.

Interface Requirements

SharePoint 2010 provides many templates to suit a particular site requirement. For example, a group of individuals might require a Group Work Team site because its "look and feel" is closer to the way they work than using say a Projects Work Database site or a Blog site.

As you gather information through user requirements and make decisions through the planning of sites and site collections, you can make a match between what the user requires and the site templates that have been included in SharePoint. If the site templates are not available, or a template is available but branding through an editor is desired, this can be recorded and identified as a task. (Branding SharePoint requires a detailed appraisal and can potentially create another project.)

> **Note**
> The SharePoint 2010 interface is a massive topic area because it relates to accessibility, and that means it relates to the Web Content Accessibility Guidelines. For more information on this and what has been done to address SharePoint accessibility, go to *http://blogs.msdn.com/b/sharepoint/archive/2010/03/09/accessibility-and-share-point-2010.aspx*.

Test Requirements

The primary requirement for testing is that the acceptance tests are designed to demonstrate that the system behaves in accordance with the requirements expressed in the Requirements or System Specification. SharePoint acceptance tests must be based on the user requirements specification, using a "Validation and Verification of SharePoint" process. This means that it is possible to create tests for virtually every statement in the User Requirements section. However, for any test to be valid, the original requirement must be defined in such a way to make it testable.

Let's look at a user requirements request. A user states a requirement as "I want Google Search to be implemented in SharePoint." Even though it is indeed possible to plant Google's search function within a SharePoint environment, there would still be a requirement to test whether the experience an individual has using SharePoint search is worse or better than using the Google search features in SharePoint.

Moving into Hardware Testing, Software Testing, Connectivity, and Performance

SharePoint includes connectivity to systems that might or might not be under the SharePoint administrator's control. For example, Active Directory might be managed by an Active Directory team, and SQL servers and clusters might be managed by SQL DBAs. This causes the scope of testing to expand—now testing includes not only tests of the hardware or software, but tests of resiliency, robustness, support, and maintainability. Taking this further, if SharePoint is presented on three environments—say, the Test, Stage, and Production platforms—providing performance tests might be different depending on the type of infrastructure, network connectivity, and other configuration.

Therefore, the test requirements need to cover user experience, software, hardware, connectivity, and performance. The last type of test, performance, needs to be defined clearly with the user requirements. Make sure that these, when collated, can set against a known criteria in SharePoint. For example, if the test is testing the speed of uploading from a client desktop, at the end of the Applications section of the User Requirements document you should state what needs to be tested.

Chapter 12

After user requirements have been gathered and detailed test requirements have been formulated, these can be prioritized. If you get a recurring theme of "Confirm that Excel Services connect to the spreadsheet for Department X" submitted as user requirements, the speed and performance of Excel Services should be tested. Of course, there will be detailed tests; however, these should be designed as tasks relevant to the implementation of the requirement, not added to the System Specification document. This is because, as pointed out earlier, the System Specification document points to subsets of SharePoint, which in themselves are defined as separate tasks with their own test schedules.

The "Test Requirements" section of the System Specification should detail the kinds of tests I discuss next, assuming it is a high-level document related to the implementation of Share-Point 2010.

Note

It is very important to test the database layer of SharePoint (the SQL layer) because this represents a significant portion of SharePoint performance and is likely, if left unchecked, to present latency issues.

Upgrading from 32-Bit to 64-Bit

For those upgrading to SharePoint 2010 from a SharePoint 2007 32-bit environment, you should be aware that in the 64-bit version, you must still carry out additional tests to identify performance issues. For example, you should include the following as test requirements:

- Confirm paging loads on the Web front-end servers. If this is high, consider adding memory as required to those servers.

- Confirm the recycling of the application pool, and test to find out whether there is a possibility of fragmentation because this will help reduce the potential impact of Web parts overconsuming memory.

- Get your users to understand the principles of large lists (through governance, education, and training programs). This has been addressed in SharePoint 2010 with the addition of the Large List Throttling feature (mentioned earlier in the "Performance Requirements" section), though this will not completely stop users from setting high values for the number of items returned in a list view.

- Examine the Health Analyzer to provide more tests, and adjust that to see the thresholds on your SharePoint environment. The Health Analyzer in SharePoint 2010 Central Administration allows administrators to confirm levels of operation in SharePoint are adequate. This component also allows you to set customized alerts, making it possible to create SharePoint administrative tests by setting the alerts at various values of tolerance, for example.

There are two types of tests that can be applied to SharePoint: acceptance testing and integration testing (described on page 209 in this chapter). Acceptance testing is the most common, and it includes testing of user requirements and technical requirements. This kind of testing is designed to capture the supportability of any aspect of SharePoint under normal or abnormal operations.

The client will need some kind of proof that the requirements specified in the SharePoint 2010 Quality Plan have been achieved. During the recording of these client requirements and the agreements reached, a number of decisions will be made regarding the basic level of testing necessary to prove, validate, and verify the solution you provide.

When recording testing requirements, make sure that you provide two sets. The first set is for the client, and it contains high-level detail and a list of tests that will be carried out to meet requirements consistent with the client vision statement. The second set of tests cover the user requirements and a list of the interfacing technical teams. Interfacing technical teams (for example, Active Directory, SQL Server, and Exchange) in a disconnected and multi-disciplined environment will need their connected platforms tested against the integration of SharePoint into those platforms.

If SharePoint development is included in the Test Requirements section, you should ensure that the test schedule is documented against whatever product is being applied to SharePoint. In other words, developer testing of a product being customized for SharePoint could be a significant project; for example, branding of a SharePoint MySite would require a number of tests of usability, accessibility, and more.

Table 12-3 indicates the kind of testing that should be considered. A method of using this table is to create a table of the test headings, and for each one, specify what would be tested and what requirement it would relate to (either a user or technical requirement).

Table 12-3 **Types of Testing**

Test	Description
Correct Function Tests	For example, test that a user who is a contributor to a site can access the site and upload a file into a document library. I'm aware that people might say, "This test is far too basic," but I have had clients who insist on ensuring that SharePoint can prove "It does what it says on the tin."
Incorrect, Abnormal, or Error Path Tests	These tests confirm that when the user carrying out an operation fails, she will be informed why she has failed. Reasons for failure can be ascertained by testing the Web part functionality where there is validation applied and confirming that what you are testing is the result of that validation failure.

Test	Description
Performance	Timing-related tests verify that specified SharePoint actions are performed within specified times.
	Capacity and volume tests check whether Share-Point was loaded with the maximum allowable values for storage or loading. Tools are available that allow you to populate site collections, sites, document libraries, or lists with test data; however, unless you have a significant amount of space, capacity testing might be difficult.
	Endurance tests investigate the ability of SharePoint to perform continuously over a period of time and should always be done against SharePoint, especially if the system is to be available for 24 hours a day.
Operability	These tests determine whether the user can carry out particular operations based on the current documentation available.
Graceful Degradation	These tests determine where SharePoint operations can be brought to a stop.
Security	These tests involve site access, Web application access, and the testing of relevant permissions assigned. For example, there might be customized permissions applied in SharePoint, and these would require testing.
Recovery	These tests confirm whether backups can be carried out on a farm and whether site and granular backups can be carried out. These tests include tests related to recovery, and they would be timed.
Availability, Reliability, and Maintainability	These tests measure the robustness of SharePoint and failovers. For example, load balancing is tested on the SharePoint Web front ends, the availability of service applications is tested, and how much work it takes to maintain all of the enabled service applications is determined.
Configuration	These tests check the configuration of SharePoint components.
Documentation	Verify the provision of documentation concerning the installation of SharePoint components. Check that the configuration carried out is fully documented. Check that any alterations to production or staging environments are documented through configuration management.
Installation	Test the installation process by carrying it out in a test environment, and then repeating the process and documentation.

> **Note**
> You can apply most of the tests listed first to the test environment and then run the same tests in terms of user acceptance again in the stage environment, which will make life easy when deploying the features in the production environment. Then you and the client would at least be comfortable that you have met agreed-upon and have coordinated it all without any detrimental effect to the production environment.

Integration Testing

If the SharePoint implementation you are doing is a small farm topology, your integrated tests will be a lot smaller than if SharePoint sits in a multifarm topology and in a disconnected environment.

You need to have integration tests because, at a hardware level, you will be able to iron out any network connectivity, security, or bandwidth issues. At the software level, you will be able to ascertain which services enabled in SharePoint, for example, are taking up valuable resources. You will also be able to test how client applications such as Excel, Word, Visio, PowerPoint, and Outlook are interacting with SharePoint. These applications in particular are integrated with SharePoint—for example, Visio Services in SharePoint allows for the display of a fully functional Visio diagram that includes external database connectivity. Therefore, your integrated test for this would not only be a test of Visio, it would be a test of the diagram and the network connectivity to whatever back-end database was connected.

Table 12-4 lists the types of integration testing you should conduct.

Table 12-4 **Types of Integration Testing**

Test	Description
Subsystems level	SharePoint Services configuration tests, search tests, user profile tests, and so on.
Hardware and software components in SharePoint	Site-level components, Web parts enabled on major portals, and enabled features. This includes SQL Server, DNS Server, SharePoint farm servers (for example, WFEs, application servers, query servers, and index servers) And load balancing.
Equipment external to the system	This can be any hardware component that is connected to the SharePoint platform to provide a service. For example, this can be an internal server connected to a camera passing real-time information into a SharePoint site through a Business Data Connection (BDC).

Test	Description
Any of the above items, where one or more components are supplied via third party.	What you are testing here is not just the configuration of the equipment, it's the response of the support arrangements in place with the third party, including some other tests in line with acceptance testing.

Design Constraints

The technical authority might decide to impose design constraints on hardware and software. These constraints fall into four categories:

1. Software constraints, which include requirements for compatibility and interoperability

2. Hardware for which a specific vendor must be chosen

3. Human constraints—for example, skill levels expected of SharePoint administrators

4. Development process aspects, which cover, for example, the use of recommended methods and tools in the development process. The client might not allow the use of SharePoint Designer 2010, for example. This means modifications to training will need to be made.

> **Tip**
> **Human constraints should be listed in the Human Requirements section.**

The design constraints you will face are based on the areas that are described in Table 12-5. Not all of these design constraints will get entered in your SharePoint Project Plan. However, it's important that you understand the distinction and ensure the relevant constraints are documented against the relevant area in the System Specification document.

Table 12-5 **Design Constraints**

Software Design Constraints	
Standards	For example, production standards for the implementation of service accounts, naming formats, management of password placement and recording.
Packages	Written as a statement. Any specific packages that might be required, including the justification for including them.
Database	Written as a statement. The user might require SharePoint to connect to a specific database or special content system—for example, to an Oracle, Lotus Notes, or SQL database. These need to be listed, including the justification for including them.
Operating System	The user might require SharePoint to be installed on top of a specific existing operating system instead of a new server-provided operating system. Details should be stated.
SharePoint Installation Guide	References to the SharePoint installation guide that details the process of the installation from the pre-requisites through to the creation of site collections and associated services configurations.
Hardware Constraints	
Hardware Standards	A statement is required regarding any standards for the build of servers, the preparation for the operating system installation, and any monitoring equipment to be used, including equipment for network connectivity, load-balance connectivity, and environmental equipment (for example, communication rooms, or data center configuration).

Summary

When completed, SharePoint System Specifications provide a fully understood platform and allow the Build phase to proceed. With a completed System Specification, the client and users can collectively sign off on the user requirements, technical requirements, and all the planning and decisions captured in the relevant services that warranted further investigation— for example, managed metadata.

The System Specification is the top-level document that links the requirements documentation together and is defined as a configurable item. Generally, changes to any of the subsection requirements can have an impact on the higher level decisions in the System Specification. For example, if there is a requirement to include Visio 2010 diagrams in the SharePoint 2010 project at a later stage, this must be factored into the Performance, Availability, and Testing Requirements sections.

You should build a System Specification as part of the Plan phase and build it up using details from the user requirements, including all the technical requirements derived from gathering information from the planning worksheets, which you can access from my blog (*http://spsscopeschedule.geoffevelyn.com*).

The SharePoint System Specification is an evolutionary document because the information in it links to the creation of the SharePoint platform and forms the soul of the SharePoint installation that will be created in the Build phase. Chapter 14, "Releasing SharePoint to the Client," lists the tasks in this penultimate stage of a SharePoint 2010 implementation, where the hardware gets provisioned and the software gets installed and configured.

Planning and Implementing the SharePoint One-Stop Shop

Learning from the Inside Out

A business manager once said to me, "I have a whole bunch of people who want to learn SharePoint over a week."

I said, "OK, what aspect of SharePoint?"

He said, "What do you mean? All of it, of course. It can't be that hard!"

I had to explain to the business manager the reasons why learning everything related to SharePoint would be impractical, would be difficult in the extreme over a week, and would not solve any user information challenges. Here are the key reasons why:

- No one can be a SharePoint Superman. No one (except maybe a few people on the planet) knows absolutely everything about SharePoint.

- Not everything in SharePoint can be taught (therefore, one person can't gain complete knowledge—unless that person is a savant!). Some things in SharePoint take time to learn and require experience for them sink in. That's why there are different skill sets, such as SharePoint administrator, developer, and architect.

- Everyone has different needs. Not every member of the organization does exactly the same thing every day with SharePoint.

- SharePoint is not a silver bullet. This goes back to planning and user requirements. SharePoint is a scalable platform whose design is based on user requirements. The Plan, Build, and Deploy phases of implementing SharePoint are therefore iterative. The user is continually learning based on those changes, and SharePoint is continually evolving. It will not meet every single user requirement now and for the future on day one of deployment.

> **Note**
>
> In the Plan phase of your SharePoint environment, you need to build the user and technical requirements. After you have these, you will have a mass of subject material concerning how SharePoint will be supplied, supported, and managed; you will also know what features will be implemented and how the users will be trained to use those features. For more information detailing the Plan, Build, and Deploy phases, be sure to read Chapter 3, "Content of Your SharePoint 2010 Project Plan."

A SharePoint One-Stop Shop is very important to a SharePoint 2010 implementation project. As the project takes shape, you will be gathering requirements, creating specifications, collecting information from meetings, and building the project contacts. This information will have to be centralized and made available to those who need to collaborate; storing this information in a SharePoint site (a One-Stop Shop) is a perfect way to ensure this takes place.

> **Note**
>
> The SharePoint 2010 One-Stop Shop can initially be created on a separate machine made available for the project team. As the environments get created and information gets moved onto the platform, the One-Stop Shop can be moved to a home accessible to all (after the production environment is created).

Naturally, the function of the SharePoint 2010 One-Stop Shop is not simply to hold information concerning the implementation project; it exists also to educate users about the project. Having access to this information will cause users to become engaged with SharePoint, learn what the product is, understand how it has been deployed, and know what services and roles are implemented in managing the platform. It also exists to store items such as FAQs, policies, guidelines, and governance.

You could, therefore, have a SharePoint site that is dedicated to "everything SharePoint" in the company. Such a site might enable users to learn SharePoint from the inside out. And because they access a SharePoint site itself to get information about the SharePoint product, you can easily provide many mechanisms to educate and inspire users to come to grips with all types of features in SharePoint. For example, you might create blogs to store articles to describe how to carry out certain functions in SharePoint 2010.

The One-Stop Shop should hold all topics concerning the use of SharePoint in the organization. This can include technical information for the support teams through the use of SharePoint blogs and RSS feeds to external sites such as MSDN, TechNet, and Subject Matter Expert (SME) blogs and Web sites. This information can be made accessible to technical staff so that they can learn how SharePoint has been configured, reference relevant service account settings, and store information about the installation of features and products.

When creating the SharePoint One-Stop Shop, you need to divide it into sections such as Project, How To, Learning, and Admin. In the section titled, "Components of the One-Stop Shop" on page 217, I'll describe these four areas in greater detail.

> ## Tip
>
> You might want to make it easier for users to get to the One-Stop Shop. For example, if the One-Stop Shop had a site named *SharePoint* and you wanted the users to be able to type **SharePoint** in the browser and go directly to the site, the quickest and easiest way is to create a DNS entry called *SharePoint* and create a Web application with a new site collection associated with it. If your SharePoint One-Stop Shop is a site within a site collection, you can use a vanity URL (a Web application with a redirect to the location of the site), but note that you should not store this in a SharePoint content database and it will require manual maintenance on each Web front-end server in the farm.
>
> For more information on redirection using a vanity URL in SharePoint, I recommend reading the article at *http://www.toddklindt.com/blog/Lists/Posts/Post.aspx?ID=48*.

Also, you should update organizational best bets and keywords to target specific blogs, wiki pages, or published portal pages as guidance documentation to solve common tasks users face in SharePoint. For example, let's say you have a blog about how users get access to SharePoint content. Many organizations having SharePoint will have distributed ownership on their sites, meaning the procedure is to request access from the owners, who then set the permissions on the user sites.

On this site, if users complain that they see an Access Denied message when they want to access particular content and want to know what the process to solve the issue, the process should state who the users should contact to request access to the content instead of having directives such as "Click Site Actions, go to Advanced Permissions," and so on. So users can then type in a keyword to search; assuming the best bet keyword has been assigned to the content, users will then find the blog instructing them how to get access to the content. By providing guidance such as this, you educate the user base as well as reduce the time and costs to get the issue sorted out if the process would normally have been to go to the Help Desk for assistance.

Everything Cannot Be Learned

Remember when you started using SharePoint for the first time? What captured your fancy? The software components? The connected environment (for example, Active Directory or Exchange)? The Reporting and Business Intelligence platforms such as PerformancePoint Server? The workflows and business process? Document management? Records management? Collaborating remotely through SharePoint Workspace 2010? Site management and permissioning? Access database services? Visio services? Word collaboration services? Or perhaps metadata, content types, InfoPath forms—I could very easily go on!

What I am saying is that no single person knows the whole of SharePoint—because it is a centralized and connected platform, there is no limit to its extensibility. And because the platform can easily be customized, future development is based on a user requirement or the addition of third-party tools.

For example, I described the features of SharePoint to a client concerning document management. Following the discussion, the client wanted document libraries to be enhanced by being connected to a third-party application they were using that automated an internal process. After some investigation and through gathering user requirements, a developer was required to ensure custom coding is done to enhance the document libraries.

The actual deployment of that custom feature is not the end of that particular development life cycle because someone has to learn how to use the feature, support the feature, and manage the feature. If the original developer is no longer available, someone else needs to be able to understand what that developer originally did. Okay, so we have configuration management to help us out with this because the developer likely documented the code, provided training information, and so on.

The key concept here is that, in the SharePoint platform, you can't possibly be expected to learn everything. A good strategy for helping users in an organization learn SharePoint is to ensure that information and management challenges are exposed so that multiple users can recognize and learn concepts. Here are some examples of statements that express information and management challenges:

- I want to learn how to implement version control for my documents.

- I want to learn how to tag information so that others can find it.

- I want to be able to find someone in the organization so that I can collaborate with them.

For example, if you have a team that focuses on project management and you need features in your SharePoint site that provides project management tools, ensuring the relevant components are understood and managed is critical to the success and the long-term use of the project management site. Therefore, user requirements should define which users require calendars, project Gantt lists, issue-tracking lists, and so on. Those are the items that users need to be trained in—they don't need to be trained in "everything SharePoint."

Everyone Has Different Needs

A member of an organization who works in the accounting department has different requirements and needs than a member of the organization who is on the communications team. These users' needs are different; therefore, some elements of their training and education will be different (and if necessary, customized to meet their requirements). The One-Stop Shop should ideally be designed to suit all generic requirements. For example, members of an organization might want to know any or all of the following:

- How to modify navigation on their site

- How to create a survey

- What the policies are regarding setting site permissions

The solutions for all of these user needs can be found in the One-Stop Shop if you were successful in understanding the client's needs. These needs are captured in the user requirements. The user requirements documentation details what the users want from their sites, the content in the site, the features required, how users work with those features, and (critically) what users want to do with SharePoint. As you gather the user requirements, you will see a common trend in the pain points the users come up against. For example, a majority of users are likely to want to use Project 2010 with SharePoint. Therefore, you need to focus on providing information about key tasks people might perform in Project 2010 and SharePoint.

Components of the One-Stop Shop

Let's recap. To provide a basis of education for users concerning SharePoint, your implementation of the new platform needs to include a central point where users can go to find information about it. In time, as the business grows with SharePoint and power users emerge, roles can be expanded so that the business takes more control of the One-Stop Shop and therefore be even closer to managing SharePoint users.

The One-Stop Shop can easily be started from a Blank Site template or a Team Site template. In any case, this central location should at least have the following areas:

- **A Landing Zone** A "welcome" section. The landing zone displays up-to-date information concerning key aspects of the SharePoint instance status, Web application and site collections lists, site owners lists, and a framework of the service (how the sites are set in terms of taxonomy). It should also provide procedures and policies, a statement of operations, new site requests, new keyword best bet requests, and key governance statements.

- **How Do I** A blog site. This site should include FAQs and training information, and questions and answer discussion areas for the SharePoint administrators to review. This holds, in particular, a list of blogs answering popular queries from the users and detailing step-by-step instructions to help users solve issues as well as to provide ideas to users.

- **Training and Education** An online class. The education area describes the training strategy, classes, courses available, requirements, and so on. It also can provide access to online classes for end users. The user visits the classroom to work through and learn how to use SharePoint by using webcasts, podcasts, online videos, and interactive workshops. Activity can be tracked by users subscribing to the service so that they are aware of their progress and can match their requirements to the training modules provided.

  More information about training is available at *http://www.microsoft.com/learning/en/us/training/sharepoint.aspx#2010sec3*.

- **Admin** A blog site. This is an area for the SharePoint administrators, interfacing teams, and affiliated technical staff. The Central Administration site provides most of this data, but the Admin page provides more of a "human" face and expands on Central Administration by providing information to educate technical visitors as well as simply inform them. Also, the Admin area provides a central base of operations for SharePoint administrators and ensures that they also control the One-Stop Shop. The following items can be provided in the Admin area:

  - **Admin Blogs** An up-to-date account of any software or hardware issues or information that would be useful concerning the administration of SharePoint.

  - **Task List** A list holding jobs for the administrators to carry out. This can be a task list stating the monitoring jobs to be carried out, say, on a daily basis and then linked back to the Admin blogs. So a blog appearing in Admin blogs could be related back to a task.

- **Logs**   A view to the Monitoring logs in Central Administration. You can monitor slowest pages and most active users against sites and services and then return statistics such as the following:

    ○ Average Duration (seconds)

    ○ Minimum Duration (seconds)

    ○ Maximum Duration (seconds)

    ○ Average Database Queries (Count)

    ○ Minimum Database Queries (Count)

    ○ Maximum Database Queries (Count)

    ○ Number of Requests

> **Note**
>
> You can additionally monitor and report on all timer jobs, search reports, and much more and have this displayed in the Admin site.

- **Growth Rates**   An updated growth rate mapper. This enables you to see the size of the content databases. Who better to provide this information to than the SQL teams?

- **Site Lists and Dynamic Analysis Trends**   Displays the state of your sites and information concerning all sites across all environments. Help desk staff can then use this area to identify what site owner is responsible for what site and potentially how that owner can be reached.

> **Tip**
>
> There are several automated tools created to aid you in providing reports that would normally be time-consuming to get out of SharePoint. An example of this is GELISTALLSITES, which allows you to list not only all or some sites of a site collection, but also shows who has specific rights on those sites. For example, it helps you to find out who owns what site. This information is output to a text file that can then be fed into a SharePoint site. For more information, check out *http://gelistallsites.codeplex.com*.

> Additionally, tools such as the following are available from more established development firms:
>
> - Quest (*http://Quest*) provides tools a site administrator can use to manage SharePoint farms, including migration, recovery, reporting, and security tools.
> - AvePoint (*http://avepoint.com*) provides backup, recovery, migration, and archiving tools.
>
> There are quite a few more firms that provide software solutions in specific or multiple areas of SharePoint. When selecting any additional product, ensure that the product is fully tested and vetted for use before committing to it and the organization that's responsible for creating and supporting the product.

- **Project Implementation Area**   The home of the SharePoint implementation proj-ect. The Project section is a Projects Web Database that houses all the information relevant to SharePoint 2010 implementation planning.

This site is further discussed in Chapter 6, in the section "Using SharePoint 2010 Sites for Proj-ect Reporting," on page 115.

Summary

This short chapter introduced you to the concept of providing a central base of opera-tions for your SharePoint technical team to operate from, a place for users to visit to find out anything related to SharePoint, and a home for information related to the SharePoint implementation project. By building this site with the users, you will aid them in learning about the product and provide the organization with a point of presence for the SharePoint implementation.

In organizations where I have implemented the One-Stop Shop, users have seen a major productivity increase and the support desk has seen a major reduction of calls. Prior to implementing the One-Stop Shop, many calls for support were being made to an already busy SharePoint team. A few key concepts to keep in mind are that the One-Stop Shop is on a continual life cycle of updating and reviewing, and anything that happens in Share-Point that users need to know needs to be reflected on it.

CHAPTER 14

Releasing SharePoint to the Client

We have now reached the Build phase. This is when the SharePoint 2010 platform gets created based on the designs, investigations, and decisions of the Plan stage. Although installing SharePoint might sound easy—I mentioned earlier the attitude I sometimes encounter of "Hey, it is simply a bit of software on a DVD, so how hard can it be to install it?" You know from reading this book thus far that the software specifications related to production go into detail concerning service application structure, topologies, performance, and resilience. This detail is much broader in scope than the level of detail you'd need if you were just looking at SharePoint.

You now know that it is not just SharePoint you are installing. You need to include and review all the services that make up SharePoint 2010—for example, Visio Services, Word Services, Excel Services, Metadata Services, User Profile, and Search.

The Build phase involves not just installing the software, but configuring the settings and services required for your solution, deploying customizations, and creating the sites you need.

This chapter is short, though, simply because I am not going to say, "Here's how you configure the hardware." There are copious articles online informing you how to do that. In any case, this isn't a book designed to say "Click here. Click there."

There are two parts of the Build phase:

1. Build the pilot system, which includes the Development, Test, and Stage (or User Acceptance Testing) environments

2. Build the production system.

Build the Pilot System

The pilot environment of SharePoint is the first level of the build based on the software specification you created using the guidelines in Chapter 12, "Producing the System Specification." To build the pilot environment, you need to install hardware, install software, and configure the key elements of SharePoint (Search, User Profiles, and so forth). If you have any third-party features or solutions, they must be installed and configured at this stage, and if you have any integration products they must also be installed and configured.

When building the pilot system, note that there are three milestones. The first is the building of the pilot, the second is confirming the users' acceptance of it, and the third milestone is the confirmation that the build of the Production system in the Build phase can go ahead. To begin the pilot build, make sure that you have listed all the components to install and that you have all the relevant documentation and steps. Also, be prepared to alter the documentation and to note any inconsistencies within the installation.

You need to ensure that there is a record for specific configuration settings for each of the features needed to be configured. For example, Search Services might require a specific account. The service account and the password would need to be recorded. I suggest, then, that configuration settings, accounts, and passwords be recorded in a special document. Therefore, you should create a "Variables and Settings" document, which should be split into the following areas:

- Farmwide variables and settings—for example, DNS zones, the product key, an install service account, the Central Administration port, and so on

- Service application variables and settings, which includes accounts and settings relevant to the service applications (such as the user profile, Search Service, Secure Store, and so on)

- Special service settings, including Web application pool accounts, network load-balancing cluster IPs, IP addresses for servers in the farm, and so on

- Site variables and settings, including host names, site descriptions, and primary site collection administrators

- User accounts, including all key service accounts and descriptions

You can also use planning and decision worksheets, as discussed in Chapter 12.

Make sure all documentation has version control in place. If you do not do this, you will not have a good basis for approving the tests of the build, you will start getting confused about the current status of the build, and you will not be able to move into building the Production environment.

I prefer to neglect the configuration of *nearly every* service application at this stage; I configure only those deemed necessary from the user requirements. If the organization will be using Microsoft Office 2010, I configure Word and Excel services. If there is a requirement for Microsoft Visio and Access, I also turn on the services related to those applications. The reason I turn these on and configure them is to identify any issues related to resource usage.

> **Note**
>
> You can make the argument that all service applications should be turned on, because by doing that you can identify what services should be placed on their own servers and what configuration should be applied. I urge caution in adopting this approach—unless you have a method of testing performance and all the service applications, you do not gain any useful results from that exercise.

When the pilot is created, it is vital that you, as project manager, ensures tasks are set to *test* SharePoint, *test* the service applications, *test* any installed features and solutions, and *test* any custom integration. *All* tests must be documented, with the results of each test detailed. When these tests are completed, they must be demonstrated to the technical authority and the project manager by the individuals responsible for carrying out the tests, so that sign-off can be achieved—that's milestone 1.

> **Note**
>
> The pilot build performance might not be at the same level as the performance levels on the Production platform. Therefore, tests on the pilot are for basic functionality. The Production platform performance levels must be greater than the performance levels for the pilot system, because the Production environment must be suitable for the client's needs. This means you need to ensure tests related to performance are repeated for the Production environment.

So milestone 1 is that the pilot system is built and approved. When that is completed, the pilot build documentation can be used to create the Development, Test, and Stage environments. This should be a relatively easy exercise if all the documentation from the pilot build is completed and approved. When this is complete, you are ready to start the tasks for milestone 2.

Milestone 2 is that the users and business have approved the relevant environments in place. Therefore, to reach milestone 2, you need to know who the key stakeholders are (and they might not be the client). When you have approval from all the users and the business, you have reached the final milestone in related to building the pilot system.

The final milestone, milestone 3 is a decision point (called a *decision gate*) where you decide whether the Production platform is "Go" or "No-Go." This is known as a decision gate because it's a point at which the entire project could be halted.

There can be many reasons (detailed in the following list) why the Production platform is a No-Go, and they might not even be technical reasons:

- The project is placed on indefinite hold because of internal company issues, such as issues related to resources, budget, both, or another consideration.

- The location of the Production environment is not ready, and network connectivity has become an issue.

- Some serious organizational issues stop you from being able to deploy to the Production platform. For example, further compliance information has a global impact on the organization, and this forces you to rethink how certain services are configured.

There could also be technical reasons why the build cannot go to production:

- The disk sizing was incorrect.

- There are serious performance-related issues on the environments that are not Share-Point related.

An example I experienced was a situation in which the environments were connected into a central domain, but performance issues with Active Directory resulted in the equipment urgently needing to be replaced. This problem forced all projects to be stopped until the issue was resolved. Sometimes, even if the pilot system is approved, things can happen in the span of time between that and the approval process for the Production platform.

To ensure that you do not hit a No-Go situation, you should have in your SharePoint 2010 Quality Plan a good Risk Management log that records all the outside influences that might affect a SharePoint build being placed into a Production environment. By doing this, you assure the client you understand the implications of any holdup and you are prepared to mitigate issues. Maintaining the Risk Management log ensures that if there is a No-Go situation you have alternatives to try, and it can reduce the chances of any No-Go issues arising because preventive action was taken before you got to that point. Risk management is discussed in Chapter 3, "Content of Your SharePoint Project Plan."

If there is a No-Go decision, you need to halt the project until the issue is corrected. This needs to be recorded as part of your configuration management (CM) process. You, as project manager, need to convene a review with the client and technical authority. This is to ensure that they are fully aware of the delay and what impact the delay might have on the project (for example, users might require the Production environment to be in place on a specific date; therefore delays could mean financial penalties, loss of productivity, or loss of face). When the issue is corrected, the next phase can take place, which is the build of the Production system.

Build the Production System

In addition to the points made related to the building of the pilot system, several other steps occur in the build of the Production system. You might not even have the hardware available to proceed, which means it needs to be purchased. This process takes time, and the project manager needs to itemize the required hardware in the SharePoint System Specification.

> **Note**
> **The disaster recovery system needs to be created alongside the Production system.**

To build your Production system, you need to have the documentation from the building of the pilot system). This documentation is quite refined by now because it was used to successfully build the pilot system, and then to build the Development, Test, and Stage environments.

That said, you still document and record any issues that arise as you build your Production environment. For example, if you need to modify the Production environment, the relevant modifications must be delivered to the Test and Stage environments first, and then tested and validated there. By using the techniques discussed in Chapter 10, "SharePoint Configuration Management," you need to manage changes to the Production environment.

As you move into the build of the Production system, the installation of software becomes very important. Let's look at the key areas of installing SharePoint via software. Note that these key areas do not necessarily run back to back, but they are presented in the general order of installation.

To help you out, I've provided Table 14-1. The first column lists the tasks; the second column has a description or a link that provides you with an explanation of what the task means and how to configure the component, settings, and features. People responsible for the tasks listed are the SharePoint architect, administrator, database administrator, and interfacing teams. If you have a team, you should meet with your team members and review each of the tasks so that everyone is clear about the process and has the correct level of resources available. Again, just like you did in the "Variables and Settings" document, you should document each of the areas in turn.

> **Note**
>
> This is a truly massive and complex area—each task requires investigation, documentation, configuration, and testing. Information that covers SharePoint 2010 installation is available at *http://technet.microsoft.com/en-gb/sharepoint/ee518643.aspx*. I strongly suggest you refer to this information as well as the links I provided in Table 14-1. Because each task needs careful consideration, you must ensure that you have documentation concerning the location, installation, configuration, and testing of each of the tasks. You should also attempt to get sign-off by your project manager, technical authority, and interfacing team members for most of these tasks.

Table 14-1 Tasks and Resources

Task	Resource
Install operating systems and pre-requisites (the .NET Framework and so forth)	*http://blogs.msdn.com/b/opal/archive/2009/10/25/sharepoint-2010-pre-requisites-download-links.aspx.*
Set up a load-balancing solution	Read the information at the following URL because you will need to decide whether to use network load balancing (NLB) or hardware load balancing (such as NETSCALER technology): *http://www.share-pointjoel.com/Lists/Posts/Post.aspx?List=0cd1a63d-183c-4fc2-8320-ba5369008acb&ID=209.*
Install Windows SharePoint Services Install Microsoft SharePoint 2010	*http://technet.microsoft.com/en-gb/sharepoint/ee518643.aspx.*
Install SQL Server	*http://technet.microsoft.com/en-us/sqlserver/ff625277.aspx.*
Install any failover/disaster recovery software	You might be using other technologies for backup and restore tasks as well as SharePoint internally provided solutions. You might be using mirroring technology (for example, a third-party tool called Acronis, which is available at *http://www.acronis.com*) that allows you to take complete mirror copies of the entire server in minutes. This is useful for disaster recovery in situations where you don't have storage area network (SAN) drives. If you have SAN-based disks, you might need to perform further configuration. See the article: *http://technet.microsoft.com/en-us/library/cc764269.aspx.*

Task	Resource
Configure Web front end servers Configure index and query services Configure search applications (if it's a large farm deployment) Configure application servers (if the topology requires them)	*http://technet.microsoft.com/en-gb/sharepoint/ee518643.aspx.*
Document as needed	This is a very important task. Each of the tasks in this table should be documented. If necessary, create a master document and have each of the preceding tasks linked to it using a referencing system if you do not have a SharePoint site to store the resulting documentation. If you do have a SharePoint site, store these in your Microsoft Project 2010 database site. (More information is available in Chapter 6, "Gathering the Resources for SharePoint Implementation.")

As you are installing the preceding software to support the hardware in place, you need to configure the software. Table 14-2 lists some key configuration points of SharePoint 2010, which I'll refer to as the "Configure SharePoint Features and Settings tasks." Again, while these are shown in a particular order in the table, more than one task can take place at the same time. Your SharePoint architect, administrator, developer, and interfacing teams working with the project manager need to make decisions about the timing of these tasks. As with the previous set of tasks, each of these tasks can be considered as having a software location (if necessary), configuration, and testing process. As such, you must ensure that each are adequately documented and tested thoroughly.

Table 14-2 Configure SharePoint Features and Settings

Task	Resource
Configure site templates	*http://technet.microsoft.com/en-us/library/cc263094.aspx.*
Apply branding and design elements	For information about creating a custom master page in SharePoint 2010, check out the following link: *http://www.heatherwaterman.com/blog/Lists/Posts/Post.aspx?ID=23.* For information about creating a starter master page, see the article by Randy Drisgill at the following location: *http://blog.drisgill.com/2009/11/starter-master-pages-for-sharepoint.html.* You can also see Randy Drisgill's branding tips at *http://blog.drisgill.com/2009/11/sp2010-branding-tip-1-applying-custom.html.*
Configure e-mail settings	*http://technet.microsoft.com/en-us/library/ee956941.aspx.*

Task	Resource
Configure analytics, diagnostic logging, and usage and health data collections	*http://blogs.technet.com/b/sharepointexperts/ archive/2010/05/03/web-analytics-in-sharepoint-2010- insights-into-reports-and-metrics.aspx.* *http://technet.microsoft.com/en-us/library/ee748636.aspx.*
Configure antivirus software and firewall protection	Microsoft Forefront Security for SharePoint integrates multiple scan engines from industry-leading vendors and content controls to help businesses protect their Microsoft SharePoint collaboration environments by eliminating documents containing malicious code, confidential information, and inappropriate content. For more information, go to *http://technet.microsoft.com/en-us/forefront/ bb734828.aspx.*
Configure blocked files	*http://technet.microsoft.com/en-us/library/cc262496.aspx.*
Configure security	*http://technet.microsoft.com/en-us/sharepoint/ee518672. aspx.*
Configure user profiles	*http://technet.microsoft.com/en-us/sharepoint/ee518672. aspx.*
Configure audiences	*http://technet.microsoft.com/en-us/library/cc263065.aspx.*
Configure Secure Sockets Layer (SSL)	*http://technet.microsoft.com/en-us/library/cc424952. aspx#section8.*
Set Web application quota templates, and choose site-collection quotas	*http://technet.microsoft.com/en-us/forefront/default.aspx.*
Configure Claims authentication, Kerberos authentication, Kerberos authentication for the claims to Windows token service	*http://technet.microsoft.com/library/ee806886(office.14). aspx.* *http://technet.microsoft.com/library/ee806870(office.14). aspx.* *http://technet.microsoft.com/library/ee806887(office.14). aspx.*
Determine self-service site provisioning	*http://technet.microsoft.com/en-us/library/cc261685.aspx.*
Configure permissions and information policies	Permission policies provide a centralized way to configure and manage a set of permissions that applies to only a subset of users or groups in a Web application. For more information, go to *http://technet.microsoft.com/en-us/ library/ff608071.aspx.*

Task	Resource
Configure any software being integrated with SharePoint 2010	One link I can give you is the Reporting Services integration (shown first). However, there are lots of service applications that can be configured at this point.
	Reporting Services: *http://technet.microsoft.com/en-us/library/ee748636.aspx*.
	Visio Services: *http://technet.microsoft.com/en-us/library/ee663485.aspx*.
	Excel Services: *http://technet.microsoft.com/en-us/library/ee424405.aspx*.
	Managed Metadata: *http://technet.microsoft.com/en-us/library/ee530389.aspx*.
	Business Connectivity Services: *http://technet.microsoft.com/en-us/library/ee661740.aspx*.
	Access Services: *http://technet.microsoft.com/en-gb/library/ee662542.aspx*.
	Secure Store Service: *http://technet.microsoft.com/en-us/library/ee806889.aspx*.
Configure Recycle Bin retention and Site Delete Confirmation	*http://technet.microsoft.com/en-us/library/cc287766.aspx*.
Deploy custom solutions and features	For a developer's perspective on this topic, go to *http://technet.microsoft.com/en-us/library/cc263205.aspx*.
	If the custom features and solutions are available (and they should be because you would have already pushed them into the Test and Stage environments and they have been tested), deploying these solutions can be done as described at the following location: *http://www.dotnetmafia.com/blogs/dotnettipoftheday/archive/2009/12/02/adding-and-deploying-solutions-with-powershell-in-sharepoint-2010.aspx*.
Document as needed	This is a very important task. Again, just as with the tasks listed in the previous table, each of the tasks in this table should be documented. If necessary, create a master document and have each of the preceding tasks linked to this document using a referencing system if you do not have a SharePoint site to store the resulting documentation. If you do have a SharePoint site, store these in your Project 2010 database site. (More information is available in Chapter 6.)

Chapter 14

If you've come this far, you are past the Build phase and into the Deploy phase. Table 14-3 lists the post-Build tasks. You now need to configure some of the key elements of Share-Point, such as Search, Document Management, Alerting, MySites, and Site Collections. You can do this working with the user requirements. Again, I've itemized the key areas of concern in Table 14-3.

Table 14-3 Post-Build Tasks

Task	Resource
Configure Search	The article found at the following link describes post-installation steps for configuring the search system in a single-server deployment. Some steps differ depending on whether the product was installed with the Standalone or Server Farm installation option. This article provides the steps for both cases: *http://technet.microsoft.com/en-gb/library/ee808863.aspx*.
	Other configuration points to cover for Search include the following:
	• Install and register filters
	• Configure content locations
	• Modify noise-word and thesaurus files, and create custom search queries
	• Perform maintenance for indexing
	• Configure Best Bets and keywords for search
	• Configure search scopes
	• Establish and implement search monitoring and a tuning plan
Configure Document Management	A significant section. The following tasks are key examples, but this is not an exhaustive list. See the following article for an overview, including topics concerning metadata routing, storage planning, navigation, and more: *http://technet.microsoft.com/en-us/library/cc262215.aspx*.
	Ensure that you examine the user requirements in the Content section to identify all different types of repositories required (for example, calendars, surveys, and so forth). Identify any custom requirements and have them defined as separated tasks in this section.
Create Folder Structure	Assign roles for security, choose a publishing process, and add an approval routine.
Create Document Profiles and Custom Profiles	Plan document profiles, emphasize subjects with keywords, and enable Web discussions.
Move Documents into the Workspace	Move multiple individual documents, and import existing folders.
Other Post-Configuration tasks	Configure alerts. Configure personal sites.

Configure SharePoint 2010 for extranet use as desired	*http://www.microsoft.com/downloads/details.aspx?displaylang =en&FamilyID=eb4bff25-baba-4112-b518-f2fc442d5467.*
Deploy updates to client machines as needed	You may need to apply updates to client workstations that will be used to access SharePoint 2010. Doing this at this stage will confirm that the hardware and software requirements at client workstation level are adequate. Also, confirm your browser support and the Office versions as applicable. For more information, go to: *http://technet.microsoft.com/ en-us/library/cc262485.aspx* or *http://technet.microsoft.com/ en-us/library/cc263526.aspx.*
Document as needed	This is a very important task. Again, just as with the tasks in Tables 14-1 and 14-2, each of the preceding tasks should be documented. If necessary, create a master document and have each of the preceding tasks linked to this document using a referencing system if you do not have a SharePoint site to store the resulting documentation. If you do have a SharePoint site, store these in your Project 2010 database site. (More information is available in Chapter 6.)

Now that you have built the SharePoint 2010 Production platform, this is by no means the end. You must ensure that you have fully tested and evaluated the Production environment to the satisfaction of the client and users. You must include training in this process as well. The documentation you have completed will provide traceability and proof that the configuration you have applied has been fully validated and tested.

Test SharePoint 2010 Production

Tests for SharePoint 2010 should include tests based on usage patterns, business scenarios, search and indexing, solutions, integrations, security, and hardening. All of these tests require full documentation, and for each test the result must be signed off on by the client or a client representative. Of course, you would not get a business user to sign off on things relevant to hardening because that person would not understand the results. You need to identify the person who is accountable for each of the relevant technical areas. (You should speak to the technical authority to identify who that person is.)

Note that the sign-off you get from each person is *not* the true sign-off on the Production environment. The client will perform the final sign-off and approval, and they will need to see that there is sufficient sign-off on each of the areas I mentioned earlier.

For further information concerning testing, see Chapter 12. You'll also find more information concerning validation and verification of SharePoint at *http://sharepointvandv.geoffevelyn.com.*

Training Users When Production Is Ready

You need to make sure users are able to handle SharePoint from the basics up. You do not want a situation like this:

"I created a document that needed to be dispersed to the sales team. We created a SharePoint site to do that. When I finally went to log onto it, permissions were all wrong so I could not even upload a document. I had to go back and forth to IT and the client, and I ended up e-mailing the document to the sales team. I wouldn't say I'm frustrated; I stopped using it."

You must create an ongoing strategy that engages the organization and allows them to participate in education and learning SharePoint. There are four levels of training you need to provide:

- System administrator

- Developer

- End users

- Support training

For each of these levels of training, you must identify the attendees, build the relevant training to suit them, and schedule the training for the relevant area.

It is very important that the long-term strategy of SharePoint in the organization be a self-service and self-perpetuating service offering, where SharePoint wants and needs are managed and coordinated from the inside of the organization. You need to be able to hook into the current training strategy of the organization (if available) and speak to them about how important it is to have people trained in the platform.

Training for developers is more complex; thus, if you do not have any developers and there is a requirement for bringing in additional developers, you need to recruit a SharePoint developer who will be part of the organization or recruit one on a contractual basis for the relevant post. (See Chapter 8, "SharePoint Customization.") If you do have developers but they do not know how to create customized solutions, it is crucial they attend the relevant training to learn how SharePoint operates from its application programming interface model.

Training for end users can be split into power users and end users. Power users can also be termed SharePoint Champions. These people have been trained either by internal Share-Point administrators or training organizations to an acceptable organizational standard. They are then introduced to the organization as SharePoint Champions and are used to provide information or cascade training to their relevant teams.

There are major benefits to this approach. First, these users have core knowledge that will help reduce calls to help desks and keep SharePoint administrators from being flooded with calls requesting support. Second, they provide a positive view of SharePoint to users and administrators within the organization. These people can invoke change in the way that people work because they work in the same fields as the end users. This means you can define which additional features should be made available to power users—for example, SharePoint Designer. This might aid in basic modifications and customizations being carried out in house. (Note this might still be seen as a disadvantage in some companies where control of SharePoint is crucial. Governance needs to clarify whether power users should use SharePoint Designer. This topic is covered in Chapter 8, "SharePoint Customization.")

Support training is provided to interfacing team members and help desk staff who need to understand how to support SharePoint. This training is useful in organizations that don't have a lot of SharePoint administrators or in organizations that require extra human presence in case something happens when the SharePoint administrators are not available. Additionally, for a global implementation of SharePoint, this is vital because all SharePoint administrators working across multiple geographical time zones need to be singing from the same hymn sheet.

> **Note**
> Going forward, even after the implementation is complete, the training and education of the users is crucial to ensuring the long-term success of SharePoint. You need to make sure users know this is the case and how to achieve continual and standardized results. Review Chapter 13, "Planning and Implementing the SharePoint One-Stop Shop," for more information. Also, building a training and education strategy is vital; you need to create a training process that allows SharePoint to grow with user acceptance. Users will themselves shape this training as they continue to use SharePoint and as the product expands and scales upward. For a review on Training and Education Planning, see Chapter 11, "Making Sure SharePoint Meets User Requirements."

Summary

Releasing SharePoint to the client marks the completion of the Build phase of the SharePoint 2010 implementation and is a key deliverable of the platform to the client. Acceptance by the customer is required at many points during this process. When this process is completed, the project moves fully into the Deploy phase (which covers post implementation, operations, optimization, and business review).

This chapter detailed the tasks necessary to build a pilot system. Through the creation and enhancement of relevant documentation and the business sign-off on the pilot system, you are able to build the Development, Test, and Stage platforms. Once these are completed, another sign-off is required before you again use the same documentation (now refined) for the creation of the Production platform.

To manage this process, you should use the techniques detailed in Chapter 10 to ensure, for example, that you have versioned copies of the information required to build all the relevant environments and configure the relevant SharePoint software components and services.

This chapter is not the definitive source for releasing a SharePoint implementation to an organization, nor is it meant to be. In fact, such a resource simply doesn't exist. There are far too many variables when implementing SharePoint 2010 in any environment, especially in large and complex ones. But this book provides you with a standard approach. At a minimum, you must do the following:

- Educate your staff, and support the end users.

- Plan the SharePoint environments, topologies, capacity, security, and performance levels.

- Configure the platform and all connected technologies.

- Test all SharePoint environments: Production, Stage, Pilot, and Development (if required).

- Ensure your SharePoint implementation is robust, reliable, and maintainable. Put monitoring and disaster recovery plans in place and test them.

- Continually monitor SharePoint, both technically and from the business perspective.

CHAPTER 15

SharePoint Is Implemented, Now What?

W HEN implemented, SharePoint 2010 must be released to the client following procedures designed to ensure that implementation meets the requirements as laid out in the SharePoint Quality Plan, and that all related tasks within the Deploy stage are completed.

There are several procedural documents that should also be completed:

- Inspection and Testing of Hardware

- Inspection and Testing of Software (Server Operating Systems)

- Inspection and Testing of SharePoint

- Requirements and System Specifications for SharePoint:

  ○ Production, Stage, Test, and Development Environments

  ○ User Requirements and Client Requirements

These documents make up a packet that the client and technical authority receive, known as *delivery documentation*. To hand off this packet to the client and technical authority, you need to implement a sign-off process. In this sign-off process, you (as project manager) review these documents with the client and technical authority so that they can take ownership of the documentation.

Here is a list of resources you will need:

- **The SharePoint 2010 Project Plan**   You need to review this document with the client so that you can verify that all the relevant milestones have been achieved.

- **The SharePoint 2010 Quality Plan**   Because this document indicates who does what and how they do it, you should review it with the client during the sign-off process. The Quality Plan includes key details about the project, including details related to risk management, configuration management, subcontract management (if the project uses external consultants), verification, and validation.

> **Note**
>
> All information relevant to the SharePoint 2010 implementation must be made available centrally on a site in SharePoint—and the best place is within the SharePoint One-Stop Shop. (The One-Stop Shop is discussed in detail in Chapter 13, "Planning and Implementing the SharePoint One-Stop Shop.") For example, you could have a subsite of the One-Stop Shop called Project Implementation based on a part of a SharePoint 2010 project Web database. The Project Implementation subsite needs to be accessible to members of the project team and other appropriate personnel, as defined by the client and technical authority.
>
> Additionally, all documentation should be considered as part of configuration management. If there were a change to the SharePoint platform, certain documents might need to be extracted, reviewed, and updated in a timely manner through separate implementation projects. That means, for example, the Production environment System Specifications for SharePoint could be updated under a version control process in a centrally managed site. This prevents documentation for the implementation from being ignored, and it informs anyone taking on SharePoint projects in the future how these projects were carried out and, more important, by whom they were carried out.

Get Signoff and Work Through the Closure Checklist

To implement SharePoint is to complete the Deploy phase. The Deploy phase includes tasks relevant to ensuring there are smooth operations, that the environment has been optimized, and that a review is carried out to confirm that the SharePoint implementation meets both client and user expectations. This review is part of the delivery documentation sign-off described above. The answers to all the following questions must be "Yes" to call your SharePoint 2010 implementation a success:

- Have the requirements been met? Have all the points in the SharePoint 2010 Quality Plan been signed off on? Has the Project Startup Checklist been completed? Have all the tasks in the Project Plan been completed as agreed?

- Has the technical authority signed off on all the testing? All tests must have been carried out, and documentation must be available that confirms the technical authority has signed off on them.

- Have all quality checks been completed? You must provide the client with confirmation that optimization of SQL Server, Web front ends, search services, and all other defined service applications have been completed. You must also confirm that planning for any additional capacity has been factored in and documented and that the client is aware of any related requirements. Confirm also that performance reviews are in place to monitor storage, performance, growth, trends, and so forth.

- Have user acceptance tests been completed? If that is the case, you would have documented the user feedback from these tests. The business representative or technical authority must sign off on the user requirements related to these acceptance tests.

- Has training and knowledge transfer been completed? Have you identified the staff to be trained? Have the schedules for training been created? Has the strategy for training four levels of staff been defined (Administrator, Support, End User, and Developer)?

- Is SharePoint governance in place (including resources)? Has the Governance Committee been created? Has the SharePoint owner been identified? Have plans been created that cover operations, management, policies for use (for example, acceptable

Chapter 15

use policies and site policies such as permissioning, auditing, image use, and so forth)?

- Have team members and appropriate client personnel signed off on Service-Level Agreements (SLAs)? Have uptime and performance levels been defined and communicated to the technical authority? Have maintenance windows been created? Have key business users been identified and communicated to regarding backup windows? Have key services been identified, and are support arrangements in place? Have governance plans been updated?

- Have disaster recovery plans and business continuity plans been defined? Have backups been performed? Have the client and technical authority signed off on the documentation of the backup and recovery processes and the timing of them?

> **Note**
>
> For more information, I recommend reading the TechNet article that describes key decisions in choosing disaster recovery strategies for a Microsoft SharePoint Server 2010 environment. Go to *http://technet.microsoft.com/en-us/library/ff628971.aspx.*
>
> Additionally, transaction log shipping is described at *http://msdn.microsoft.com/en-us/library/ms187103.aspx,* and mirroring is described at *http://technet.microsoft.com/en-us/library/ms189852.aspx.*

SharePoint sign-off is not a one-way street. You are getting the client to agree that the implementation you have carried out matches their requirements. At the same time, you are getting the client to understand their responsibilities to the system that has been implemented. You do this because SharePoint passes from being your implementation project to being part of the business and part of the organization's information technology framework.

You should use the Project Closure Checklist to verify various facets of the project have been completed, and at the same time show the client that a Project Startup Checklist lists the same exercises that were carried out in the end. Too often, SharePoint implementation projects provide the client with no method of identifying what processes or procedures were adhered to and where to get information about on-site work, finances, archiving, and so forth.

Figure 15-1 shows the Project Closure Checklist. Feel free to use this and modify it to include anything else you want to ensure completion of.

SharePoint Project Closure Checklist				
TITLE		**PROJECT NUMBER**		
Aspects to Consider	**Y**	**N**	**N/A**	**Reference**
Deliverables				
Do SharePoint project files record the issue of project deliverables?				
Have all internal copies of the deliverables been distributed?				
Do the project files record the clients acceptance of the deliverables?				
File Management				
Is the filing complete with all references to all project material?				
Has all temporary material, including disks and files been removed?				
Has the software used on the project, including soft copies of the deliverable documents been backed up and referenced in the files?				
Archiving				
Have the master copies of the project deliverables been archived to the SharePoint One-Stop Shop?				
Have the project files been archived?				
Loan Items				
Have all client/sub-subcontractor loan items been mustered/returned?				
Has the client/sub-subcontractor returned all loaned items?				
Have lease items been returned?				
Subcontractors				
Has the subcontractor work been completed?				
Have all subcontractor invoices been received, authorized and sent to Finance?				
Has a subcontractor performance report been completed?				
On Site Work				
Have all project material been returned from the client's office?				
Have all passes been returned to site reception?				
Finance				
Has our final invoice been issued to the client?				
Commercial				
Has the client agreed to the closure of outstanding Teaming/Confidentiality Agreements?				
Project Closure				
Have any support or warranty arrangments been established?				
Where appropriate, have staff CVs been updated?				
Has the potential for follow-on work been explored with the client?				
Has a Client Questionnaire been sent to the client?				
Have all quality assurance non-conformances been closed out?				
Has a Project Experience Questionnaire form been completed?				
Has this completed form been copied to the central Project Management Office (PMO) or to the client?				
PROJECT MANAGER NAME		**DATE**		

Figure 15-1 SharePoint Project Closure Checklist.

Chapter 15

The preceding Project Closure Checklist is a version I use to complete SharePoint implementations and can easily be adapted. Again, as with the Project Startup Checklist, you should include in the Reference column any relevant document or communication used (for example, e-mail correspondence related to the checklist item).

Confirm the Resources Necessary for Business As Usual

You should verify and have client agreement that the human resources required to support the environment are in place and are satisfactory for "Business As Usual" (BAU). This is very important because the level of user satisfaction with support is directly related to this. If you have a low level of SharePoint administrative support, users will find out the hard way, especially when trying to get answers from a very busy administrator left to look after four separate environments and handle the requests from 10,000 users.

After you have confirmed the correct level of support exists for your SharePoint implementation, describe that level of support in the governance plan for SharePoint. Be sure to set processes that ensure the growth of SharePoint is monitored, and that there are processes to set the level of resources needed to manage and support that growth.

Why is it important to ensure you have the correct level of support for SharePoint? Here's an example: consider a scenario in which SharePoint has been implemented in a large organization. It was implemented with little user involvement, and it features a lowly SharePoint administrator who was promoted into being the SharePoint master to look after several SharePoint farms. The rules of site ownership are not set; users assume that permissions are set by technology—in other words, by the SharePoint administrator.

So you have a "stretched" SharePoint administrator who increases the security level of certain content simply because a user requests it. And because of the administrator's preconceived ideas about setting permissions (ideas coming from Windows Server Land), it can get worse. For example, suppose a user wants full access to something and says to the administrator, "Give me Full Control rights." So the SharePoint administrator, in the absence of any stated policies, gives Full Control to whatever the user wants and does so with no traceability or control—SharePoint Wild West ensues.

Does this sound a bit extreme? It really isn't. In my experience, personnel in quite a few organizations assume that anything that has the word "Admin" attached to it means technical administration, not business administration. Normally, this situation can be fixed with education, governance, and an understanding that data collaboration and data ownership is on the business side (meaning the business side takes control of permissions because SharePoint owners are from the business side and educated about how to manage a

SharePoint site). Correct levels of support are not determined just by throwing people without SharePoint skills into decision-making positions. You need to ensure that you have people with the right skills in place and also ensure that the balance is correct.

You must not only define human resources to support the product, but you need to ensure that you have created a Terms of Reference (TOR) for each resource and that the person has agreed to the TOR.

See the section "Training and Education Planning" on page 180 in Chapter 11 for more information about project strategies that ensure the organization has well-trained people in place when you are ready to hand off SharePoint.

To create an effective framework for ongoing administrative support of your SharePoint 2010 implementation, your handoff of the SharePoint 2010 platform needs to include the following:

- Review of the platform (when is it used, outputs)

- Mention of who owns SharePoint

- Business continuity and disaster recovery plans

- Future needs (normally captured at the Business Analyst level and specified as part of the implementation)

Establish and Maintain Governance

As part of handing SharePoint off to the client, the client takes the mantle of ensuring their vision of SharePoint is maintained and enhanced. This is where governance comes in. Establishing and maintaining SharePoint governance involves establishing rules and managing, scoping, and structuring the platform to ensure SharePoint continually meets user requirements. The people who do this are part of the SharePoint Governance Committee.

For more information about defining a governance plan for SharePoint, read Chapter 9, "SharePoint Governance."

To maintain governance, you need continual communication among those who drive the SharePoint strategy for the organization. Simply sending out documents or asking people to collaborate on SharePoint without face-to-face get-togethers is not enough. Meetings will need to be held. Those meetings can be used to drive actions because governance meetings are attended by decision makers. For infrastructure meetings, you have the technical authority, who is a decision maker concerning the infrastructure. The best way to ensure meetings occur regularly is to have proactive people acting as chairpersons and to have the SharePoint architect or administrator schedule the meetings.

Meetings and administrative activities that should take place include the following:

- Weekly operations meetings should be held so that those responsible for managing SharePoint on a technical level can report on the current week's SharePoint activities, infrastructure issues, changes, modifications, and enhancements and to describe the following week's highlights. Which individuals attend these meetings depends on the level of support you have for the components defined in SharePoint and who you have designated to look after those components. For example, you might have the SQL team responsible for the database and a network team responsible for the infrastructure. To help you decide this, ask the technical authority or manager of each team, who should be communicating with the SharePoint technical support team.

- A monthly business review should be held. This is a Governance Committee meeting in which committee members review user trends, issues, pain points, success stories, and key policies (for example, policies related to acceptable use, operations, the logical framework, and training guides).

- A monthly technical or infrastructure review meeting should take place. This is a good way for the interfacing teams that work with SharePoint administrators, architects, business analysts, and developers (with administrator attendance being mandatory) to carry out a review of the network infrastructure, confirm network connectivity, and discuss security, disk space, memory, performance, and so forth The information exchanged in this meeting can then be used to report to the technical authority any forecasts concerning additional capacity planning or other areas of concern.

> ### Tip
> If the infrastructure team has the necessary tools to monitor their environments, including SharePoint, reporting information from those tools could be stored at a central site and then be presented as a standard operations meeting, for example.

- Continually review the environment concerning migrations, solutions, service packs, and hotfixes. The SharePoint administrator needs to be on the ball and continually monitor for hotfixes relevant to their SharePoint environment. Good places to check for related news is the SharePoint Team Blog at the following location: *http://blogs.msdn.com/b/sharepoint*.

Summary

This final chapter of the book explained what it takes to ensure that SharePoint, once implemented, is part of the organizational life cycle. Processes in the way people work as individuals in an organization can be applied to SharePoint through the business side of the organization rather than through the technical side. This approach results in faster user adoption, better training, and enhanced productivity.

A SharePoint implementation is a combination of quality planning and project planning. Here's a final review of the key points:

- SharePoint acquisition is not about technology, but about business processes.

    Many people believe that a new shiny SharePoint platform is a magic potion that will fix whatever glitches there are in the way people work in the organization. They assume that after installation profits will be up, downtime will be decreased, and productivity will go through the roof.

    This is often not the case. If the current process for tracking an invoice or managing customer relations is inefficient, simply putting SharePoint in place will merely speed up a bad process. For example, customers will still wind up getting duplicate mailings, but they'll be delivered in two days rather than three! The first step in any SharePoint implementation must be to find out how things are really being done in a department and not what the training manual describes as the process. This is a process that can be summed up as "Making sure SharePoint meets user requirements," and it's the topic of Chapter 11. When you've assured that it does, changes can be made to design the optimal process to achieve success using the new technology.

- SharePoint acquisition is more about people than technology.

    SharePoint adoption requires that users alter the way they have always done things. This require users to leave their comfort zone. Because people don't usually like change, they tend to resist, complain, and sometimes even leave the company. Unless the users are involved from the beginning, they see a new acquisition like SharePoint as something done to them and they feel powerless. The people in an organization who are doing the most work with the current system are invaluable assets in the task of trying to make their job more efficient. Make sure that you define SharePoint governance, engage with your users (both from the business and technical sides of the organization), and look critically at user requirements from both camps.

- Wisely choose and train a cross-organizational team to set goals and priorities.

  The best and the brightest from each department make good working partners with senior management when choosing new systems. That way, no one gets surprised by the costs in terms of money or effort when implementation time comes around. Creating a cooperative atmosphere, of course, is key to making this work.

  Buy-in doesn't happen automatically. Often, the attitude of people lower in the organizational hierarchy is that their presence is merely window dressing and that the senior managers will make the final decision regardless of their input. A skilled facilitator is necessary to get past this distrust. You need an evangelistic project manager to make this happen. Or, depending on the scale of the technology release (that is, if SharePoint and other new technologies are involved), you might need a program manager to enhance client understanding and create a vision using the SharePoint project mantra.

- Establish good protocols for interviewing the client and users.

  It's easy for the user or client to be overwhelmed by slick SharePoint presentations, particularly when the presenter is talking about things that most people don't completely understand. Showmanship can get in the way of demonstrating real capabilities. Unless the review team is judging each vendor against the same list of needs, with the same understanding of the significance of each rating, "likeability" can win over capability.

  Make sure you use people who can be interactive with the users. Business analysts are very important in helping you elicit responses from the client and users. The purpose of interviewing is to enable both sides to learn—the client and users learn about the platform, and the interviewers learn about what the client and users do and what they need from SharePoint.

  Generating a list of requirements is hard work. If the team hasn't bonded before these discussions, a power struggle ensues, with each faction holding out for its own "essential" specifications. An outsider with no ties to any internal group is usually better able to bring about consensus than someone from the inside. The overarching goal is to produce a list of standards that support the mission of the enterprise. The more immediate goal is to create unity that transcends the narrowness of each participant's vision of that mission. The team meeting that follows each presentation must reinforce the common purpose while giving everyone a chance to voice their understanding or lack of it, as well as their concerns.

- Obtain "real" agreement on user and client requirements.

  Creating SharePoint requirements means finding multiple solutions to multicriteria problems. Every business wants a high-quality, easy-to-use SharePoint implementation that happens instantly and costs next to nothing! Of course, that doesn't exist. It's the actual frontline users who will be responsible for making the new system add value to the enterprise. Even if the management team does not provide their requirements, the project will proceed faster, more efficiently, and with a better result if the frontline people have a real voice in the selection of features and other specifics about the platform. Getting their buy-in at the start seems like a delay, but it results in a shorter, better project in the long run.

- Identify system requirements without alienating the users.

  Getting agreement on system and user requirements is an art as well as a science. It involves establishing productive communication between people who encounter many obstacles to achieving clarity. It is a frustrating process, but when done right, it is the foundation for success. When the people who will be most affected by the change are motivated to help the project succeed and see the project's value to them as well as to the company, the requirements will be an exciting design adventure, not a boring and confusing chore. The key is training the parties in terms of communication and team effort. With both your knowledge and practical exercises, you can build a team that will succeed.

- Work with the users and client during implementation.

  Success means everyone succeeds. The users, company management, implementation partners, and SharePoint and hardware vendors must all achieve common success—if they don't, all will fail. When the entire company teams agrees on vendors and implementation partners, the road is much smoother. When the vendors, implementation partners, and company teams are adversaries, the road leads to disaster. Everyone must believe that success requires everyone to succeed.

- Prepare the users to adapt to the changes required by the new system.

  Change management is a process, not an event. It should occur continuously throughout the course of the procurement and implementation. Management should not assume that everyone is going to accept the new system without a great deal of preparation.

  The selection and implementation teams will be consumed for a significant amount of time with bringing the project to completion. However, their efforts won't even appear on the mental radar screen of most users unless there is a deliberate effort to raise awareness of the coming change. Because people don't like change in general, it's hard to introduce a particular change without changing the initial attitude people have about the concept. This is the first and most essential level of change management.

After that has been addressed, people are more apt to be open to the detailed changes that will be required. Use SharePoint governance and create training and education strategies to ensure that users will continually engage with SharePoint. As SharePoint grows and becomes more of an enterprise platform, the more users will feel comfortable with it, become more productive, and feel that they have a stake in the future of SharePoint in the organization.

Index

D

E

About the Author

Geoff Evelyn enjoys over 25 years in Information Technology with over 10 years of experience in SharePoint, covering development, design, and implementation. He specializes in SharePoint information systems design, architecture, implementation, planning, governance and automation—all in the land of SharePoint.

Geoff headed the team that introduced SharePoint to the Scottish Highland University in 2001 and then over 30 other Scottish colleges. He went on to help implement, manage, and govern SharePoint in many global companies. Geoff is a Fellow of Institute of Analysts and Programmers and a member of the Institute for the Management of Information Systems, and has published many articles and guides on SharePoint, all available on his website, *www.stationcomputing.com*.

What do you think of this book?

We want to hear from you!

To participate in a brief online survey, please visit:

microsoft.com/learning/booksurvey

Tell us how well this book meets your needs—what works effectively, and what we can do better. Your feedback will help us continually improve our books and learning resources for you.

Thank you in advance for your input!

Stay in touch!

CPSIA information can be obtained at www.ICGtesting.com
Printed in the USA
BVOW081856160512

290389BV00007BB/86/P

9 780735 648708